Alien V

CW01560611

Crashed UFOs, M

Richard Dolan Press
Rochester, New York 14619
USA

Richard Dolan Press and logo are
registered trademarks of Richard Dolan Press

Wood, Robert
    In Search of Alien Viruses: Crashed UFOs, MJ-12 & Biowarfare /
    by Robert Wood, Ph.D.
    311 p. cm.
    Includes index.
    ISBN-13: 978-1490929149
    1. Unidentified Flying Objects

    I. Wood, Robert II. Title

First published in the United States by Richard Dolan Press

Cover image of budding HIV retrovirus, from Wikimedia Commons.
Back cover image, adapted from illustration by Bill McDonald (see Appendix Illustration 2).

Alien Viruses

Crashed UFOs, MJ-12, & Biowarfare

Dr. Robert M. Wood

with
Nick Redfern

Richard Dolan Press

Table of Contents

Prologue

by Dr. Bob Wood

Any sufficiently advanced technology is indistinguishable from magic.[1]

I don't believe in magic...but I have seen it at the Magic Castle in Hollywood. Magicians are trained to know how to fool people using the real world of science, and since they fool so many people successfully, some of them may become arrogant. When trained physicists feel they can replicate most of the known phenomena, they too can become arrogant, until they encounter some data that are anomalous, that "don't fit." Some scientists are inclined to discard the data and preserve the order they thought they knew, and make statements like, "Space travel is utter bilge."[2] Others attempt to classify the anomalous data and see if theories can be modified to accommodate them. These new theories then become the science of tomorrow. The apparent "magic" has been explained with new equations.

All living creatures have unique characteristics for their species. Some "lower order" insects like bees have remarkable skills at finding nectar; different bird species are highly adapted to finding their own kind of food. The societal aspects of ant colonies are well known. Some of them use techniques that we, as "intelligent life," have difficulty explaining. So, what characterizes "intelligence"? I choose that it is "logic and the attendant mathematical lore that goes with it." So, intelligent life in the universe[3] is expected to be logical and probably to be able to understand equations, and to design useful tools. Now, one could argue that ant colonies are sophisticated, and that their society is complex. However, if we found ant colonies on another planet, I doubt we would declare them intelligent. They, and the birds and the bees seem to survive more because of sophisticated instinct than logic.

Fred Hoyle, a brilliant cosmologist, once wrote a science fiction book called "The Black Cloud"[4] which described the psychic attack on Earth of a cloud of particles (each of no consequence by itself) dooming Earth. Since some alleged aliens have been reported as having psychic abilities, it is conceivable that they might be able to do all this logic and mathematics psychically, thereby suggesting lack of a logical thought process. However, I would argue that the logic and math exists in their society even though they may not put it on paper. For example, the process of remote viewing has been enhanced by a logical treatment of the procedures, and random number generators are yielding a wealth of impressive data in both time and space.[5]

Therefore, in discussing alien societies and motives, I'm going to assume that it is reasonable to assess their motives, means and opportunity on a logical basis, and that they have access to no different set of equations or physics or biology than we do. If their society is older, they could logically be able to understand our universe more clearly with even better concept and attendant equations than we have. In summary, my perspective is that it is logical to assume that the laws of nature apply equally everywhere.

Alien diseases and the science fiction classics

The public, the government, and the media have all been influenced by two powerful stories, both made into movies, and they have affected how we potentially view alien creatures. The first one, the famous *War of the Worlds*[6] by H. G. Wells, has been made into at least one famous radio broadcast[7] and two movies. Here the invading Martian aliens (big, destructive, seemingly mechanical) attempt to kill everyone in sight until at the end they die, killed by one of our own infections.

In the second classic story, *The Andromeda Strain,*[8] an exploratory craft is brought back to earth ahead of schedule for classified reasons, and crashes in a rural area, and those who investigate, including the town's doctor, are killed by a deadly pathogen, which turns out to be classified as a virus having a fascinating structure and mechanism of action. We have been preparing for this event for decades, so with multi-levels of biologic security at the disease control center, and by clever reasoning, we are able to defeat the disease just before it kills everyone in the story, and subsequently, the earth's population. This too has been made into a movie very effectively.[9] In Chapter 17, you will read about how there was unusual interest in this story by our biological warfare folks.

These stories have major significance towards the perception of UFOs by the Government and by the public. *The War of the Worlds* left the impression, partly because of media hype, that millions of people were panicked by the potential threat of aliens. Actually, according to historians, two people died, one from a heart attack and one from running a red light.[10] Those who were upset were limited to those who were near the alleged landing locations of the aliens. Nevertheless, the image stuck: aliens will cause panic if they are here. This assumption, in my opinion, significantly influenced governments to suppress the genuine potential extraterrestrial sightings and indeed -- the early indications that we thought they were extraterrestrial.[11] Therefore, avoiding panic became one of the centerpieces of policy for UFO management by the U.S.

The second book, *The Andromeda Strain* is also significant in that it deals with the potential panic, but introduces a reality found today for the study and control of communicable diseases in both mostly unclassified (Center for Disease Control, Atlanta) and classified (Fort Detrick, Maryland) research institutions run by the Government. Similar highly sophisticated multi-level containment facilities exist in industry for research. The sophistication of these facilities transcends those in *The Andromeda Strain,* both here and in the former Soviet Union at Biopreparat and indeed at Porton Down, to be introduced in Chapter 15.

Leaked classified documents describe a robust UFO recovery program since the 40s

The concerns for the containment of alien pathogens probably began with the Cape Girardoux alien, allegedly held up for a photo by two federal agents.[12] We have no data on whether they became ill after the recovery event; however, *The Majestic Documents*[13] include three rather specific and significant references to crash recoveries. The first is the *Interplanetary Phenomenon Unit* preliminary report on the Roswell crashes signed July 16, 1947. The second is the *1ˢᵗ Annual Report* (published after March 1951, based on an internal reference), dealing with extensive review of all the technology from UFOs to date. The third is the Special Operations Manual, or SOM 1-01, entitled *Extraterrestrial Entities and Technology, Recovery and Disposal.*[14] The first two of these leaked documents appear to be drafts of final versions, whereas the SOM 1-01 is a final, proofread, professionally produced field manual printed in 1954 on a hot lead printing press.

The quotations from these three documents unite the discovery of lethal pathogens with the application to biological warfare for all to see. The storage of tissue samples at Ft. Detrick makes it very clear that these issues will not be studied by those without proper security clearances, and that the leading edge research undoubtedly went right to classified facilities and has stayed there. It would be very reasonable to conjecture that the understanding of retroviruses probably BEGAN there, and leaked into the outside literature years later. This might explain why the search for "retro-virus" prior to 1951 in the open literature has been fruitless. In addition, the hyphenated version of the word has never been found in the unclassified literature. Some skeptics have argued that this suggests that the document is a fake because of this error. However, a careful evaluation of the 17 pages of the *1ˢᵗ Annual Report* reveals 37 hyphenated verb, adjectives and nouns. The author of the report clearly favored the use of hyphens when in doubt.[15] Each reader can decide whether the author of the *1ˢᵗ Annual Report* was "hyphen-happy." In addition, the authenticity of the date of this report is enhanced by the forensic linguistic aspect that in the 40s, the use of hyphens for compound words was much more common than it is today.

It would be reasonable to imagine that the study of all epidemics (epidemiology) would be often if not mostly classified. The preceding history and quotations suggest to the ambitious student of biological warfare that the creation of a super weapon might well be possible. In the military research of the late 1940's weapons of mass destruction were quite in vogue, both in the USA and the USSR.

What facilities deal with biological warfare and epidemiology?

The facilities designed for safely studying pathogens include increasingly effective types of filtering systems that prevent the intrusion of specific sized particles, with the higher the number of the level indicating the smaller the size of filtration methods employed. The facilities are divided in Biosafety Levels. Note the following is from Ft. Detrick's own literature:

"Appropriate precautions should be observed in collection, handling, shipping, and processing of diagnostic samples. Both the Centers for Disease Control and Prevention (CDC, Atlanta, Georgia.) and the U.S. Army Medical Research Institute of Infectious Diseases (USAMRIID, Fort

Detrick, Frederick, Maryland.) have diagnostic laboratories operating at the maximum Biosafety Level (BL-4; see The U.S. Biological Warfare and Biological Defense Programs manual, for further discussion of BLs). Viral isolation should not be attempted without BL-4 containment."

The facility USAMRIID at Ft. Detrick, MD consists of four levels of biosafety:

Biosafety Level I—minimal biohazard, Study of low risk infectious elements such as pneumococcus and salmonella

Biosafety Level II—moderate biohazard, examples of infectious agents studied: hepatitis, influenza, Lyme disease.

Biosafety Level III—high biohazard, multiple vaccinations required, examples of infectious agents studied: anthrax, typhus, human immune deficiency virus.

Biosafety Level IV Maximum security— examples of infectious agents studied: Viral Hemorrhagic Fevers: Ebola, Hanta, Lassa virus—all highly virulent with no known cure.

Other U.S. facilities include the well-known Center for Disease Control, Atlanta that interacts with the media and public, and the Dugway Proving Ground, an Army facility in Utah reported to be a storehouse for and testing of biological weapons. Would it be reasonable to assume that there are black ops here with unknown organisms of uncontrollable lethality? Are there black ops with EBE-related pathogens at Area 51 as well? For a first-hand report from a worker at Area 51, read Chapter 23, "The Area 51 Revelation."

In the United Kingdom, the oft-mentioned facility for biological warfare is Porton Down, and my colleague Nick Redfern will be mentioning their possible role in alien crash retrievals in Chapters 15 and 16. It is also a covert facility with BL-IV capability.

In the former Soviet Union, the leading facility is Biopreparat, assisted by support facilities of the Anti-Plague Institute in Rostov, Vektor in Novosibirsk, the Bacterial Warfare Facility at Oblensk and Compound 19 in Sverdlovsk. In all, there were 47 facilities located across the former USSR that deal with various aspects of biological warfare and epidemiology.

In addition, the Pasteur Institute in Paris should be mentioned. They did early good work during World War II on Nazi biowarfare plans, and have a non-trivial capability. They were arguably the most instrumental in identifying HIV-1, since many researchers and professors consider Montagnier of Pasteur more persuasive than

Gallo of the U.S. National Institutes of Health in this identification.

Have some past epidemics been due to alien viruses?

Our current perception of population on Earth has been that of a steady increase, with occasional reductions due to plagues, wars or famine. Epidemiologists study this history in more detail, as evidenced by this record:[16]

- Native South Americans use curare or amphibian toxins in poison darts.
- Soldiers catapult corpses and dead animals into besieged cities.
- 1346: Tatar forces besieging Kaffa (now Feodossia, Ukraine) catapult plague corpses into the city.
- 1347-1351: Bubonic plague (the Black Death) kills 25 million people in Europe.
- June 24, 1763: Capt. Ecuyer, a British officer under the command of Gen. Sir Jeffrey Amherst, distributes smallpox-infected blankets to Indians during the French and Indian War in North America.
- 1881: Louis Pasteur develops bacterial vaccination. (Rabies is a virus).
- 1918-1919: Spanish flu kills 50 million people around the world.
- 1925: Geneva Protocol for the Prohibition of Use in War of Asphyxiating. Poisonous or Other Gases and of Bacteriological Methods of Warfare.
- 1932-1945: Japanese establish biological weapons program, known as Unit 731, at Pin Fan, Manchuria and other cities in China. Human experiments were used and 3,000 prisoners died.
- 1941: Japanese attack the city of Changteh with cholera. It is estimated 10,000 civilians and 1,700 Japanese soldiers die.
- 1942: British test anthrax on sheep on the Scottish island of Gruinard. The uninhabited island is still believed to be contaminated and is still off-limits.
- 1942: United States begins research into biological weapons.
- WWII: Czech resistance uses anthrax as a weapon against German occupiers by spreading spores on envelopes.
- 1960s: Vietcong smear excrement on pungi sticks used as booby traps; the United States develops a biological warfare arsenal.
- 1968: U.S. conducts biological weapons tests at Johnston Atoll in the South Pacific.
- 1969: U.S. and U.K. officially end their offensive biological weapons program.
- May 1971-February 1973: United States destroys biological weapons stockpile.
- 1973: Soviet Union begins Biopreparat biological weapons program.

- March 1975: Biological and Toxin Weapons Convention comes into effect.
- 1978: Bulgarian agents assassinate Georgi Markov in London, using a Ricin pellet and attempt to assassinate Vladimir Kostov.
- 1978-1980: Natural anthrax epidemic in Zimbabwe. Estimated 10,000 cases
- April 2, 1979: Anthrax accident at Sverdlovsk, Russia. More than 66 civilians and an unknown number of military personnel are killed. Records seized by KGB.
- 1980: World Health Organization eradicates smallpox. Officially, two labs have the virus, the Centers for Disease Control in Atlanta and the Ivanovski Institute in Moscow. It is believed biowarfare units may still have smallpox stocks.
- 1980-1988 Gulf War (Iran-Iraq): Iraq uses chemical weapons and works on biological weapons.
- 1984: Soviet Union reportedly creates super plague.
- 1985-1989: Ken Alibek (Kanatjan Alibekov) develops Alibekov Anthrax, a weapons grade strain.
- 1989: Valdimir Vladimir Kostov defects to the U.K. and reveals Soviet biowarfare program.
- 1990-1991: Gulf War (Desert Storm) Iraq prepares biological weapons for possible use.
- April 11, 1990: U.S. and U.K. demand that the Soviet Union cease their biological weapons program. Gorbachev later 'officially' cancels the program.
- January 1991: U.S. and British experts inspect a Biopreparat facility.
- 1991: Ken Alibek quits Biopreparat and defects to the United States, now works at Ft. Detrick.
- 1992: Boris Yeltsin 'officially' cancels Russia's 'offensive' weapons program.
- 1993: NATO creates working groups on biological warfare defense.
- 1995: Aum Shrinikyo releases Sarin gas in the Tokyo subway. Aum also researches biological weapons, tries to obtain Ebola.
- 1995: U.S. accuses Russia of continuing its bioweapons program and helping Iran develop a biowarfare program.
- 1996: United Nations Special Commission on Iraq (UNSCOM) inspectors destroy Iraqi biological weapons.
- 1997: Soviet scientists publish details of genetically altered anthrax in Vaccine.
- February 1998: FBI arrests two men, including Larry Wayne Harris in Nevada, alleging they are carrying anthrax. They are later cleared.
- March 1998: United States orders that all troops receive anthrax vaccination.

• Spring 1998: Canada orders troops in the Gulf to receive anthrax vaccination.

More recently, a modification in April 2005 has authorized any influenza that could cause a pandemic (worldwide epidemic) will fall under the Quarantinable Communicable Diseases. While it is true that any one of these epidemics noted earlier COULD have started from an alien pathogen, we need to look at the evidence, beginning with those few cases where there seems to be some.

Three examples of possible death from alien pathogens

Case1: The SED Technicians. First on my list is the death of the four SED (Sandia Engineering District) technicians (alluded to in the *Interplanetary Phenomenon Unit* and *1st Annual Report*, discussed in detail in Chapters 4 and 5.

Case 2. The Chihuahua, Mexico Crash, August 1974. Chapter 17 provides comprehensive detail about the specifics of this crash, with exceptional detail.

Case 3. Varginha, Brazil death of Corporal Chereze. Chapter 19, titled Somaliland and Varginha, describes this case also in remarkable detail, together with other witness reports of possible contact with aliens.

Pathogens are biological agents with the potential to induce disease and illness in their host(s). Four kinds of pathogens dominate in causing human disease:

1. Fungi are complex cells that digest food externally and absorb the nutrient into its cells. Life threatening fungal infections in humans most often occur in immunocompromised patients or vulnerable people with a weakened immune system, although fungi are common problems in the immunocompetent population as the causative agents of skin, nail or yeast infections. The typical fungal spore size is 1-40 micrometer in length.

2. Bacteria. Although the vast majority of bacteria are harmless or beneficial to one's body, a few pathogenic bacteria can cause infectious diseases. The most common bacterial disease is tuberculosis, which affects just about 2 million people mostly in sub-Saharan Africa. Pathogenic bacteria contribute to other globally important diseases, such as pneumonia. Pathogenic bacteria also cause infections such as tetanus, typhoid fever, diphtheria, syphilis

and Hansen's disease. Bacteria can often be killed by antibiotics because the cell wall in the outside is destroyed and then the DNA. They typically range between 1 and 5 micrometers in length.

3. Viruses. Virus means poison in Latin, and is a microscopic particle, which may infect the cells of a living organism. Some notable pathogenic viruses cause smallpox, influenza, mumps, measles, chickenpox, Ebola, and rubella. Some viruses we do not know how to cure, such as an HIV-like retrovirus or a Viral Hemorrhagic Fever like Hantavirus. Viruses typically range between 20-300 nanometers in length.

4. Prions are infectious pathogens that do not contain nucleic acids. Prions are short for proteinaceous infectious particles. Prions are abnormal proteins whose presence causes some diseases such as scrapie, bovine spongiform encephalopathy (mad cow disease) and Creutzfeldt-Jakob disease.

Each of these pathogens has a range of sizes depending on their molecular structure. Generally, they are listed in order of smaller size, with the smallest of bacteria being about 400 nm, which is the very largest size for the virus: viruses from 400 nm (Ebola is 200 nm in diameter) to 20 nm prions. Recently, research is suggesting that some of the more lethal pathogens are not viruses but are prions. Special microscopes are required to study pathogens as small as prions.

Prions are very different from bacteria and viruses. The discovery that prion diseases were transmissible led researchers to the natural conclusions that the infective agent had to be a bacterium or a virus. When, however, infectious tissue remained infectious after treatment with both heat (which destroys most bacteria) and ultraviolet light (which should inactivate viruses) the conclusion was that some other kind of infectious agent was responsible. In 1982, neurologist Stanley Prusiner of the University of California provided the first direct evidence that the infectious agent was a protein, for which he received the Nobel Prize in 1997. Nobel laureate Carleton Gadjusek discovered kuru in New Guinea, in a cannibalistic tribe, brought cerebral matter from infected patients back to Ft. Detrick and Patuxent Wildlife Research Center, where they were injected into apes and other lower forms of life—then the apes escaped from Ft. Detrick and prion-based diseases spread throughout North America.[17]

Logical basis for Homo sapiens involvement

The steady growth of prion-based diseases in the world ("mad cow" in cattle, scrapie in sheep, transmissible mink encephalopathy (TME), chronic wasting disease (CWD) in elk, kuru in cannibals and Creutzfeldt-Jakob Disease (CJD) in humans) have caused tremendous apprehension in the cattle, game, and meat packing industry in the UK, Canada and the U.S. Our smarter scientists would have seen these coming years ago, and the "classified world" could easily have contemplated a research program to understand fully the causes of these diseases to prepare to control them. Anyone wanting to understand how to vaccinate against new diseases would find that studies of infected cattle might be helpful. "Our" (Homo sapiens) concerns deal with preventing epidemics and panic as well as gaining control of the human immune virus or potential alien threat pathogens, both retroviruses and Viral Hemorrhagic Fevers. Additionally, in the case of military application, their merit would be considered for biological warfare. Knowing perfectly well that an open unclassified project would have caused the very panic we would be trying to prevent, a covert monitoring project would have made a lot of sense. Get big choppers, make them as silent as possible, install the latest in laser cutting tools, anesthetize the targets with accurate darts, pick them up, get the bovine samples, and drop the carcasses near where they got them, and do it all in 15 minutes or so. Presumably, it would also be easy to spot the sick ones by using an infrared signature discrimination technique if required. Such procedures allow a group so motivated to exploit a wide variety of ecosystems. Evaluation of some of the drugs and technology administered seems to demonstrate a link to current day German pharmaceutical laboratories. Chapters 7 and 20 respectively report on the specifics of animals & biological warfare and the AIDS-cattle mutilation controversy.

New pathogens, new diseases?

This book provides three examples from the past of apparent alien-caused illnesses, followed by death. It is evident that some of the best microbiologists of the world would have been working to understand causes and controls.

What is the ideal pathogen to use against inhabitants of earth? What would its characteristics be?

1. Rapid incubation period
2. Rapid onset and death
3. Stable pathogen, difficult to kill
4. Overwhelms or bypasses the immune system
5. Biologically sophisticated "Surgical Strike" on the immune systems
6. Selective in action—should be defeated by sophisticated countermeasures known to attacker

Today there are new threats and challenges emerging upon our society. Many people are aware of AIDS (autoimmune deficiency syndrome), HIV (human immune deficiency virus), "mad cow" disease (Creutzfeldt-Jakob Disease (CJD) and chronic fatigue and immune dysfunction syndrome (CFIDS).

Logical basis for extraterrestrial biological entity involvement. Since many UFO researchers, including myself, consider that the UFO data suggest many more than one alien race, there would be of course a large number of motives to contemplate. However, some races seem to be protective of our interests and might be motivated by the same objectives as Homo sapiens. Other EBEs, however, could be assumed to be contemplating how best to take over the planet with viruses or prions, thereby reducing the turmoil and property damage. "Their" concerns might be (1) the detailed understanding of earth-based genetics, perhaps for breeding purposes or (2) for the development of long-term lethal pathogens and their vaccines for removing Homo sapiens from this particular planet. Prion-based diseases are invariably fatal, but the disease takes years to decades, e.g. CJD. This would be a good 'extinction disease', as it is categorically fatal, jumps species, and the pathogen is nearly indestructible. Clearly, their first visits in the 40s were relevant to causing some Homo sapiens deaths. They could want to perfect the optimum procedure to kill all the Homo sapiens except those that would be vaccinated.

Conclusion of the Prologue

We have postulated that there is no magic, the laws of science are the same everywhere, and that the common element of intelligence is logic and the attendant equations. Therefore, there is no genuine caveat: "You're not smart enough to understand our science." This is even true in the presence of psychic phenomena. We just don't know the concepts and the attendant equations yet.

Two fiction stories involving pathogens have substantially influenced our UFO/alien policy, and leaked classified documents describe a robust UFO recovery program since the 40s. There are major hints from these documents about infections, death, mutilations, biological warfare, and pharmaceutical research as well as the ever-present psychological warfare programs.

At least three countries have major laboratories for handling potential alien pathogens and biological warfare. BW and the study of alien pathogens are intellectually entwined. Therefore, is it reasonable to ask whether it is possible or likely that some of our recorded epidemics are due to alien viruses? Several alien crashes have been followed by local deaths. There is even the logical possibility that the Hantavirus was the original pathogen from the Roswell deaths of four technicians. There are modern concerns that new pathogens are neither understood nor controllable, causing diseases about which we need more data. In particular, retroviruses, Viral Hemorrhagic Fevers (VHFs) and prions warrant attention because the diseases they cause are poorly understood compared those caused by bacteria and fungi.

Anyone wanting to understand how to vaccinate against new diseases would find that studies of infected cattle might be helpful. The evidence strongly suggests that both "our" people (earth covert military forces) and alien craft are mutilating animals, mostly cattle for similar but different reasons. "Our" concerns deal with preventing epidemics and panic as well as gaining control of the human immune virus or potential alien threat pathogens. "Their" concerns might be the detailed understanding of earth-based genetics, perhaps for breeding purposes **or** for the development of long-term lethal pathogens and their vaccines for removing Homo sapiens from this particular planet.

Alien pathogens, including bacteria, viruses and prions, have played and are playing a critical role in our global society, and are being studied both by our covert forces and by the aliens themselves.

The book you are about to read presents fascinating detail about specific events that link to impressive human stories of the covert study of alien viruses.

Prologue Notes:

[1] Arthur C. Clarke, *Profiles of the Future*, 1961

[2] Sir Richard Wooley, British Astronomer Royal, 1956, one year before Sputnik

[3] Shklovskii and Sagan, *Intelligent Life in the Universe*, 1966

[4] Fred Hoyle, *The Black Cloud*, 1957

[5] For example, go to www.princeton and look for the Princeton Engineering Anomalies Research publications.

[6] H.G. Wells, *War of the Worlds*, 1898

[7] Orson Welles, 1938, *War of the Worlds*, on the Mystery Theater

[8] Michael Chrichton, *The Andromeda Strain*, Knopf, 1969

[9] One in 1971 and one in 1992.

[10] Hadley Cantril, *The Invasion from Mars*, Princeton Univ. Press, 1940

[11] For example, the *letter from George Marshall to FDR* dated March 1942 after the LA "air raid".

[12] *The Secret* DVD, Wood and Wood LLC, 2003

[13] Wood, Robert M. and Ryan S., *The Majestic Documents*, 1998 and www.majesticdocuments.com

[14] *Majestic-12 Group Special Operations Manual 1-01* dated April 1954

[15] List of 37 hyphenated words in the 1st Annual Report: other-world visitation, long-range flight, human-like (occupants), post-1947 incident, un-published documents, bio-medical intelligence, multi-layered security, psy-op development, over-all intelligence, stand-by fighters, all-encompassing defense, well-functioning (order), micro-circuitry, low-power transmission, electro-magnetic research, retro-virus, high-temperature alloys, electro-hydrodynamic technology, super-aerodynes, out-weighed, inter-active program, mid-air collision, body-bag, air-borne release, south-westerly (sic) course, small-disturbance theory, three-dimensional body, Indo-China, air-sea rescue, Wright-Patterson AFB, near-miss incidents, cylindrical-shaped aircraft, right-angle course (this hyphen is at the end of line), dogfight-style encounter, elliptically-shaped object, low-level flights, on-and-off (periods).

[16] The source here is a former Soviet scientist who studied these matters.

[17] For a nice perspective of the spread of prion diseases, see Colm Kelleher, *Brain Trust*, Paraview Pocket Books, 2004

Introduction

By Nick Redfern

W hen Bob Wood asked me if I would be interested in ghostwriting a book for him on his phenomenal amount of research into the connections between crashed UFOs, Roswell, MJ-12, and alien viruses, I thought about the proposal both long and hard. After all, in 2005 Simon & Schuster had published my book *Body Snatchers in the Desert* that offered a distinctly down-to-earth explanation for the Roswell event. However, I have always taken the view that, as none of us can say with one hundred per cent certainty what happened at Roswell on the fateful day in July 1947, it behooves us – indeed it is *vital* - to look at *all* of the available evidence pertaining to this particular aspect of the UFO controversy with an unbiased mind - and an open one, too.

Bob has been carefully and quietly looking into the potentially very disturbing angle of crashed UFOs and its connection to a lethal alien virus, for a full decade. In that time, he has uncovered an absolute wealth of data, documentation, testimony and materials that, until now, has largely remained unseen. And, he has quite literally gone where no researcher has gone before in his quest, having tirelessly pursued this seldom-trod path with utter diligence and complete dedication. His findings will interest you, they will astound you, and they may even make you concerned for our future as a species, and about our interactions with the intelligences behind the on-going UFO presence on our world.

And so, I have no hesitation in offering Bob both my support and my admiration, for having had the determination and the sheer guts to delve deep into an area that many lesser souls have either steered clear of, or have openly derided and dismissed as being of no consequence. The results of Bob's in-depth work and eye-opening discoveries should be read by anyone and everyone interested in the controversial world of the crashed UFO.

Preface

According to *Article IX* of *The Treaty on Principles Governing the Activities of States in the Exploration and Use of Outer Space, Including the Moon and Other Celestial Bodies*, that was collectively signed at Washington, London, and Moscow on January 27, 1967, and that was entered into force on October 10 of that year:

"In the exploration and use of outer space, including the Moon and other celestial bodies, States Parties to the Treaty shall be guided by the principle of co-operation and mutual assistance and shall conduct all their activities in outer space, including the Moon and other celestial bodies, with due regard to the corresponding interests of all other States Parties to the Treaty. States Parties to the Treaty shall pursue studies of outer space, including the Moon and other celestial bodies, and conduct exploration of them so as to avoid their harmful contamination and also adverse changes in the environment of the Earth resulting from the introduction of extraterrestrial matter and, where necessary, shall adopt appropriate measures for this purpose.

"If a State Party to the Treaty has reason to believe that an activity or experiment planned by it or its nationals in outer space, including the Moon and other celestial bodies, would cause potentially harmful interference with activities of other States Parties in the peaceful exploration and use of outer space, including the Moon and other celestial bodies, it shall undertake appropriate international consultations before proceeding with any such activity or experiment. A State Party to the Treaty which has reason to believe that an activity or experiment planned by another State Party in outer space, including the Moon and other celestial bodies, would cause potentially harmful interference with activities in the peaceful exploration and use of outer space, including the Moon and other celestial bodies, may request consultation concerning the activity or experiment."[1]

The concern expressed within the above-extract about "adverse changes in the environment of the Earth resulting from the introduction of extraterrestrial matter" was, and, indeed, still is, a very real one.

In an article titled *Alien Infection*, writer Leslie Mullen noted: "When diseases like SARS, Mad Cow Disease and Monkey-pox cross the species barrier and infect humans, they dominate news headlines. Just imagine, then, the reaction if potentially infectious pathogens were found in rock samples from Mars. As we look toward exploring other worlds, and perhaps even bringing samples back to Earth for testing, astrobiologists have to wonder: could alien pathogens cross the 'planet' barrier and wreak havoc on our world? Even though there is no proof of bacterial or viral pathogens anywhere except Earth, there is already a worried advocacy group called the *International Committee Against Martian Sample Return*, and science fiction novels like *The Andromeda Strain* depict nightmare alien infection scenarios."[2]

Sample Return Missions Scare Some Researchers was the headline that appeared on www.space.com on April 9, 2000. "Researchers, environmentalists and policymakers want NASA to consider carefully its plans to visit and bring back samples from Mars, Europa, and other solar system bodies," it was reported. According to Norine Noonan, director of the Environmental Protection Agency's research arm, who also had then-recently chaired a NASA-sponsored panel on planetary protection: "This is a very serious issue, and there are clearly many concerns."

It was added: "NASA's longstanding policy is to both protect the Earth and preserve planetary conditions for future biological and organic constituent exploration...In recent years, NASA has commissioned the National Research Council to conduct several studies on the potential for contaminating other worlds. Now that the space agency also is considering a variety of sample return missions, researchers are becoming increasingly aware that they must put clear standards in place to protect against the highly unlikely but possible introduction - and escape - of extraterrestrial life to Earth. While minimal, the risk level 'is not zero,' warns one NRC study."[3]

Science writer Robert Roy Britt stated on November 27, 2000 that: "A group of scientists says it has collected an alien bacterium 10 miles above Earth, plus signatures of other extraterrestrial microbes even higher in the atmosphere. ...The bacterium was collected at that altitude by a balloon operated by the Indian Space

Research Organization. Chandra Wickramasinghe, who leads a study into the results, called the microbe a previously unknown strain of bacteria and said it likely came from a comet. Wickramasinghe and a colleague, Fred Hoyle, say the findings support an idea they pioneered, called panspermia, which holds that the seeds of life are everywhere in space and are the source for life on Earth."[4]

In June 2003, *National Geographic News* revealed: "In a letter to the British medical journal *The Lancet*, Chandra Wickramasinghe, from Cardiff University in Wales, and other scientists, propose that SARS may have originated in outer space then fallen down to Earth and landed in China, where the outbreak began. It sounds like a headline from a supermarket tabloid, but the idea may not be as outlandish as it first appears. One hundred tons (90 metric tons) of space debris fall on Earth every day; some scientists believe as much as one ton (0.9 metric ton) of bacteria from space is part of that daily deposit. Particles carrying the SARS virus could have come from a comet, the researchers say, and released into the debris trail of the comet's tail. The Earth's passage through the stream would have led to the entry of the culprit particles. 'We're not saying this is definitely what happened,' said Wickramasinghe, who is also the director of the Cardiff Center for Astrobiology, a research effort that seeks evidence of extraterrestrial life. 'But the theory should not be ruled out.'"[5]

One of those that recognized the potential threat posed by lethal viruses of exotic origins is Joshua Lederberg, who was born in New Jersey in 1925, and who obtained his B.A. with honors in Zoology at Columbia. In 1947, Lederberg was appointed Assistant Professor of Genetics at the University of Wisconsin, where he was promoted to Associate Professor in 1950, and subsequently to Professor in 1954. Stanford University Medical School entrusted to him the organization of its Department of Genetics and appointed him Professor and Executive Head in 1959. Lederberg's lifelong research, for which he received the Nobel Prize in 1958 at the age of thirty-three, has been in genetic structure and function in micro-organisms, and he has been actively involved in artificial intelligence research, in computer science, and in NASA's experimental programs seeking life on Mars.

An 8-page paper written by Lederberg for *Science* on August 12, 1960 titled *Exobiology: Approaches to Life Beyond the Earth* states in part: "...The introduction of microbial life to a previously barren planet, or to one occupied by a less well-adapted form of life, could result in the explosive growth of the implant. With a generation time of 30 minutes and easy dissemination by winds and currents, common bacteria could occupy a nutrient medium the size of the earth in a few days or weeks."[6]

More disturbing extracts state: "The most dramatic hazard would be the introduction of a new disease, imperiling human health. What we know of the biology of infection makes this an extremely unlikely possibility...However, a converse argument can also be made, that we have evolved our specific defenses against terrestrial bacteria and that we might be less capable of coping with organisms that lack the proteins and carbohydrates by which they could be recognized as foreign...at present the prospects for treating a returning vehicle to neutralize any possible hazard are at best marginal by comparison with the immensity of the risk."

By the mid-1960s, Lederberg was writing a column for *The Washington Post* newspaper. And several of those columns are of both note and relevance to the issues presented within the pages of this book. On September 24, 1966 Lederberg wrote a feature for the newspaper titled *A Treaty on Germ Warfare* that dealt with his worries about biological warfare. In part, Lederberg said: "The United States has vehemently denied the military use of any biological weapons or any lethal chemical weapons. However, research on these weapons has continued through and from World War II. The Army has a well-known research facility at Fort Detrick, Md., and a testing station at Dugway, Utah...The large scale deployment of infectious agents is a potential threat against the whole species: mutant forms of viruses could well develop that would spread over the earth's population for a new Black Death...The future of the species is very much bound up with the control of these weapons..."[7]

Co-written by Lederberg with Carl Sagan and Elliott C. Levinthal, *Contamination of Mars* is an 18-page paper that was published by the Smithsonian Institution in June 1967, and that largely concentrates upon ascertaining the potential hazards that the human species might pose to the planet Mars by way of introducing hostile organisms into the planet's eco-system. The paper contains an intriguing entry that focuses on the way in which hostile organisms might be released if a spacecraft crashed on the surface of Mars.

According to *Contamination of Mars*: "One serious contingency for release of contained micro-organisms is a crash-landing, and, particularly, a spacecraft impacting Mars with a velocity about 6 km/sec will be totally pulverized. But experience with missile impact indicates that even at impact velocities of 0.6 km/sec or less, a significant fraction of the missile's mass is not in the impact crater and is unrecoverable. The shells and grenades used in bacteriological warfare indicate that contained microorganisms will survive such impacts...In the case of a hard landing, and particularly, of a hypervelocity impact of a spacecraft on Mars, spacecraft fragments will be distributed over a wide area. In a period of minutes – less than the time for many unshielded terrestrial organisms to accumulate an ultraviolet mean lethal does on Mars – fragments travelling in parabolic trajectories at 6 km/sec will cover a lateral distance ~ 1000 km."[8]

Published in *The Washington Post* on August 31, 1968, a feature from Lederberg titled *The Infamous Black Death May Return To Haunt Us*, dealt with the nature of the Black Death that decimated Europe in the 14th Century, and drew parallels between biological warfare research in the 20th Century and the fears about the regulation and control of such research, a theme that Lederberg often returned to.[9]

Printed in *The Washington Post* on September 7, 1969, Lederberg's *Mankind Had A Near Miss From A Mystery Pandemic* told a story of highly unsettling proportions:

"In the aftermath of the six-day war in the Middle east last summer, direct air transport from Uganda to Germany and Yugoslavia was disrupted. Shipments of "green monkeys," for use in preparing vaccines, were diverted to London airport before transhipment. In the process, a group of at least eight monkeys acquired a disease heretofore unknown to medical science. The disease remains unnamed but might be called Marburg-virus, for it infected at least thirty-two people and killed five of them in Marburg, Germany, and infected two in Frankfurt."

Lederberg continued: "The origin of Marburg-virus is unknown. The threat of a major virus epidemic – a global pandemic – hangs over the head of the species at any time. We were lucky on this occasion, but it was a near miss. It could easily have established a very large focus of infection in countries like India or China or South Vietnam, and in our present knowledge of virology we would have been ill-equipped to stop it from dominating the earth, with a half-billion casualties."[10]

On July 13, 1969, Lederberg wrote a letter to *The New York Times* and castigated the newspaper for discussing the possibility that the astronauts that returned from the *Apollo 11* Moon-landing mission, Armstrong, Aldrin and Collins, offered, "a tangible risk of global infection by lunar microbes." Lederberg explained that the lack of an atmosphere effectively rendered it almost impossible for the Moon to harbor deadly microbes or viruses that could have an effect on our planet. He stressed, however, that the issue of having to "protect the Earth against possible infection from Mars," was one that *definitely* needed resolving and required more study. [11]

Published in the *Post* on August 16, 1970, a two-page feature from Lederberg titled *Engineering Viruses For Health Or Warfare* addressed the issue of modified and created viruses for use in warfare and similar modifications for health purposes. Lederberg stated in part: "We now begin to realize that the intentional release of an infectious particle, be it a virus or bacterium, from the confines of the laboratory or of medical practice must be formally condemned as an irresponsible threat against the whole human community."[12]

When the Space Shuttle *Columbia* broke apart during reentry on February 1, 2003, more than 80 on-board science experiments were lost in the fiery descent. On February 24, 2006, however, it was revealed that Texas State University-San Marcos biologist Robert McLean had salvaged some unexpected surprises from the wreckage: namely, a strain of slow-growing bacteria that had survived the crash, a discovery which may have significant implications for the concept of panspermia, which is the scenario of life "hitchhiking" on rocks ejected from meteorite impacts on one world, and that could travel through space and seed other worlds with life under favorable conditions.

Notably, found within the wreckage of *Columbia* was a bacteria called Microbispora: a slow-growing organism normally found in soil, that McLean determined had probably contaminated the experiment prior to launch. "This organism appears to have survived an atmospheric passage, with the heat and the force of impact," McLean said. "That's only about a fifth of the speed that something on a real meteorite would have to survive, but it is at least five or six times faster than what's been tested before. This is important for panspermia, because if something survives space travel, it eventually has to get down to the Earth and survive passage through the atmosphere and impact. This doesn't prove anything; it just contributes evidence to the plausibility of panspermia."[13]

It was revealed in the British *Observer* newspaper on March 5, 2006 that on July 25, 2001, "blood-red rain" fell over the Kerala district of western India, and continued for the next two months. All along the coast it rained crimson, turning local people's clothes pink, burning leaves on trees and falling as scarlet sheets at some points. Godfrey Louis, a physicist at Mahatma Gandhi University in Kottayam, stated: "If you look at these particles under a microscope, you can see they are not dust, they have a clear biological appearance." Indeed, Louis concluded that the rain was made up of bacteria-like material that had been swept to Earth from a passing comet.

Milton Wainwright, a microbiologist at Sheffield, is currently testing samples of Kerala's "red rain." "It is too early to say what's in the phial," he said. "But it is certainly not dust. Nor is there any DNA there, but then alien bacteria would not necessarily contain DNA."

Louis added: "If anybody hears a theory like this, that it is from a comet, they dismiss it as an unbelievable kind of conclusion. Unless people understand our arguments - people will just rule it out as an impossible thing, that extra-terrestrial biology is responsible for this red rain."[14]

From *The Journal of the American Medical Association* on August 5, 1988, *Medical Science, Infectious Disease And The Unity Of Humankind* comes a two-page paper dealing with Joshua Lederberg's concerns about super-viruses wreaking havoc across the globe; and that it is, perhaps, an appropriate issue with which to bring this *Introduction* to a close. As Lederberg noted in the final paragraph of this paper: "The microbe that felled one child in a distant continent yesterday can reach yours today and seed a global pandemic tomorrow." Without doubt, that is a sobering and disturbing thought.[15]

And it is a thought made even more sobering and disturbing by the fact that - according to a wealth of data uncovered by Robert Wood, and presented here, under one, unified cover for the first time - elements of the United States Government, Intelligence Community, and Military may have secretly known at least sixty years ago that extraterrestrial-originated viruses of an utterly lethal nature were a very real threat to the human species, if not to life on Earth as a whole.

The story that follows is a strange and controversial one, and encompasses incredible tales of shadowy whistleblowers; leaked, and apparently-still-classified, documents of the highest classification; *Deep Throat*-style sources buried within the heart of the world of international espionage; crashed UFOs; dead alien bodies held in cryogenic storage within secure official facilities; and a cover-up of manifestly epic proportions that had its origins in the harsh deserts of New Mexico in the summer of 1947, and that extends to the heart of the White House itself. As will now become apparent.

* * *

Preface Notes

1. *The Treaty on Principles Governing the Activities of States in the Exploration and Use of Outer Space, Including the Moon and Other Celestial Bodies*, October 10, 1967.

2. *Alien Infection*, Leslie Mullen. See: www.astrobio.net/news/modules.php?op=modload&name=News&file=article&sid=570

3. *Sample Return Missions Scare Some Researchers* (author not credited). See: www.space.com/searchforlife/planet_protection_000407.html

4. *Alien Microbe Reported Found in Earth's Atmosphere*, Robert Roy Britt. See: http://www.space.com/scienceastronomy/planetearth/alien_bacteria_001127.html

5. *Far-Out Theory Ties SARS Origins to Comet*, Stefan Lovgren, *National Geographic News*, June 3, 2003. See:
http://news.nationalgeographic.com/news/2003/06/0603_030603_sarsspace.html

6. *Exobiology: Approaches to Life Beyond the Earth*, Joshua Lederberg, *Science*, Vol. 132, No. 3424, August 12, 1960.

7. *A Treaty on Germ Warfare* by Joshua Lederberg, *Washington Post*, September 24, 1966.

8. *Contamination of Mars,* Joshua Lederberg with Carl Sagan and Elliott C. Levinthal, Smithsonian Institution, June 1967.

9. *The Infamous Black Death May Return To Haunt Us*, Joshua Lederberg, *Washington Post*, August 31, 1968.

10. *Mankind Had A Near Miss From A Mystery Pandemic*, Joshua Lederberg, *Washington Post*, September 7, 1969.

11. *New York Times*, July 13, 1969.

12. *Engineering Viruses For Health Or Warfare*, Joshua Lederberg, *Washington Post,* August 16, 1970.

13. *Texas State Research Sheds New Light On Panspermia*, Texas State University Press Release, February 24, 2006. See: www.astrobiology.com/news/viewpr.html?pid=19104

14. *Red Rain Could Prove That Aliens Have Landed*, Amelia Gentleman and Robin McKie, *Observer*, March 5 2006.

15. *Medical Science, Infectious Disease And The Unity Of Humankind*, Joshua Lederberg, *The Journal of the American Medical Association*, August 5, 1988.

Chapter 1
Roswell

The genesis of the astonishing story that this book chronicles largely has its roots in a controversial series of events that occurred in New Mexico in the summer of 1947, and chiefly at a place that is now inextricably and forever linked with the UFO mystery: Roswell. On July 8, 1947, the *Roswell Daily Record* newspaper announced in bold headlines that staff at the nearby Roswell Army Air Force (RAAF) base had recovered the remains of a crashed, unidentified flying object. Under the headline *RAAF Captures Flying Saucer On Ranch In Roswell Region*, the newspaper, directly quoting the base's Press Information Officer, Walter Haut, reported the following:

"The many rumors regarding the flying disc became a reality yesterday when the Intelligence office of the 509th Bomb Group of the Eighth Air Force, Roswell Army Air Field, was fortunate to gain possession of a disc through the cooperation of one of the local ranchers and the sheriff's office of Chaves County. The flying object landed on a ranch near Roswell sometime last week. Not having phone facilities, the rancher stored the disc until such time as he was able to contact the sheriff's office, who in turn notified Maj. Jesse A. Marcel of the 509th Bomb Group Intelligence Office. Action was immediately taken and the disc was picked up at the rancher's home. It was inspected at the Roswell Army Air Field and subsequently loaned by Major Marcel to higher headquarters."[1]

The military would hastily retract this statement, however, substituting it for a far more down to earth one, in which, it was asserted, the materials found "near Roswell," and brought to the base, originated with nothing stranger than a weather balloon. In an effort to add further weight to this new scenario, photographs showing Brigadier General Roger Ramey, of the Eighth Air Force at Fort Worth, Texas, surrounded by what were quite obviously mundane balloon-based materials, were taken and paraded for one and all to see. The press, unfortunately, totally bought into the cover-up, hook, line, and sinker. Stranger still: no one within the media thought to ask the military an obvious question: why were its highly trained personnel initially unable to differentiate between a

Flying Saucer and a weather balloon?[2]

And for three decades that question remained unanswered – until UFO researcher and nuclear physicist Stanton T. Friedman began digging into the mystery.

It was January 20, 1978 and Friedman was lecturing in Baton Rouge, Louisiana. While there he took part in a variety of interviews with local media. It was during an interval in one such interview at a television station in town that Friedman was introduced to the station's manager, who was a good friend of none-other than the still-surviving Jesse Marcel; and who, according to the official press release from the RAAF, was a key player in the recovery of the strange materials found out in the New Mexican desert on that fateful day back in July 1947. Thus began Friedman's intense quest – that continues to this day – to learn the truth about Roswell.[3]

When interviewed, Marcel would state that: "I saw a lot of wreckage but no complete machine. It had disintegrated before it hit the ground. The wreckage was scattered over an area about three quarters of a mile long and several hundred feet wide. I was pretty well acquainted with most everything that was in the air at that time, both ours and foreign. I was also acquainted with virtually every type of weather-observation or radar-tracking device being used by either the civilians or the military. What it was we didn't know. We just picked up the fragments." Marcel was certain, however, that the debris was unlike anything he had ever seen before or since, and added that, "it certainly wasn't anything built by us."[4]

As Friedman's research progressed, he came into contact with another investigator, William Moore, who had also uncovered strands of what sounded very much like the same event, albeit from the perspective of additional witnesses. The two began to share data, and were able to determine that the location where the crash and subsequent recovery had occurred was an incredibly isolated piece of farmland known as the Foster Ranch. Situated around seventy-five miles north of the town of Roswell, New Mexico, at the time the ranch was worked by William Ware "Mac" Brazel who, having died in the 1960s, was unfortunately and obviously not available for interview. But, there were others who remembered that heady period very well, indeed.

Brazel's son, Bill, related a highly intriguing account about the nature of the materials recovered at the ranch. It was, he said, "something on the order of tinfoil except that [it] wouldn't tear. You could wrinkle it and lay it back down and it immediately resumed its original shape. [It was] quite pliable, but you couldn't crease or bend it like ordinary metal. Almost like a plastic, but definitely metallic in nature. Dad once said that the Army had once told him it was not anything made by us."[5]

And, as time progressed, retired Major Jesse Marcel also began to divulge further data on the strange debris found out in the blistering heat of the New Mexico desert: "[It] could not be bent or broken or even dented by a sixteen-pound sledge hammer. Almost weightless, like a metal with plastic properties."[6]

Another story, and one that was of great significance to the controversy of what did or did not crash, came from Vern and Jean Maltais, a married couple who stated that a friend of theirs, Grady Barnett, who was a field engineer attached to the Soil Conservation Service, had guardedly informed them that at some point in the summer of 1947, he had stumbled upon the remains of a very unusual looking vehicle on New Mexico's Plains of San Augustin that resembled "a kind of disk [that] looked like dirty stainless steel." Sprawled around the object were a number of dead bodies of a very unusual nature: all were short, with oversized baldheads, and "oddly spaced eyes." Barnett stood staring for a while at the shocking scene, unsure of what he should do. That is, until a detachment of military personnel quickly arrived on the scene and *told* him what to do: remain silent and say nothing to anyone.[7]

In 1980, the case was taken to a whole new level when William Moore co-authored with Charles Berlitz a book on the case that was titled, quite appropriately, *The Roswell Incident*. At the time that the book was published, most of the available evidence in hand, was that which had been uncovered by Friedman and Moore. And, five years later, the still-on-going research of the pair had led to the identification of almost a hundred people who were implicated in the events of July 1947 to varying degrees.[8]

A new development of some significance occurred in July 1985, when Moore spoke at the annual symposium of the Mutual UFO Network (MUFON) at St. Louis, Missouri. Moore revealed the intriguing story of what had taken place when Friedman had carefully broached the "alien body" angle of the Roswell story with a man named Lewis Rickett, who had been stationed at Roswell at the time with the Counter Intelligence Corps (CIC).

In Friedman's own words: "When I mentioned bodies, Rickett clearly reacted and indicated that this was an area he couldn't talk about. He indicated there were different levels of security about this work - that a directive had come down placing this at a high level. He went on to say that certain subjects were discussed only in rooms that couldn't be bugged."[9]

The team of Moore and Friedman was not the only one looking into the complexities of the Roswell story. Additional data, of an equally startling nature, began to surface in the late 1980s, and continued well into the 1990s, from researchers Kevin Randle and Don Schmitt. The collective data that the pair uncovered told a provocative story: it was reportedly on the night of July 4, 1947, that a stricken vehicle from another world crashed outside of Roswell, having already disgorged a considerable amount of material on the Foster Ranch, following, presumably, some form of mid-air calamity. The object was not of a classic-saucer shape, however. Rather, it was somewhat narrow with what was described as a bat-like wing, and was around thirty feet in length – this point having been stressed particularly by CIC man Lewis Rickett.[10]

Interestingly, also according to Rickett, in September 1947 he became embroiled in the Roswell affair at a deep level when he spent a period of time working with Dr. Lincoln La Paz of the University of New Mexico. During the Second World War, while on leave from Ohio State, La Paz had served as Research Mathematician at the New Mexico Proving Ground and as Technical Director, Operations Analysis Section, with the Second Air Force. During this period his interests shifted to ballistics and then, specifically, to the study of meteorites. In 1945, La Paz joined the faculty of the University of New Mexico and founded the Institute of Meteoritics, whose Director he remained until 1966. From 1945 to 1953 he also served as Head of the Department of Mathematics and Astronomy and, from 1953 to 1962, as Director of the Division of Astronomy.[11]

At a time when meteorites were widely viewed as curiosities, La Paz had the vision to recognize their scientific significance. He established active meteorite research programs at the University of New Mexico and described numerous new meteorites, many of which he had personally recovered. La Paz also, almost single-handedly, established the outstanding meteorite collection at the University of New Mexico and his research resulted in the publication of over 120 scientific articles and books, and he also helped establish the journal *Meteoritics* and served as President of the Meteoritical Society. La Paz died on October 19, 1985 in Albuquerque, New Mexico.[12]

The story that Rickett told as it related to Roswell, was that he and La Paz were assigned to specifically determine the "speed and trajectory" of the vehicle that had crashed. Interestingly, the pair found what was interpreted to be a "possible touchdown point," where, perhaps, the vehicle had made an emergency landing before complete disaster struck. This site was described as being around five miles from where rancher Brazel located the strange materials on the Foster Ranch. Notably, at the site of the touchdown, the sand had reportedly been crystallized as the result of what was deemed to be exposure to an extraordinarily high temperature. Significantly, Rickett recalled that La Paz had prepared an official report on their collective findings for the attention of cleared personnel in the Pentagon, that offered the theory that what had crashed was some form of "unmanned interplanetary probe."

That La Paz was not briefed in advance on the fact that bodies were also apparently recovered (hence his conclusion that the device was "unmanned"), suggests strongly that, as Rickett had advised Friedman, "there were different levels of security" surrounding Roswell, and that "need-to-know" was an overwhelming factor in the extent to which official players in the story were briefed, or were *not* briefed, on aspects of what had occurred.[13]

Randle and Schmitt concluded, based on the testimony of their sources, that as many as five alien bodies were found in the desert, one of which might have survived the initial crash. Notably, no less a source than Edwin Easley, who was the Provost Marshal at Roswell, made comments about "the creatures;" while Sergeant Melvin E. Brown stated that, "They looked Asian but had larger heads and no hair. They looked a yellow color."[14]

Chillingly, a death-threat was made to the family of Frankie Rowe, whose father served with the Roswell Fire Department at the time of the crash, and who was implicated in the controversy. According to Rowe, her father guardedly confided in her family that he was a witness to both unusual materials and strange bodies, as well as one, solitary being that had survived the desert impact: "The one that was walking was about the size of a 10 year old child, and it didn't have any hair...it seemed so scared and lost and afraid." Rowe adds that after the events in which her father was implicated had occurred, a number of military personnel came to the family home and made it abundantly clear that if anyone so much as said a word about the Roswell events, "they might just take us out to the middle of the desert and shoot all of us and nobody would ever find us."[15]

Glenn Dennis, a mortician at Ballard's Funeral Home in Roswell, has made provocative statements on Roswell, too, and has signed a sworn affidavit, asserting that a friend of his at the Roswell Army Air Force base, a nurse, had secretly confided in him that an autopsy of one of the Roswell bodies had been undertaken on-base: "She went into this room to get some supplies and saw two doctors in there with a gurney and these small bodies that were in a rubber sheet or body pouch. Two of the bodies had been very badly mangled, like maybe the predators had been eating on them...one of the hands was severed from the body, and when they flipped it over, there were little tiny suction cups on the inside of the fingers...The heads were large, eyes were set in. The skulls were soft like a newborn baby's; they were pliable. The ears, instead of one canal, had two canals, no lobes or anything, just a little flap over each canal. The mouths were just very small slits. Their face and nose were concave."[16]

Reporter Johnny McBoyle's account fits the pattern of events, too. McBoyle is known to have seen what was described as a "big crumpled dishpan" at the crash-site, and had reported back to Roswell's KSWS Radio Station that: "The Army is there and they are going to pick it up. And get this – they're saying something about little men being on board." McBoyle would later decline to elaborate upon his knowledge of what it was that had occurred in the New Mexican desert.[17]

What was perhaps one of the most significant contributions to the crashed UFO controversy surfaced on November 29, 1983 from Dr. Robert Irving Sarbacher, of the Washington Institute of Technology Oceanographic and Physical Sciences, who wrote the following to UFO researcher and co-author of the book, *UFO Crash at Aztec*, William Steinman:

"Dear Mr. Steinman: I am sorry I have taken so long in answering your letters.

"However, I have moved my office and have had to make a number of extended trips. To answer your last question in your letter of October 14, 1983, there is no particular reason I feel I shouldn't or couldn't answer any and all of your questions. I am delighted to answer all of them to the best of my ability.

"You listed some of your questions in your letter of September 12th. I will attempt to answer them as you had listed them.

"1. Relating to my own experience regarding recovered flying saucers, I had no association with any of the people involved in the recovery and have no knowledge regarding the dates of the recoveries. If I had I would send it to you.

"2. Regarding verification that persons you list were involved, I can say only this: John von Neuman was definitely involved. Dr. Vannevar Bush was definitely involved, and I think Dr. Robert Oppenheimer also.

"My association with the Research and Development Board under Doctor Compton during the Eisenhower administration was rather limited so that although I had been invited to participate in several discussions associated with the reported recoveries, I could not personally attend the meetings. I am sure that they would have asked Dr. von Braun and the others that you listed were probably asked and may or may not have attended. This is all I know for sure.

"3. I did receive some official reports when I was in my office at the Pentagon but all of these were left there as the time we were never supposed to take them out of the office.

"4. I do not recall receiving any photographs such as you request so I am not in a position to answer. 5. I have to make the same reply as on No. 4.

"I recall the interview with Dr. Brenner of the Canadian Embassy. I think the answers I gave him were the ones you listed. Naturally, I was more familiar with the subject matter under discussion, at that time. Actually I would have been able to give more specific answers had I attended the meetings concerning the subject. You must understand that I took this assignment as a private contribution. We were called "dollar-a-year men". My first responsibility was the maintenance of my own business activity so that my participation was limited.

"About the only thing I remember at this time is that certain materials reported to have come from flying saucer crashes were extremely light and very tough. I am sure our laboratories analyzed them very carefully.

"There were reports that instruments or people operating these machines were also of very light weight, sufficient to withstand the tremendous deceleration and acceleration associated with their machinery. I remember in talking with some of the people at the office that I got the impression these "aliens" were constructed like certain insects we have observed on earth, wherein because of the low mass the inertial forces involved in operation of these instruments would be quite low.

"I still do not know why the high order of classification has been given and why the denial of the existence of these devices.

"I am sorry it has taken me so long to reply but I suggest you get in touch with the others who may be more directly involved in this program.

"Sincerely Yours, Dr. Robert I. Sarbacher."[18]

Despite the wealth of testimony and data that surfaced between 1947 and the late 1990s, the Government steadfastly ignored all of the claims made about Roswell. That is, until 1994, when, in response to questions asked by the late Congressman for New Mexico, Steven Schiff, the United States Air Force conceded that a mundane weather balloon was *not* the culprit behind the Roswell controversy, after all. Rather, asserted the Air Force, the device that had come down on the Foster Ranch was a balloon that originated with a classified operation known as Mogul, and that utilized balloons to carry radar reflectors and acoustic sensors aloft for the purpose of determining the state of Soviet nuclear weapons research.[19]

Then, in 1997, and in a very surprising move, the Air Force addressed, in a full-length report, the controversy surrounding the allegations that unusual bodies were found in the New Mexico desert. The Air Force's conclusions were that people had mistakenly seen crash-test-dummies utilized in parachute-based experiments. The fact that such experiments did not even begin until the early 1950s did not faze the Air Force in the slightest, who arrogantly proclaimed that firsthand witnesses to the bodies had *all* mistaken the year in question due to what officials ingeniously termed "time-compression."[20]

32

But, despite the best efforts of the Pentagon, the mystery of Roswell continues to rumble and reverberate, for one prime reason: aside from a brief FBI Teletype of July 1947 that discusses the case in terms that do not make it at all clear what was actually recovered, *no* officially-declassified documents have *ever* surfaced into the public domain that reveal the truth about Roswell. Indeed, the Air Force and the Pentagon conceded that even they could not find *any* files confirming the Mogul and Crash-Test-Dummy scenarios, and that all such theories offered by the Air Force were simply that: theories, and nothing else.

At an *unofficial* level, however, documents on Roswell *have* surfaced, and they tell the story of the still-classified events that occurred deep in the deserts of New Mexico in July 1947. Collectively, this material has become known as the MJ-12 Documents. According to the documentation, in the immediate wake of the Roswell affair a super-secret group was established by President Harry Truman – variously referred to as MJ-12, Majestic 12 or Majic 12. Staffed by the elite of the intelligence world, the military, and the scientific community, it was the task of MJ-12 to investigate the truth behind the Roswell events and the larger, collective UFO mystery, and to carefully ensure that the shocking truth never reached the eyes or ears of the public or the media.

What you are about to read is the story of those documents, of their origins and content, of the military and intelligence insiders who leaked them to the UFO research community, and of the biggest and darkest secrets of all: namely, that we are not alone in the Universe, and that our unearthly visitors may possibly pose a direct, and very lethal, biological hazard to the human species.

* * *

Chapter 1 Notes

1. *Roswell Daily Record*, 8 July 1947.

2. *The Roswell Incident*, Charles Berlitz and William L. Moore, Granada Publishing Ltd., 1980.

3. *The Roswell Incident: Beginning of the Cosmic Watergate*, Stanton T. Friedman and William L. Moore, MUFON Symposium Proceedings, 1981.

4. *The Roswell Incident*, Charles Berlitz and William L. Moore, Granada Publishing Ltd., 1980.

5. *The Roswell Investigation: New Evidence, New Conclusions*, William L. Moore, 1982.

6. Ibid.

7. *Crash at Corona*, Stanton T. Friedman and Don Berliner, Paragon House, 1992.

8. *The Roswell Incident*, Charles Berlitz and William L. Moore, Granada Publishing Ltd., 1980.

9. *Crashed Saucers: Evidence in the Search for Proof*, William L. Moore, MUFON Symposium Proceedings, 1985.

10. *The Truth About the UFO Crash at Roswell*, Kevin D. Randle and Donald R. Schmitt, M. Evans, 1994. *UFO Crash at Roswell*, Kevin D. Randle and Donald R. Schmitt, Avon, 1991.

11. Ibid. *The Roswell Incident*, Charles Berlitz and William L. Moore, Granada Publishing Ltd., 1980. For background on Lincoln La Paz, see: http://www.math.osu.edu/history/biographies/lapaz

12. www.math.ohio-state.edu/history/biographies/lapaz

13. *The Truth About the UFO Crash at Roswell*, Kevin D. Randle and Donald R. Schmitt, M. Evans, 1994. *UFO Crash at Roswell*, Kevin D. Randle and Donald R. Schmitt, Avon, 1991.

14. Ibid. *Alien Liaison*, Timothy Good, Random Century Ltd., 1991. *Alien Contact*, Timothy Good, Morrow, 1992.

15. *The Truth About the UFO Crash at Roswell*, Kevin D. Randle and Donald R. Schmitt, M. Evans, 1994. *UFO Crash at Roswell*, Kevin D. Randle and Donald R. Schmitt, Avon, 1991.

16. *Roswell in Perspective*, Karl Pflock, The Fund for UFO Research, 1994.

17. *Roswell in Perspective*, Karl Pflock, The Fund for UFO Research, 1994. *The Truth About the UFO Crash at Roswell*, Kevin D. Randle and Donald R. Schmitt, M. Evans, 1994. *UFO Crash at Roswell*, Kevin D. Randle and Donald R. Schmitt, Avon, 1991. *The Roswell Incident*, Charles Berlitz and William L. Moore, Granada Publishing Ltd., 1980. *Crash at Corona*, Stanton T. Friedman and Don Berliner, Paragon House, 1992.

18. Letter from Dr. Robert I. Sarbacher to William Steinman, November 29, 1983.

19. Report of Air Force Research Regarding the Roswell Incident, Colonel Richard L. Weaver, United States Air Force, 1994. *The Roswell Report: Fact vs. Fiction in the New Mexico Desert*, Colonel Richard L. Weaver, United States Air Force, 1995. *Results of a Search for Records Concerning the 1947 Crash Near Roswell, New Mexico*, General Accounting Office, July 28, 1995.

20. *The Roswell Report: Case Closed*, Captain James McAndrew, United States Air Force, July 4, 1997.

Chapter 2
Majestic

The origins of the MJ-12 story can be traced back to 1980. It was in September of that year that *The Roswell Incident*, written by William Moore and Charles Berlitz, was published. In an effort to bring the book to the attention of the media and the general public, Moore embarked on a promotional tour that included an interview with WOW Radio in Omaha, Nebraska. After the interview was concluded, the radio station received a telephone call from a man asking to speak with Moore. As luck would have it, Moore was still on the premises.

The caller identified himself as a colonel from nearby Orfutt Air Force Base. "We think you're the only one we've heard that seems to know what he's talking about," the colonel told Moore. Not only that: the colonel wanted to meet Moore personally "for coffee and a chat." Moore, however, was due to embark on the next leg of the tour and advised the colonel that he would call him back at the earliest opportunity.

Interestingly, however, after concluding an interview for Albuquerque's KOB Radio shortly afterwards, and before he had the opportunity to return the call from Orfutt AFB, Moore was told there was a call waiting for him. Again, the message was the same: "We think you're the only one we've heard that seems to know what he's talking about." This, of course, grabbed Moore's attention, and he wasted no time at all in arranging a meeting with the mysterious caller – that occurred in an Albuquerque restaurant a few days later.

The elderly man that Moore would ultimately meet (and who Moore would always publicly refer to as the "Falcon" to protect his identity) claimed to represent a group of individuals within the U.S. Intelligence community that desired an end to the overwhelming secrecy that surrounded the UFO issue. Not only that: this same group was looking for a reputable and suitable figure within the UFO research community that would be willing to work with them, and assist in the controlled release of certain materials and documents to the public as part of a carefully planned and executed program to acclimatize the world to the idea that aliens were among us.

Moore considered this utterly unique scenario and finally a deal was reached: he would come on board. After all, Moore was himself determined to uncover the truth about UFOs, and he saw this as an ideal way of uncovering that same truth. But there was a catch: the man told Moore that he and his colleagues would require Moore to do some work for them. This would include reporting to the Falcon on the results of Intelligence-based disinformation operations against American citizens.

At the close of the meeting, the Falcon handed Moore a manila envelope that he thought Moore would find "interesting." It contained a one-page, seemingly official, and highly classified, document titled *Collection Requirements for Project "Silver Sky,"* the subject matter of which was a series of significant UFO encounters that had occurred in New Mexico in 1969 – and all within 50 miles of the town of Roswell, no less. After the strange meeting, Moore began to research the document but found, to his concern, that it was without any shadow of a doubt, a complete fabrication. And at the next meeting with the Falcon, in October 1980, an angry Moore informed the Falcon of his conclusions with respect to the document and demanded to know what was going on.

The Falcon claimed that this was merely a "test" to see if he, Moore, was trustworthy and to determine if he could be considered a good, rigorous investigator. The last thing the group wanted at that stage, said the Falcon, was to have someone shouting their mouth off to one and all. Instead, Moore did exactly what they hoped he would do: he researched the document carefully and quietly, and said nothing to anyone else until given the go-ahead to do so. Moore, the Falcon said, had passed the test.[1]

And, as a direct result of this odd situation, and over the course of the next four years, Moore found himself embroiled in what was truly a cloak-and-dagger world: he would be required to drive or fly to selected, secret locations where he would be provided with, by shady characters within the world of espionage and intelligence, what were purported to be ultra-classified documents on crashed UFOs, dead aliens, live aliens, and secret UFO projects of a dizzying nature. A number of those same documents would refer to a secret group that seemed to be a key player in the American Government's UFO program. That group was MJ-12.[2]

Among the more significant documents that Moore received was one that has become known as the *Carter Briefing Document*. Reportedly, it is a series of notes compiled as part of a briefing for former United States President Jimmy Carter, after his election in 1976. The documents tell a story that would become very familiar to Moore: one of crashed UFOs, alien contact, Top Secret projects designed to hide the truth from the public, and attempts by the military and the world of intelligence to understand what it was that lay at the heart of the UFO puzzle.[3]

Moore also received copies of what were purported to be interdepartmental CIA papers of the mid-to-late 1970s, supposedly prepared by senior figures within MJ-12; as well as various other documents of a similar nature that reinforced the central themes of the story: the crash and retrieval by the U.S. military of an alien spacecraft at Roswell, New Mexico, in 1947, and the establishment of the MJ-12 group. But without any shadow of a doubt, the most significant document that Moore received from his intelligence contacts was one that was sent to a colleague of Moore: Jaime Shandera, a Los Angeles-based television producer who had been working with Moore on this operation.[4]

It was December 11, 1984 when Shandera received in the mail a manila envelope that contained a 35mm roll of film that, when developed, told an astonishing story. Classified *Top Secret/Majic Eyes Only*, the document can essentially be broken down into two parts. The first is a 1952 briefing for President-elect Eisenhower informing him of the reality of the UFO crash at Roswell; and the second is a 1947 memorandum from President Harry Truman to Secretary of Defense James Forrestal, authorizing the establishment of MJ-12.

According to the documents, the membership of MJ-12 included Rear Admiral Roscoe Hillenkoetter, who was the first Director of the CIA; Rear Admiral Sidney Souers, the first Director of Central Intelligence; the Commanding General of Air Materiel Command: General Nathan Twining; and Dr. Vannevar Bush, who was the head of the Joint Research and Development Board, and who, in 1983, Dr. Robert Sarbacher had informed researcher William Steinman was a central player in the crashed UFO saga.[5]

Moore and Shandera (along with Stanton Friedman) worked quietly and carefully for more than two years as they sought to determine the truth behind the documents; however, in the summer of 1987 and after British author Timothy Good highlighted them in his book *Above Top Secret: The Worldwide UFO Cover-Up* (having received them from a source that he, Good, refuses to name three decades later), the team of Moore-Shandera-Friedman made their copy of the documents available to the media and to the UFO research community.[6]

According to the 1952 document: "On 24 June, 1947, a civilian pilot flying over the Cascade Mountains in the State of Washington observed nine flying disc-shaped aircraft traveling in formation at a high rate of speed...little of substance was learned about the objects until a local rancher reported that one had crashed in a remote region of New Mexico located approximately seventy-five miles northwest of Roswell Army Air Base..."

The most controversial and sensational aspect of the Roswell event, namely the reported recovery of alien bodies at the crash site, was also addressed within the pages of the *Eisenhower Briefing Document*:

"On 07 July 1947, a secret operation was begun to assure recovery of the wreckage of this object for scientific study. During the course of this operation, aerial reconnaissance discovered that four small human-like beings had apparently ejected from the craft at some point before it exploded. These had fallen to earth about two miles east of the wreckage site. All four were dead and badly decomposed due to action by predators and exposure to the elements during the approximately one week time period which had elapsed before their discovery. A special scientific team took charge of removing these bodies for study."

Moreover, it was stated with regard to the origin of the aliens: "Since it is virtually certain that these craft do not originate in any country on earth, considerable speculation has centered around what their point of origin might be and how they get here. Mars was and remains a possibility, although some scientists, most notably Dr. [Donald] Menzel, consider it more likely that we are dealing with beings from another solar system."[7]

Were the documents real? Were they disinformation? Or were they nothing more than a hoax? After the MJ-12 papers surfaced into the public domain, a wealth of research was undertaken into their contents, as well as forensic analyses of the style, typeface and format. Stanton Friedman is certain that the documents are genuine, leaked documents.[8]

The FBI and the Air Force have both publicly stated that, in their collective opinion, *all* of the MJ-12 papers are fabrications. Two decades later, the debate concerning the *Eisenhower Briefing Document* and the *Truman Directive* continues to rumble on.[9]

In 1994, *another* MJ-12 document surfaced. Known as the *Special Operations Manual* and titled *Extraterrestrial Entities and Technologies – Recovery and Disposal*, and dated April 1954, it focuses upon the recovery methods that should be employed with regard to crashed UFOs, as well as methods of deception to keep the public and the media ignorant of the facts. The *Manual* is discussed in-depth in a later chapter.[10]

But for what is without doubt the most significant story in the saga of MJ-12, we have to turn our attention to a man named Timothy S. Cooper, of Big Bear Lake, California. In July 1991, the famed crashed-UFO researcher Leonard Stringfield published his penultimate document on his lengthy research titled *UFO Crash/Retrievals: The Inner Sanctum, Status Report VI*. The report, running to 142-pages, was Stringfield's longest and most comprehensive study of data and testimony on the crashed UFO controversy.

Contained within the pages of *The Inner Sanctum* were various accounts provided to Stringfield by Cooper, who was then a relative newcomer to the UFO research scene. Cooper had been quietly and carefully researching the issue of crashed UFOs for several years, and had provided Stringfield with some startling data that he, Cooper, had acquired from a number of sources in the military and in the intelligence community.[11]

Those sources included Albert Bruce Collins, who, in the 1940s, had been assigned to both the University of Chicago and Los Alamos. Collins had knowledge of crashed UFO incidents in that period, along with "bizarre biological experiments" and "unusual research into nuclear powered aircraft" that had been undertaken by the military in the deserts of New Mexico at the same time. Cooper also spoke with a former nurse who was stationed at Los Alamos in the mid-to-late 1940s, and who had confirmed to Cooper her knowledge of a number of strange bodies that had been brought to the base on various occasions from 1945 to 1947. All were small in height, with "deformed," hairless heads.[12]

"Dr. Epigoni" was another source that Cooper had spoken with by 1991, and whose story Stringfield related within the pages of *The Inner Sanctum*. Again, Epigoni (who Cooper said had worked with Albert Einstein, Edward Teller, and Robert Oppenheimer) confirmed that, yes: UFOs *had* crashed to Earth.[13]

By far the most interesting of Cooper's sources, however, was a man that Cooper called "Bob," and who had claimed to Cooper, in a September 9, 1990 interview, that while stationed at Holloman Air Force Base in 1948, he had been ordered by a Colonel Paul Helmick to "print a typed report of 50-pages that included some black and white photographs." Cooper added to Stringfield that: "Bob told me that the report basically contained information about the crash or landing of a UFO at White Sands Missile Range. What he saw in the photos was amazing. The depicted a saucer-like craft on the ground...the craft was shiny and metallic with no apparent markings nor any visible propulsion system."[14]

Cooper would later provide Stringfield with the cover-page of a document that he had acquired from one of his sources that was dated July 16, 1947, and that was titled: *Air Accident Report on "Flying Disc" aircraft near the White Sands Proving Ground, New Mexico*. Again, this reinforced the crash of a UFO in New Mexico in the summer of 1947. It also reinforced the significant fact that Cooper was cultivating interesting sources of data within the military and intelligence communities. Stringfield published a copy of the cover-page of the *Air Accident Report* in his final paper on crashed UFOs. Titled *UFO Crash/Retrievals: Search for Proof in a Hall of Mirrors, Status Report VII*, it was published in February 1994. Stringfield died in December 1994.[15]

It was during this period of time that Cooper was also speaking with researchers Stanton T. Friedman and Timothy Good, and providing them with copies of seemingly official documentation on MJ-12 and crashed UFOs that he had secured from a number of clandestine sources in the official world. Once again, the documents reinforced the scenario of one or more UFO crashes in New Mexico in 1947. It was as a result of Cooper having contacted Friedman that Robert Wood subsequently came to know Cooper.

As Robert Wood explained: "I had known [Stanton Friedman] since 1969 as a careful UFO investigator. When I retired in 1993 from research and development management at McDonnell

Douglas, Stan initiated contact with me, knowing that I might have more time for UFO research. At about the same time, Walt Andrus asked if I would be willing to serve as the Director for Research for MUFON International."

Wood continued: "Stan receives many inquiries, and he had had correspondence with Timothy S. Cooper of Big Bear Lake, who had reported receiving documents in his mailbox and from other sources having to do with the covert U.S. UFO program. Stan asked me if I would be willing to drive to Big Bear Lake to meet Tim since I was closer than he was in Canada."[16]

And so, as a result, on September 17, 1996, Robert Wood wrote thus to Cooper:

"Stan has shared with me some of your transmittals to him, and they have, in my opinion, a rather strong ring of authenticity. As you may know, no document can be deemed totally authentic in the absence of an original. Therefore, the issues of provenance are of great importance, especially in the context of the remarkable documents you have been receiving.

"Therefore I would be eager to chat with you for an hour or two over lunch or whatever you like about the documents that you have been getting, factors relating to revealing the identity of your source, worries you may or may not have about being watched, etc., what authenticity you think each of the documents you have received should get, and other things you would like to discuss."[17]

One week later, on September 24, Wood met Cooper in person for the first time. Wood's comprehensive notes elaborate upon the issue of Cooper and how he became embroiled in the crashed UFO controversy. Notably, those same notes reveal that Cooper's source for the story of the UFO crash at the White Sands Proving Ground (now the White Sands Missile Range), New Mexico in 1947, and cited in Leonard Stringfield's *Status Report* of 1991, was none other than his own father, Harry B. Cooper, who had a lengthy career in the U.S. military:

"The story of his relationship with his father began when his father mentioned some interesting things that he had done in the Army, enough to tweak Timothy's interest in buying and reading *The Roswell Incident* by [Charles Berlitz and William] Moore. His father saw it, and said that there was a lot in there that was accurate. And so he told him his story. He was the person in charge of the reprographics building at Holloman, and one day Colonel [Paul] Helmick [who by then had been identified as the former command- ing officer with the Alamogordo Army Air Force] came with a document pouch locked to his wrist and two MPs with Tommy- guns. They stayed outside.

"All other personnel were sent home, and then Tim's father was told that they were going to run six (or was it ten?) copies of this document, which had photos requiring half tones, even though it might take all night. The photos were apparently Graphic 8 x 10s. They showed a number of silvery objects in the sand and many trucks and personnel. The document was dated the summer of 1947 but the time when this happened was in 1948. The report was addressed to the Commanding General of the Air Materiel Com- mand at Wright Field.

"[Cooper's father] produced the copies and was told when Helmick left that he was to forget everything. Tim had promised his father never to tell anyone this story. However in later conversation with Len Stringfield, he revealed it, changing enough of it (he thought) to keep his father from being identified. Unfortunately, he had left a copy of Len's book with his mother; and when his father was visiting one day he saw the book, and read the story, and became extremely upset because of potential loss of pension and benefits. This remains to this day a major source of friction. I promised Tim that I would make no effort to pursue his father."[18]

In 2004, Nick Redfern secured copies of Harry B. Cooper's official military record, that demonstrated Cooper, Sr., served in the Marine Corps from September 26, 1941 to December 24, 1945; and in the Air Force from October 11, 1947 to July 13, 1960. During the latter service, Cooper *was indeed* stationed at Alamogordo in 1948, and later at March Air Force Base, California; and Wiesbaden Air Base, Germany, which was his last tour of duty. Harry B. Cooper died on September 2, 2000 and is buried in Riverside National Cemetery, California.[19]

But what of the sources who provided Tim Cooper with the many and varied MJ-12 documents? It transpired that Cooper's chief source of documentation was a mysterious and enigmatic figure that called himself Thomas Cantwheel.

Robert Wood is a meticulous recorder of data; and after the meeting he prepared an in-depth summary of his question-and-answer session with Cooper. As Wood noted: "We began the discussion by my giving him a list of the questions I wanted to cover, and before I knew it Tim Was reading from an investigative report folder that he had on Cantwheel. He said that some of this was put together by a friend of his who was a private investigator."[20]

Robert Wood's files demonstrate that, even as far back as 1996, Cooper was privately stating that he had considerable doubts that "Thomas Cantwheel" was the real name of his source. Indeed, Wood's notes taken at the time reveal that no one with the last name of Cantwheel had *ever* been issued with a United States Social Security number, and no one named Cantwheel (Thomas or otherwise) had ever been listed within any United States telephone directory. But if Thomas Cantwheel was not the real name of the source of the data, then who was he? And why had he specifically selected Cooper to be the recipient of what would turn out to be hundreds of pages of documents?[21]

According to Bob Wood's notes on this question: "[Tim Cooper] thinks Cantwheel knew his father to some extent when they were both at Holloman, with Cantwheel being an important counterintelligence officer. He implied that his father didn't know who Cantwheel was, or if he did, he wasn't going to say. Tim chose Stan because of the positive impression he made in a TV appearance."[22]

But even if Cantwheel was unwilling to divulge his real identity, Cooper had been able to ascertain enough data to build up detailed background data on his source. Wood's notes reveal that Cantwheel was very elderly, possibly even in his early nineties; he had a Southern accent; had enlisted in the Army in the 1930s; and later joined the Counter-Intelligence Corps. In addition, Cooper told Wood that Cantwheel had said that, in 1942, he had joined an ultra-secret organization known as the Interplanetary Phenomenon Unit, and stayed with that same organization until 1958. He also asserted that he had worked with the CIA and FBI and retired in the early 1980s. Cantwheel was careful to add, however, that he served in an "active reserve" status until 1989, and as an "inactive reserve" until the mid-1990s. Interestingly, Cooper had learned that Cantwheel, who claimed to be suffering from terminal cancer, had very possibly himself resided in Big Bear Lake until July 1995. And as Cooper had noted, Cantwheel resembled the late actor Henry Fonda in appearance, but with a beard.[23]

But what made a definitive identification of Cantwheel even more difficult to ascertain was the very real possibility that by the time Robert Wood met with Cooper, Cantwheel had already died. Indeed, on February 29, 1996, Cooper had received a letter from Cantwheel dated exactly one week previous that began: "Dear Mr. Cooper: By the time this letter reaches you, I will have left this world. I have cancer and don't have much time."

In that same letter, Cantwheel divulged more data on what it was that had motivated him to speak with Cooper. And, he also revealed one particular startling fact: that some of the documents that he had provided to Cooper were not genuine documents. They were not fakes, either, however. Rather, the documents were, as Cantwheel preferred the term "constructs." A copy of Cantwheel's letter of February 29, 1996 was provided to Wood and explains the facts in his, Cantwheel's, own words:

"There are many things to tell you about the 1947 New Mexico discoveries that I was personally involved with, but, the grave beckons me most earnestly and will not wait any longer.

"First, I'm sorry that I did not seek you out earlier and have open face-to-face chats instead of sending you mail drops. There was good reasons [sic] for this which I will not go into. Secondly, my health does not allow me to get out, especially in the winter. Thirdly, I have poor eyesight and cannot drive a car anymore.

"I have been following your research into the White Sands case since 1990 though you were not aware of it. You're [sic] liaison with the late Springfield [Note: this should be Stringfield], and Friedman, was brought to my attention by my intelligence contact at Fort Meade. You are correct in assuming that there was more than one UFO (incorrectly actually, we know what they are) incident at White Sands aside the Corona case wrongly called the Roswell incident (even though Marcel and Cavitt did find debris that was taken to the Roswell air base). Your father was correct in regards to the classified intelligence report and the secrecy at Holloman AFB."[24]

Cantwheel then turned his attention to the documentation that he had supplied Cooper with: "In regards to the documents, I must assume that you have had them investigated by the so-called 'experts' by now and have determined that some were obvious fakes. Sorry about that. The others were copies and Xeroxed from originals. These came from my personal files.

"As for the manner in which you received them, it was necessary to construct them in a way so as to protect you from criminal prosecution. But, I assure you that the names, dates and places are valid. I think I provided you with enough leads to help you find valuable information that can be found in any library. I hope you will not think too ill of me for leading you on for so long. I believe that in good time, the intelligence community will be forced to open up more UFO intelligence files to the public. UFOs will not go away, and will only increase in intensity.

"In closing, I can only add that the UFO secret has been a costly one, not only in lost credibility by the government, but in human lives as well. During my services for CIC and CIA, I committed many distasteful and, sometime, regrettable acts of skullduggery in the interests of national security for my superiors, and now I will be rewarded for my sins. Live a long and rewarding life Tim. I add a word of caution along with it. TRUST NO ONE COMPLETELY!"[25]

On June 2, 1997, Robert Wood met with Cooper once more at Cooper's Big Bear Lake home. Again, the focus of the conversation was the documents, Cooper's on-going contacts, and Cantwheel. But the elusive Cantwheel was not Cooper's only source of MJ-12 documentation. Another was "Salina," who was alleged to be the daughter of Thomas Cantwheel.

As Ryan Wood stated: "In 1996, Tim Cooper received through the U.S. Mail a handwritten letter from Cantwheel's daughter who claimed to have been employed in the CIA for over 20 years, and [who] was a close associate [of] Deputy Director of Central Intelligence James Jesus Angleton (1954–1974). J.J. Angleton ran the Agency's most secret directorate and reported directly to DCI Allen W. Dulles until 1961.

"Salina claims that the Counter Intelligence (CI) ran all the high-level intelligence collection activities outside of normal channels within the Agency's UFO program initiated by General Walter B. Smith in late 1952. Smith brought in Angleton and Dulles as consultants for the program under what is suspected as MK-ULTRA, MJ-TWELVE, and Operation MAGNITUDE, in conjunction with a State Department intelligence unit for Psy-Op activities and active measures against the Soviets.

"Approved by President Truman under the Top Secret directive dated October 24, 1952, the United States Communications Intelligence Board (USCIB) was directed to reconstitute the USCIB's COMINT activities through the National Security Agency, in which the DCI, Secretary of Defense and State would form a 'Special Committee' to oversee the seven-man USCIB/NSA oversight committee. Salina served as a coordinator between CI and NSA COMINT operations.

"In 1999, Cooper received an alleged original carbon copy of a 1961 CI/MJ-12 directive copy from DCI to MJ1-7 concerning UFO policy and presidential KNT with a letter from former CI employee 'Scotty' outlining Salina's wish to release the directive 'in a responsible manner,' which Cooper gave to the Woods for forensic examination. A very reliable Psy-Op officer who was contracted by the CIA in the 70s has confirmed Salina's existence and employment in J.J. Angleton's CI organization.

"It is possible that MJ-12 was an informal and unauthorized group acting outside of normal intelligence channels, classified above the president, and CI maintained control of it at least until Angleton's dismissal in 1974. It is also possible that the Office of Technical Services (OTS) created and administered MJ-TWELVE, the same office that ran MK-ULTRA and related operations."

Cooper also had three other sources, as Wood noted:

"Source S-1 got his name because the return address and many of the documents had a -1 on the first page. The return address is Las Vegas, Nevada, and he mailed information on three different occasions during the summer with postmarks of Big Bear Lake and Fort Meade, Maryland with return addresses of Las Vegas and a suspiciously torn (not there) return address. The materials supplied included some typed personal cover letters to Tim Cooper. Other photographs arrived as undeveloped film and upon developing were pictures taken of a TV displaying the [Ray] Santilli [Alien Autopsy] film.

"At about 10 pm, 16 September 1999, Tim Cooper met at his front door a man carrying an arm load of documents. He apparently came from a maroon vehicle. He said he was the same person as the one who had called a few days earlier and had been sending him other materials. He apparently was source 'S-2.' He said that he was with Army Intelligence, and had been assigned as a liaison officer with Foreign Technology Division at Dayton. Tim and S-2 spoke for approximately 2–3 minutes with S-2 highlighting some of the contents identified on the previous page. Description withheld to protect identity of source S-2.

"The history of Source S-3 is that Tim Cooper received one letter postmarked from Sacramento, California with the Police Officers Association return address (Pig Bowl). Enclosed was a one-page memo that authorized the creation of the Interplanetary Phenomenon Unit, a part of the Counter Intelligence Corps (CIC)."[26]

Ryan Wood is a key player in the MJ-12 story, and it was Robert Wood who had brought son Ryan into the controversy in 1996:

"About this time I had been sharing some aspects of these document authentication issues with my son Ryan, whose computer skills and creative marketing skills transcended mine. We therefore became partners, with the initial objective of writing a book together that might reveal the history of the United States as reflected by the data in questioned UFO documents.

"However, the document drops to Tim Cooper provided so much more data base and so many difficult authenticity challenges that we set the book idea aside and began to concentrate on the challenge of validating the documents and dealing with the many concerns expressed about their validity. Ryan and I began to become systematically familiar with questioned document procedures and retained selected professionals to deal with these issues. In addition, we visited the U.S. Government Printing Office and obtained basic information relevant to printing techniques available to our Government.

"We made an early decision to share these documents (with Tim Cooper's permission) with others to begin the authentication process, and also to share them with the public in order to bring forward confirming reports if they were indeed genuine and authentic. Generally, we have limited our focus to those documents that are classified Majestic, MAJIC, or MJ-12 or other documents or projects that seem to intimately relate to these."[27]

And now, with the background on Timothy Cooper and his sources, and the way in which Robert Wood came into contact with Cooper all in hand, let us examine the documentation that Cooper obtained.

* * *

Chapter 2 Notes

1. *Out There: The Government's Secret Quest for Extraterrestrials*, Howard Blum, Simon & Schuster, 1990. *Project Beta: The Story of Paul Bennewitz, National Security, and the Creation of a Modern UFO Myth*, Greg Bishop, Paraview-Pocket Books, 2005.

2. Ibid.

3. *The MJ-12 Documents: An Analytical Report*, William L. Moore and Jaime Shandera, Fair Witness Project, Inc., 1990.

4. Ibid.

5. *Above Top Secret: The Worldwide UFO Cover-up*, Timothy Good, Sidgwick & Jackson, 1987. *Alien Contact: Top Secret UFO Files Revealed*, Timothy Good, Morrow, 1993.

6. Ibid.

7. *Top Secret/Majic: Operation Majestic-12 and the United States Government's UFO Cover-Up*, Stanton T. Friedman, Marlowe & Company, 1996. *Eisenhower Briefing Document* available at: www.majesticdocuments.com by downloading: http://209.132.68.98/pdf/eisenhower_briefing.pdf. *Truman Memorandum* available at www.majesticdocuments.com by downloading: http://209.132.68.98/pdf/truman_forrestal.pdf

8. Ibid.

9. *Body Snatchers in the Desert: The Horrible Truth at the Heart of the Roswell Story*, Nick Redfern, Paraview-Pocket Books, 2005.

10. *SOM1-01 Majestic-12 Group Special Operations Manual: Extraterrestrial Entities and Technology, Recovery and Disposal*; available at www.majesticdocuments.com by downloading: http://209.132.68.98/pdf/som101_part1.pdf and: http://209.132.68.98/pdf/som101_part2.pdf

11. *UFO Crash/Retrievals: The Inner Sanctum, Status Report V1*, Leonard Stringfield, published privately, 1991.

12. Ibid.

13. Ibid.

14. Ibid.

15. *UFO Crash Retrievals: Search for Proof in a Hall of Mirrors, Status Report VII*, Leonard Stringfield, published privately, 1994.

16. *Validating the New Majestic Documents*, Robert M. Wood, *Mutual UFO Network Symposium Proceedings*, 2000.

17. Letter from Robert Wood to Timothy Cooper, September 17, 1996.

18. *Questions for Timothy Cooper*, Robert Wood, September 24, 1996.

19. National Archives and Record Administration Form 13164, 2005.

20. *Questions for Timothy Cooper*, Robert Wood, September 24, 1996.

21. Ibid.

22. Letter from Robert Wood to Stanton T. Friedman, September 28, 1996.

23. *Background Investigation of Thomas Cantwheel (AKA), Preliminary*, Timothy S. Cooper, April 18, 1996.

24. Letter from Thomas Cantwheel to Timothy Cooper, February 22, 1996.

25. Ibid.

26. *Document Sources*, Ryan Wood. See: http://www.majesticdocuments.com/sources.php

27. *Validating the New Majestic Documents*, Robert M. Wood, *Mutual UFO Network Symposium Proceedings*, 2000.

Chapter 3
The Cooper Document Collection
February 1942

Collectively, the body of documentation on MJ-12 (and related organizations and operations) acquired by Timothy Cooper from his sources amounts to, literally, thousands of pages. Needless to say, it defies belief that a mere, single hoaxer could be responsible for putting together such a tremendous and staggering amount of highly complex material. Not only that: the documents are typed on numerous, different typewriters, which strongly suggests that they are not the work of one person. In addition, and of critical importance, is the fact that Timothy Cooper provided Robert Wood with many of the original envelopes (displaying postage data), in which the documentation that Cooper received from his various sources was contained.[1]

So that the reader may appreciate the enormity, content and scope of this material (as well as a greater appreciation of what MJ-12 was – and still may be), summaries of the documentation provided by Cooper to Wood are related below.

Among the most interesting examples is a collection of papers that pre-date the Roswell events of 1947 by five years; the earliest being a memo prepared on February 27, 1942 by then-President Franklin D. Roosevelt for the attention of Chief of Staff, General George C. Marshall. The document discusses the famous "Los Angeles Air Raid" of February 25, 1942, in which multiple targets of unknown origin flew over Southern California, and defied both identification and all attempts to shoot them down. To this day, even, the incident is still shrouded in mystery. Notably, the document at issue refers to "atomic secrets learned from study of celestial devices;" as well as an authorization to Vannevar Bush, ordering him to "proceed with the project without further delay."[2]

One week later, on March 5, 1942, according to another document provided to Cooper, Marshall wrote to Roosevelt informing him that in the wake of the invasion of Southern California airspace, the military "recovered an unidentified airplane off the coast of California... with no bearing on conventional explanation." Marshall continued that: "This Headquarters has come to the determination that the mystery airplanes are in fact not earthly and according to secret intelligence sources they are in all probability of interplanetary origin." Moreover, Marshall added: "As a consequence I have issued orders to Army G2 that a special intelligence unit be created to further investigate the phenomenon and report any significant connection between recent incidents and those collected by the director the office of Coordinator of Information."[3]

Two years later, classified research was still continuing: on February 22, 1944 Roosevelt prepared a "Double Top Secret" memo for the attention of a group known as the Special Committee on Non-Terrestrial Science and Technology. The document discusses the need for "coming to grips with the reality that our planet is not the only one harboring intelligent life the universe."[4]

As Ryan Wood notes: "Apparently the Special Committee on Non-terrestrial Science and Technology had been working some time in order to define a clear action. Dr. Bush had presumably presented a proposal from the Committee for an aggressive separate program to apply 'non-terrestrial know-how' to the war effort, but FDR thought that it would threaten the atomic bomb program. Thus, he carefully avoids saying 'no,' but says that we will, 'take every advantage of such wonders that have come to us,' *after* we have won the war."[5]

Chronologically, the next document that Cooper received dated from June 1947. Titled *Relationships with Inhabitants of Celestial Bodies*, it is co-written by the "father of the atom bomb," Robert Oppenheimer, with Albert Einstein. Significant is the fact that this document contains the earliest known reference to *Extraterrestrial Biological Entities* or *EBEs* – terminology allegedly used within cleared-echelons of the intelligence community to describe alien creatures – and discusses the possible nature of the alien presence, its intentions, and the human response to that same presence.[6]

A letter written by Vannevar Bush to President Truman on July 5, 1947 addresses some critically important points, as Ryan Wood notes: "Possibly as a result of the New Mexico events, Vannevar Bush writes a memo to Truman recapping the status of the earlier investigations. As an apparent follow up by FDR to Bush, FDR wrote another letter (which we don't have) in April 1944 requesting recommendations on four specific points. This letter is Bush's answer. The letter also shows an 'OK' and a Harry Truman signature. This letter is stamped with the known authentic 'original' stamp, and was probably produced by a typewriter because of the uniformity of letter spacing. We expect to show, of course, that this format was commonly used by Office of Scientific Research and Development typewriters of the era."[7]

Ryan Wood adds: "Bush restates the FDR questions for Truman's benefit, mentions the assistance of distinguished committees, alludes to the 'many meetings since the events of this summer,' transmits the full reports as appendices, and proposes a 'single mechanism for implementing the recommendations of the several committees.'"[8]

As Wood asks: "Could this be one hugely classified program called Majestic Twelve at the end of the summer? The date of the letter, 5 July, was, of course, coincident with the recoveries going on in New Mexico at that very time. Harry Truman's 'OK' may have been prophetic." Indeed, it may.[9]

A "Directive" to General Nathan Twining from Eisenhower, dated July 8, 1947 authorizes Twining, the head of the Air Materiel Command, to proceed to White Sands to "...make an appraisal of the reported unidentified objects being kept there." Interestingly, Twining's flight log shows that he *did* fly there on the 7th.[10]

Forty-eight hours later, according to the Cooper files, President Truman signed a virtually identical letter authorizing Twining to go to White Sands. "Someone," Ryan Wood concludes, "apparently thought it was so important that the Commander-in-Chief put his name on the spot without 'passing the buck.' Alternatively, Ike himself may have requested a 'back-up' memo."[11]

A three-page *Air Accident Report* concerning the recovery of an aerial vehicle of unknown origin near the White Sands Proving Ground in July 1947 was the next document provided to Timothy Cooper. In its pages, says Ryan Wood: "Twining apparently describes in first order detail the inside of a flying disc, everything from the typewriter-like keys that control the propulsion system, to a thirty-five foot doughnut shaped, one-inch tube inside the craft filled with a clear substance. The significance and consistency of the technical content has not been evaluated, although it is clear that the writing is consistent with 1947 state of the art, not modern."[12]

Also originating in the same time period is a two-page memo

prepared by Twining and dated July 18, 1947, authorizing the activation of a new laboratory to conduct meteorological research and development and upper air research in conjunction with the Electronics Subdivision of the Engineering Division of the AMC. It states in part: "In view of the close relationship and interdependence of research in meteorology and research in electromagnetic compressional wave propagation, action is being taken to reorganize the present Applied Propagation Laboratory of Watson laboratories in the Atmospheric Laboratory, and expand its functions to include research and development in meteorology and related geophysical fields."[13]

Later, the memo goes on to state that: "...funds requested for F.Y. 1949 Project 680-11, Atmospheric Research and applied scientific research of the upper atmosphere, a total sum of $6,000,000 has been specified..."[14]

Ryan Wood comments: "What a huge sum of money in 1949 to study the 'upper atmosphere.' A more logical interpretation is that we are analyzing flying saucers, their technology, why they are here, and what are we going to do about it."[15]

An August 1947 document marked for the attention of the Commanding General of the Army Air Forces discusses the control of restricted data; something that led Thomas Cantwheel to inform Timothy Cooper that: "SAC [Strategic Air Command] wanted to keep certain AAF [Army Air Force] personnel from accessing the out-going messages from Roswell AAF to SAC headquarters that would identify AAF personnel responsible for the transport of classified material to Wright Field, and the personnel who were responsible for disposition of the wreckage and bodies found near Socorro and Corona, New Mexico."[16]

Two-pages in length and written on September 2, 1947, is a *Flying Saucer Analytical Report*, prepared by Research and Development experts for General C. P. Cabell, Commanding General of the Air Materiel Command. It provides a credible glimpse into the problems that faced the first analytical team to examine crash-recovered extraterrestrial hardware. Notably, the document records that: "...some nation has reached a stage of flight development in which the present ideas are entirely obsolete..." Although this would seem to suggest the presence of an infinitely advanced technology, the research team apparently *did* have success in identifying at least *some* control surfaces and exhaust ports, and concluded that the spherical reactor (which was described as being of a hydrogen isotope type) was connected to propulsion motors.[17]

On September 19, 1947, Hillenkoetter wrote a one-page memorandum to the Joint Intelligence Committee titled *Memorandum for the Military Assessment of the Joint Intelligence Committee*, which, as will be noted, is an acronym for Majic – a term often allied to both MJ-12 and Majestic 12. Ryan Wood notes: "The four paragraphs say we need a classified intelligence project; we recovered one craft [and] captured one. It says no coordinated scientific examination is possible until we get a clear directive from the president. It also says Wright Field has a new biological laboratory [and] the Joint Research and Development Board, the FBI [and Britain's] MI5 [and] MI6 are helping.[18]

Twining's *White Hot Report: Mission Assessment of Recovered Lenticular Aerodyne Objects* is a 19-page document, and is also dated September 19, 1947. It summarizes the work of numerous scientists and engineers, contains specific technical details, offers notable political insight, and closes with a pitch for a fully funded top secret research and development intelligence gathering organization, namely: Majestic.[19]

On the following day, Brigadier General Malcolm Crow wrote to Twining, describing the preliminary results of the post-mortem examination of the events described in the previously mentioned *Air Accident Report* of July 17, 1947. This perfunctory, preliminary report is clear in its references to a recovered UFO, and refers to the "collision in full flight with [an] object other than [a] conventional aircraft."[20]

A memo to the Air Surgeon, written by a Lt. Col. Tucker on September 22, 1947, and titled *Analysis of Factors Contributing to "Pilot-Error" Experiences in Operating Experimental Aircraft Controls* is of critical importance since, as Ryan Wood has been able to determine: "Tucker and his correct period phone extension, memo format, and writing style have been verified in the National Archives. Tucker was part of the Aero Medical Laboratory, Psychological Branch. [The document] discusses two incidents on 25 March and 4 July 1947...and interactions with symbolic instrumentation with tactile manipulation of flight controls."[21]

Two days after the Tucker memo was prepared, Secretary of State

George Marshall, in a document titled *Presentation of Report to the President Re. ULAT*, wrote to President Truman thus: "It would be better to discuss the report during the meeting. This would give the members a better picture of the situation rather than having it released piecemeal." Marshall goes on to say: "I further suggest that Twining present the findings of the Majestic-12 briefing to be given be the Director of Central Intelligence with a detailed showing of visual as well as written materials."[22]

According to files provided to Timothy Cooper, not everyone was happy with that briefing, however: a memo to General Spaatz dated September 25, 1947 voices concern about the quality of the briefing given on the previous day, and requests that the presentation package be specifically improved for the National Security Council meeting scheduled for the following day. Thomas Cantwheel's comments, typed in capital letters at the bottom of the document, sum up the sentiment: "The Secretary of Defense was unhappy with briefing of the AMC and R&D briefing officers and Symington wanted Bush and Twining to meet with Truman before NSC meeting on the 26th so that a more concise and explainable report of the discovery would be made."[23]

Stamped *Majic Eyes Only* is a September 25, 1947 memo to Truman from Marshall, that, as Ryan Wood observes: "...is telling Humelsine, the secretary to President Truman, to make sure that Truman realizes that he's not going to let anything out to the public, and even suggests a 'cover story.'"[24]

Twining's *Report to the President, Parts I-V* of September 26, 1947 makes an illuminating comment: "In accordance with your instructions, advisors from State, Treasury, War, and Navy departments assisted me in a two month exploratory mission concerning the reality of other-world visitation."[25]

On the following day, September 27, Marshall wrote to his Executive Secretary, Carl Humelsine, warning him about the tragic consequences that would undoubtedly result from a public disclosure of the truth behind the UFO crashes in New Mexico. Humelsine, however, was apparently against signing such an agreement to remain quiet concerning these events because he had already heard about them through other, ultimately unidentifiable sources. As evidence of this, the memo states in part: "...(a) you are unwilling to commit yourself to any agreement regarding not communicating its contents to any other person in view of the fact that you felt you already knew certain of the things probably referred to in the memo, as suggested to you by seeing the security reference 'MAJIC' and (b) you could not feel that such a letter as this could have been addressed to you without the knowledge of the President...."[26]

A document titled *Unidentified Aircraft Sightings Over the United States, Top Secret Eyes Only, Intelligence Estimate,* and dated September 30, 1947 is a presidential briefing prepared by the Special Studies and Evaluation State-War-Navy Coordinating Committee, and the Office of National Estimates Central Intelligence Agency. The six-page document covers essential elements of information; but specifically omits any references to recovered UFO wreckage or alien bodies. Ryan Wood notes that this is not surprising, since "the briefing is about unidentified aircraft *sightings.*"

Wood further notes that: "The main headings are: estimates of Soviet capabilities, domestic capabilities, estimate of the situation, estimates of interplanetary capabilities, and conclusions." Interestingly, the document appears to be a retype and Cooper's "Source S-2" had handwritten at the bottom of the document that this was the best version available. The document was annotated thus by Harry Truman: "I want the Director of NSA to have this for future reference. October 24, 1952."[27]

On February 11, 1948, Hillenkoetter (DCI) wrote a *Top Secret Majic Eyes Only* memorandum to President Truman concerning what are described within the document as the *Majic Black Book Summaries.* Hillenkoetter wrote: "For some time, the last two months in particular, I have had our intelligence liaison organization concentrating on the possible presentation on 'Majic' for my use as well as for the other officials concerned, particularly yourself. A highly specialized organization is now engaged in the very necessary process of separating the wheat from the chaff and correlating the items with past information in order that I may be able to quickly and intelligently evaluate the importance of the product."[28]

Allegedly declassified by the CIA, but most likely released by National Archives Records Administration (NARA) due to its "approved for release" stamp, as well as the valid, lower-right-hand-corner control-number, is a CIA-Joint Objectives Intelligence Agency document dated April 12, 1949, that lists MJ-12 on the distribution list, and that focuses upon a *Project 63*, which *was* a genuine operation focusing on the secret transfer of Nazi scientists to the United States from Germany in the post-Second World War-era.[29]

A three page memo CIA Office of Scientific Intelligence document of October 30, 1950 titled *Analysis of the Corona and Oscura Peak, New Mexico Wreckage of Unidentified Lenticular Aerodyne Technology* covers flight dynamics, power plant, propulsion, construction, avionics and navigation issues. Notably, the author of the document stated that with respect to the alien technology: "construction methods are unknown at this time," and opined that the alien vehicles "travel through space by utilizing the ionizing plasma and the planets magnetic lines of force..."[30]

A document of November 4, 1953 to the Director of Central Intelligence deals with President Dwight D. Eisenhower's comments pertaining to an: "MJTWELVE Operations Plan of June 16, 1953 on the subject of instructions for the expenditures of the National UFO Intelligence Program, and more specifically, the Special Operations instructions to be issued to Unified and Specific Major Commands and Commanders." In the document, Eisenhower expresses concern about inflaming the UFO situation with the Soviets; reiterates that both the CIA and the NSA had leading roles to play in the UFO program; and confirms that both Robert Oppenheimer and Albert Einstein (described as the director of something known as *Project Jehovah*) were involved in research relating to UFO physics.[31]

The Nature of Survey document of 1955 is one-page in length and begins: "An analysis has been made of the first one-hundred publications in the AFSA Unidentified Flying Object Intelligence Reports, prepared by the U.S. Army Security Service, the U.S. Naval Security Group, and the U.S. Air Force Security Service. Additional reports were reviewed which originated from respective branches intelligence departments. These reports were produced in order to establish what material of UFO intelligence is of value in relation to the New Mexico incidents and the ongoing MAJESTIC PRO-GRAM."[32]

Ryan Wood states that with regard to the so-called *Bowen Manuscript*: "Perhaps the most stunning physical evidence for the existence of the TOP SECRET/MAJIC program is this original 339-page manuscript about flying saucers. Written by Vernon Bowen, the original is on watermarked paper with red TOP SECRET/MAJIC stampings on some of the chapters. Most of the rest of the document is marked CONFIDENTIAL. Original, handwritten marginalia shows linkages to *Project White Hot*, Twining, Vannevar Bush, *Moon Dust*, and Donald Menzel. A well-written snapshot of the public history of flying saucers from 1947 to 1954. Bowen was personally well-connected to many top people."[33]

The bulk of the files that Timothy Cooper received that date from the 1960s are contained within a future chapter that focuses upon the assassination of President John F. Kennedy on November 22, 1963. However, Cooper *did* receive additional documentation on other MJ-12-related issues that were generated within the same time frame of the 1960s.[34]

With respect to one significant document, Ryan Wood has stated that: "The fifteen page Top Secret Majic report on *Isotope Thermal Thrusters and Applications,* by John S. Martinez, is clearly over-stamped at a later time with security warnings and a period style vertical number scheme of 28710. The contents are normal physics, yet use nuclear power in thermonic reactions to generate significant power for a variety of applications for spacecraft and nuclear rockets. [The document is] well referenced with much of the information more publicly understood now in this eclectic field of nuclear propulsion. This area has a rich history of close linkage to UFOs, since it was widely understood even in 1947 that UFOs don't run on kerosene; they must be nuclear. [The] Nuclear Energy for the Propulsion of Aircraft (NEPA) [project] and the Aircraft Nuclear Project (ANP) were huge military efforts to test the feasibility of nuclear propulsion in airplanes. Although the modern day success of these programs is unknown, the earlier programs were canceled and not considered successful."[35]

The *Summary of National Investigation Committee on Aerial Phenomenon (NICAP) Cases* is a 12-page, chronological summary of the civilian *National Investigation Committee on Aerial Phenomenon* cases allegedly pulled from the Air Force's *Project Blue Book* files. Ryan Wood notes that the document states: "N.M. Cases were pulled from Project Sign files and classified (TS); 1) Corona, NM; 2) Socorro, NM; 3) WSPG, NM."[36]

Edward Teller's *Pitch to President Reagan for SDI* is a five-page, double-spaced memo written for President Reagan's approval by

Teller, who clearly shows his familiarity with the UFO subject and its threat to National Security. The document opens with a truly gripping sentence: "I wish to bring to your attention a very real and dangerous situation that threatens not only us, the world, but our very existence as a race." The document goes on to state that: "No longer can the United States be in the position which it found itself in 1947. This was realized in January 1950 when President Truman made a decision to go ahead with a defense program exceeding in scope and cost of the Manhattan Project."[37]

Timothy Cooper was the recipient of another document allegedly written by Edward Teller, titled *UFO Technology and the Imbalance of Power* that discusses a wealth of detail about the nature of official secrecy, and both the benefits and hazards of UFO secrecy during both the Cold War and the present day. Incredibly, Teller actually proposed that official secrecy surrounding UFOs should be lessened for three prime reasons: (a) to stimulate research in the field of military applications of UFO technology; (b) to promote cooperation between the USA and its allies around the world on the UFO issue; and (c) to inform the American public of "the true state of UFO reality." Teller also proposed that the majority of then-classified UFO documents should be declassified. In addition, Teller discusses the advantages of utilizing UFO technology in the U.S. military's remotely piloted vehicle (RPV) program, as well as maintaining an adequate defense against "UFO nuclear weapons."[38]

On January 30, 1996, Cooper received from his prime source, Thomas Cantwheel, a two-page memo that included a drawing of what Cantwheel claimed was an unidentified aerodyne found on July 5, 1947 south of Socorro, New Mexico by elements of the Armed Forces Special Weapons Project. The memo begins, in Cantwheel's words: "The 'loaned' aircraft was acquired in 1945 from the Air Technical Services Command (ATSC, now AEDS, Air Force Systems Command). The 'S' aircraft was designed from an aerodyne recovered in 1941 that crashed in southeastern Missouri and the one captured in 1942 in Louisiana. Reconstruction commenced in 1945 with the assistance of German scientists at Wright Field. Propulsion programs tried to duplicate the atomic power plant found in the aerodyne captured in Louisiana and integrated the magnetic drive system developed by Tesla... Efforts to conceal the true nature of flight operations were successful in that the AF devised a cover intelligence project called Blue Book... In 1958, *Project UFO* and *Moon Dust* were activated when the USA *Interplanetary Phenomenon Unit* operations ceased and CIC responsibility for UFO security was transferred to USAFOSI."[39]

The final document of both significance and relevance received by Cooper was dated November 1998 and was titled *Top Secret Jehovah*. Ryan Wood outlined the nature of the document: "Chronologically, this is the most recent document to cite the words TOP SECRET MAJESTIC. With hand written references to the 'Weird Desk' and 'A51' this document provides a glimpse into the modern world of asset code names, and instant assignations for unauthorized disclosure. The document is rich with key phrases such as Project 'KOHTPOA,' MOD and KGB officials, Dreamland, Area 54 & 17, leaks by Teller, Sagan, China problems, and contacting '33' investors. Many of the details are checkable."[40]

There are two additional documents that are integral parts of the Timothy Cooper document collection: the *Interplanetary Phenomenon Unit Summary* document of 1947, and the *Majestic Twelve 1st Annual Report* of 1952. Indeed, *so integral* are they to the crux of the story that this book tells – namely the existence of a lethal virus of extraterrestrial origins – they are discussed in full in the following two chapters.

*   *   *

Chapter 3 Notes:

1. *Validating the New Majestic Documents*, Robert M. Wood, *Mutual UFO Network Symposium Proceedings*, 2000.

2. Memorandum to George Marshall from President Franklin D. Roosevelt, February 27, 1942. Available at www.majesticdocuments.com by downloading: http://209.132.68.98/pdf/fdr.pdf

3. Memorandum to President Franklin D. Roosevelt from George Marshall, March 5, 1942. Available at www.majesticdocuments.com by downloading: http://209.132.68.98/marshall-fdr-march1942.pdf

4. Special Committee on Non-Terrestrial Science and Technology memorandum, February 22, 1944. Available at www.majesticdocuments.com by downloading: http://209.132.68.98/fdr_22feb44.pdf

5. Ibid.

6. *Relationships With Inhabitants of Celestial Bodies*, Robert Oppenheimer and Albert Einstein, 1947. Available at www.majesticdocuments.com by downloading: http://209.132.68.98/oppenheimer_einstein.pdf

7. Letter from Vannevar Bush to President Harry Truman, July 5, 1947. Available at www.majesticdocuments.com by downloading: http://209.132.68.98/bush-truman_ 5july47.pdf

8. Ibid.

9. Ibid.

10. Directive to General Nathan Twining, July 8, 1947. Available at www.majesticdocuments.com by downloading: http://209.132.68.98/ twining_eisenhower.pdf

11. Directive to General Nathan Twining, July 9, 1947. Available at www.majesticdocuments.com by downloading: http://209.132.68.98/twining_ truman.pdf

12. *Air Accident Report*, July 16, 1947. Available at www.majesticdocuments.com by downloading: http://209.132.68.98/airaccidentreport.pdf

13. Memorandum from Nathan Twining to Curtis Le May, July 18, 1947. Available at www.majesticdocuments.com by downloading: http://209.132.68.98/ meteorological-r&d_18-jul47.pdf

14. Ibid.

15. Ibid.

16. Memorandum to the Commanding General, Army Air Forces, August 12, 1947. Available at www.majesticdocuments.com by downloading: http://209.132.68.98/ cwo-marcrau_12aug47.pdf

17. *Flying Saucer Analytical Report*, September 2, 1947. Available at www. majesticdocucuments.com by downloading: http://209.132.68.98/rdlab_ analyticalrpt2sept47.pdf

18. Memorandum to the Joint Intelligence Committee from Rear Admiral Roscoe Hillenkoetter, September 19, 1947. Available at www.majesticdocuments.com by downloading: http://209.132.68.98/hillenkoetter_memo.pdf

19. *White Hot Report: Mission Assessment of Recovered Lenticular Aerodyne Objects*, September 19, 1947. Available at www.majesticdocuments.com by downloading: http://209.132.68.98/twining_whitehotreport.pdf

20. Aero Medical Laboratory Memorandum, September 20, 1947. Available at www.majesticdocuments.com by downloading: http://209.132.68.98/grow_ twining.pdf

21. *Analysis of Factors Contributing to "Pilot Error" Experiences in Operating Experimental Aircraft Controls*, Office of the Air Surgeon, September 22, 1947. Available at www.majesticdocuments.com by downloading: http://209.132.68.98/ tucker.pdf

22. Memorandum to President Harry Truman, September 24, 1947. Available at www.majesticdocuments.com by downloading: http://209.132.68.98/marshall-pres_ 24sept47.pdf

23. Memorandum to General Carl Spaatz, September 25, 1947. Available at www.majesticdocuments.com by downloading: http://209.132.68.98/af-secretary-spaatz.pdf

24. Memorandum from Secretary of State George Marshall to President Harry Truman, September 25, 1947. Available at www.majesticdocuments.com by downloading: http://209.132.68.98/marshall-truman-25Sept47.pdf

25. Twining's *Report to the President, Parts 1-V*, September 26, 1947. Available at www.majesticdocuments.com by downloading: http://209.132.68.98/twining-pres_26sept47.pdf

26. Memorandum from Secretary of State George Marshall to Carl Humelsine, September 27, 1947. Available at www.majesticdocuments.com by downloading: http://209.132.68.98/marshall-humelsine-27sept47.pdf

27. *Unidentified Aircraft Sightings Over The United States, Presidential Briefing.* Available at www.majesticdocuments.com by downloading: http://209.132.68.98/tseo_presbriefing_30sept47.pdf

28. *Majic Black Book Summaries*, February 11, 1948. Available at www.majesticdocuments.com by downloading http://209.132.68.98/hillenkoetter-truman-blackbook.pdf

29. Central Intelligence Agency-Joint Objectives Intelligence Agency Memorandum, April 12, 1949. Available at www.majesticdocuments.com by downloading: http://209.132.68.98/cia_joia.pdf

30. *Analysis of the Corona and Oscura Peak, New Mexico Wreckage of Unidentified Lenticular Aerodyne Technology*, Office of Scientific Intelligence, Central Intelligence Agency, October 30, 1950. Available at www.majesticdocuments.com by downloading: http://209.132.68.98/cia_oscurapeak.pdf

31. Memorandum from President Dwight D. Eisenhower to the Director of Central Intelligence, November 4, 1953. Available at www.majesticdocuments.com by downloading: http://209.132.68.98/eisenhower-dci_4nov53.pdf

32. *Nature of Survey*, 1955. Available at www.majesticdocuments.com by downloading: http://209.132.68.98/natureofsurveyfragment.pdf

33. *The Bowen Manuscript*, 1959. Available at www.majesticdocuments.com by downloading: http://209.132.68.98/bowen.pdf

34. See Chapter 12: *Crashed UFOs, Bio-War and the JFK Assassination.*

35. *Isotope Thermal Thrusters and Applications* (Year Unknown). Available at www.majesticdocuments.com by downloading: http://209.132.68.98/isotope_thermal_thrusters.pdf

36. *Summary of National Investigations Committee on Aerial Phenomena (NICAP) Cases* (Year Unknown). Available at www.majesticdocuments.com by downloading: http://209.132.68.98/nicap-cases.pdf

37. *Pitch to President Reagan for SDI* by Edward Teller (exact date unknown but believed to be the 1980s). Available at www.majesticdocuments.com by downloading: http://209.132.68.98/ufotechnology-teller.pdf

38. *UFO Technology and the Imbalance of Power* by Edward Teller (exact date unknown but believed to be the 1980s). Available at www.majesticdocuments.com by downloading: http://209.132.68.98/ufotechnology-teller.pdf

39. *S-Aircraft and Drawing and Memorandum* by Thomas Cantwheel, January 30, 1996. Available at www.majesticdocuments.com by downloading: http://209.132.68.98/s-aircraft.pdf

40. *Top Secret Jehovah*, Memorandum from the Central Intelligence Agency to MAJSEC, November 1998. Available at www.majesticdocuments.com by downloading: http://209.132.68.98/jehovah.pdf

Chapter 4
The Interplanetary
Phenomenon Unit
March 1942

Without any shadow of a doubt at all, two of the most intriguing and notable documents contained within the mass of material made available to Timothy Cooper are the *Interplanetary Phenomenon Unit Summary* of 1947; and the *Majestic Twelve 1ˢᵗ Annual Report* – that is undated but that *appears* to be of 1950s vintage. And, chronologically speaking, it is within the pages of these two documents that we begin to learn of the concern exhibited by the Government, military, and intelligence community in 1947 that alien beings represented a potential biological threat to the human race. Let us begin with the IPU.

Ryan Wood has stated that: "On March 5, 1942, George C. Marshall writes a top-secret memo to the President, which states: 'regarding the air raid over Los Angeles it was learned by Army G2 that Rear Admiral Anderson...recovered an unidentified airplane off the coast of California...with no bearing on conventional explanation...This Headquarters has come to the determination that the mystery airplanes are in fact not earthly and according to secret intelligence sources they are in all probability of interplanetary origin.' Marshall goes on to state: 'As a consequence I have issued orders to Army G2 that a special intelligence unit be created to further investigate the phenomenon and report any significant connection between recent incidents and those collected by the director the office of Coordinator of Information.' The memo bears correct Office of Chief of Staff (OCS) file numbers and has 'Interplanetary Phenomenon Unit' (IPU) typed on it at a later time by a different typewriter. It is logical to believe that this is the order that sets up the IPU."[1] Five years later, the IPU was apparently still operating – albeit in a highly covert fashion.

The seven-page IPU *Summary* that Timothy Cooper shared with Robert Wood tells an extraordinary story. Classified *Top Secret Ultra*, and specifically dated July 22, 1947, the document was reportedly "prepared by Headquarters Interplanetary Phenomenon

Unit, Scientific and Technical Branch, Counterintelligence Directorate, as requested by [Assistant Chief of Staff], G-2 at the express
order of Chief of Staff."

The writer of the document states that late on the night of July 3,
1947 "radar stations in East Texas and White Sands Proving
Ground, N.M., tracked two unidentified aircraft until both dropped
off radar. Two crash sites have been located close to the WSPG. Site
LZ-1 was located at a ranch near Corona, approx. 75 miles northwest
of the town of Roswell. Site LZ-2 was located approx. 20 miles
southwest of the town of Socorro...with Oscura Peak being the
geographic reference point."

The document notes further: "...personnel were mainly interested
in LZ-2 as this site contained the majority of structural detail of the
craft's airframe, propulsion and navigation technology. The recovery
of five bodies in a damaged escape cylinder, precluded an investigation at LZ-1." Interestingly, the IPU *Summary* contains a reference
to the fact that those military personnel that first arrived at site LZ-2
had initially concluded that what had crashed was a balloon from
the Army Air Forces' Project Mogul. Nearly half a century later, as
we saw earlier, the Air Force resurrected the Mogul scenario in 1994
as a part of its attempts to defuse the controversies surrounding
Roswell.

The IPU document makes it clear that the recovery of the
wreckage and the bodies was seen as being a matter of profound
significance and was handled with the utmost secrecy:

"A special radiobiological team accompanied by a SED and
security detail from Sandia Base under orders from Colonel S. V.
Hasbrouck, USA, Armed Forces Special Weapons Project, secured
the immediate area surrounding the crash site...Because of the
stringent security measures that were in place at both crash sites,
the team was not able to gain access to the several locations where
wreckage and bodies are being held. CIC member of the team was
able to learn that several bodies were taken to the hospital at
Roswell AAF and others to either Los Alamos, Wright Field,
Patterson AAF, and Randolph Field for security reasons. It is
believed that this dispersion was on the orders of General Thomas
Handy, Fourth Army Hdqrs. Remains of the powerplant were taken
to Alamogordo AAF and Kirtland AAF. Structural debris and
assorted parts were taken to AMC, Wright Field. Other remains

were transported across the WSPG to the storage facilities of the NRL. All this was accomplished by 1730 MST 7 July."

But far more serious issues quickly became apparent with respect to the recovery of the bodies, as the document records: "Ground personnel from Sandia experienced some form of contamination resulting in the deaths of 3 technicians. The status of the fourth technician is unknown. Autopsies are scheduled to determine cause of death. CIC has make [sic] appropriate security file entries into dossiers with cross references for future review."

As a result of this potentially serious "contamination," the IPU document notes, studies of the alien bodies were made by senior personnel: "As to the bodies recovered at LZ-2, it appeared that none of the five crew members survived entry into our atmosphere due to unknown causes. DR. DETLEV BRONK has been asked to assist in the autopsy of one well preserved cadaver to be done by MAJOR CHARLES E. REA. From what descriptions the team was able to learn and from photographs taken by intelligence photographers, the occupants appear in most respects human with some anatomical differences in the head, eyes, hands and feet. They have a slight build about five feet tall, with grayish-pink skin color, They have no hair on their bodies and clothed with a tight fitting flight suit that appears to be fire proof (some of the bodies looked as if they had been burned on head and the hands). Their overall stature reminds one of young children. It is believed that there were male and female genders present, but was hard to distinguish."

The IPU also learned: "The most disturbing aspect of this investigation was – there were other bodies found not far from LZ-1 that looked as if they had been dissected as you would a frog. It is not known if army field surgeons had performed exploratory surgery on these bodies. Animal parts were reportedly discovered inside the craft at LZ-2 but this cannot be confirmed. The team has reserved judgment on this issue."

In conclusion, it was stated: "Our assessment of this investigation rests on two assumptions: 1) Either this discovery was an elaborate and well-orchestrated hoax (maybe by the Russians), or; 2) Our country has played host to beings from another planet. Until more data can be acquired from other intelligence sources, it is the opinion of the team, that the investigation be expanded to include sources that might elucidate other possibilities not found by contemporary science. It is also recommended that appropriate budgets be allocated to facilitate future assignments that the unit may be called upon to perform. Until further orders, this investigation will continue."[2]

This is, without doubt, data of profound significance. But can it be validated? That there *was* an organization known as the Interplanetary Phenomenon Unit is a matter of official record. On September 25, 1980, in response to a Freedom of Information Act request initiated by researcher and author Richard Hall, Colonel William B. Guild, Director of Counterintelligence, Department of the Army, wrote: "Please be advised that the IPU of the Science and Technology Branch, Counterintelligence Directorate, Department of the Army, was disestablished during the late 1950's and never reactivated. All records were surrendered to the U.S. Air Force Office of Special Investigations in conjunction with operation 'BLUE-BOOK.'"[3]

Despite the fact that Guild was certain that all of the IPU records had been turned over to the AFOSI, no such material can be found within the declassified AFOSI files at the National Archives, Maryland that concern the Air Force's UFO investigation program known as Project Bluebook. This, of course, begs the question: where are the IPU's UFO files?

In 1984, William Steinman, the author of the book *UFO Crash at Aztec* attempted to answer that question and contacted the Army himself. On May 16 of that year, Steinman received a reply from Lt. Col. Lance R. Cornine, Department of the Army, who wrote:

"As you note in your letter, the so-called Interplanetary Phenomenon Unit (IPU) was disestablished and, as far as we are aware, all records, if any, were transferred to the Air Force in the late 1950's. The 'unit' was formed as an in-house project purely as an interest item for the Assistant Chief of Staff for Intelligence. It was never a 'unit' in the military sense, nor was it ever formally organized or reportable, it had no investigative function, mission or authority, and may not even have had any formal records at all. It is only through institutional memory that any recollection exists of this unit. We are therefore unable to answer your questions as to the exact purpose of the unit, exactly when it was disestablished, or who was in command. This last would not apply in any case, as no one was in 'command'. We have no records or documentation of any kind on this unit."[4]

Cornine's reply is puzzling. Four years previously, Richard Hall had been informed that IPU records *did* exist. We know this because Colonel William B. Guild had told Hall that the UFO records of the IPU had been turned over to the Air Force's Office of Special Investigations. Yet, by the time that Steinman was making his inquiries, it appears that someone within officialdom had decided that inquiring members of the public should be told that no such records had ever existed, which is a clear contradiction of the Army's previous stance.

Interestingly, the Freedom of Information Act has shown that the Army has on file what is known as an *FOI/Privacy Act Standard Operating Proecdure (SOP)* document that, even today, acts as a guide for Army personnel, in the event that inquiring members of the public specifically ask questions about the IPU. The Army's *SOP* reads thus:

"Periodically this office will receive requests concerning an activity described as the 'Interplanetary Phenomenon Unit' and for information on UFOs. When replying to request for UFO's records our reply should be as follows: 'This is in response to your letter of [insert date] under the Freedom of Information Act, 5USC 552, requesting information concerning Army intelligence records related to UFO encounter reports. To determine the existence of Army intelligence investigative records responsive to your request, we have conducted an in-depth check of the files and indices maintained by this office. We regret to inform you that there is no record concerning UFOs within this office and the Department of the Army."[5]

The *SOP* continues:

"If asked about the IPU, the reply is as follows: 'Please be advised that the Interplanetary Phenomenon Unit of the Scientific and Technical Branch, Counter Intelligence Directorate, Department of the Army was disestablished during the late 1950's and never reactivated. All records pertaining to this unit were surrendered to the U.S. Air Force Office of Special Investigations in conjunction with operation 'Bluebook'. There is no record system maintained within the Department of the Army to catalog, process, index or otherwise evaluate UFO information. We regret that we are unable to be of more assistance concerning this matter."[6]

Notably, the Army also has a *SOP* in place for dealing with persistent inquirers who may not be initially convinced by the Army's assertions:

"If there is a follow-on request concerning the IPU, our reply should be as follows: 'As stated in our letter of [insert date] records of Interplanetary Phenomenon Unit no longer are maintained by the Department of the Army. Once surrendered, the records became the property of the gaining office (U.S. Air Force, Office of Special Investigations) and their disposition would not be monitored by the Army. Consequently, the information you seek is not available through this office.'

"If we are questioned further concerning this unit, our reply should be as follows: 'As stated in our previous letters of [insert date] and [insert date], the Department of the Army is no longer in possession of the records you seek and we cannot locate any information on the unit. Unfortunately, for that reason alone, we are simply unable to answer your questions.'"[7]

As this *SOP* amply demonstrates, the Army recognizes that questions have been asked (and will continue to be asked) about the IPU; and, as a result, have prepared detailed guidelines for those whose task it is to respond to such inquiries. But if the UFO files of the IPU were forwarded to the Air Force's Office of Special Investigations (AFOSI), why were they not included in the AFOSI's UFO files that were declassified when the Project Blue Book files were declassified?

A clue, perhaps, can be found within the pages of the July 22, 1947 IPU *Summary* document. Specifically on the cover page, is a typed note, dated September 4, 1960 that was prepared by Lieutenant General John A. Samford, then-Director of the National Security Agency. The note states that the IPU summary has, of that date, been "re-classified as intelligence material affecting the national security and has been upgraded as above top secret with a 'need to know' basis. Only those authorized persons with Majic access may have access. Downgrading schedule to commence only with an approved Presidential E.O. [Executive Order] with approval of U.S. Majestic Intelligence and Security."[8]

In view of Samford's statement, it is highly likely that the Army is correct in its belief that the IPU's UFO files were turned over to the AFOSI. However, Samford's words suggest that after they were transferred from the Army, those same files came under the subsequent review of the National Security Agency and MJ-12, who determined that the IPU files should not be shared with Blue Book personnel. This seems to be a reasonable scenario to explain the apparent loss of the IPU's files after they left the Army.

And what of the contents of the IPU *Summary* as they relate to the critical and relevant issue of an apparent alien virus present at the New Mexico crash sites of 1947? The biggest problem that faces us is that, by Thomas Cantwheel's own admission, *some* of the documents that he supplied Timothy Cooper with were not genuine. But they were not hoaxed either. Rather, they were, by Cantwheel's own admission, created (either by his hand or by still-unidentified colleagues of Cantwheel), in a fashion "to protect you [Cooper] from criminal prosecution."[9]

It is important to note, however, that Cantwheel was careful to point out that: "I assure you that the names, dates and places are valid. I think I provided you with enough leads to help you find valuable information that can be found in any library. I hope you will not think too ill of me for leading you on for so long."[10]

In other words, a specific forensic analysis of the IPU *Summary* might be an utterly fruitless and meaningless task if this document is one of Cantwheel's "constructs." And if the document *is* such a "construct," created to provide Cooper with real data, but in a fashion designed to ensure that he could not be prosecuted for possessing and utilizing classified original documents, this may also explain why, in the original version of the document supplied to Cooper there were numerous typographical errors. *If* this document was typed by Cantwheel, and was directly based upon classified materials in Cantwheel's possession, it is highly possible that those same typographical errors were the result of Cantwheel's age and infirmity.

With that thought in mind, let us focus on the *content* of the document (that Cantwheel stressed was completely "valid") and that has a bearing on the alien virus angle of the story. As will become apparent in the following chapter, *Analyzing the 1ˢᵗ Annual Report*, there is a copious amount of data available suggesting that at least *some* of the alien bodies found at UFO crash sites in New Mexico in the summer of 1947 presented a biological threat.

But what of the references to the autopsy of a "well-preserved" alien cadaver undertaken by Major Charles E. Rea, with assistance provided by Dr. Detlev Bronk? Certainly, Bronk was an intriguing person to bring into the fold: born on August 13, 1897, Bronk was a neurophysiologist (that is concerned with the study of the nervous system), and the President of the National Academy of Sciences from 1950 to 1962, and the President of Johns Hopkins University from 1949 to 1953. *Bronk Crater*, on the surface of the Moon, is named after Dr. Bronk.[11]

Until the IPU *Summary* of July 22, 1947 surfaced, Major Charles Ethan Rea's name was unknown to the ufological community. However, diligent research has led to the discovery of a copious amount of intriguing data on the man and his career. Born in Montana in 1908, Rea attended high school in Billings and received a medical degree with distinction from the University of Minnesota in 1931. He also earned a degree in pathology from the University of Chicago, and joined the surgical staff at the University of Minnesota, where he stayed until his retirement in 1978. Renowned for his volunteer work, Rea was actively involved in the 1950s and 1960s with a Twin Cities school for children with mental disabilities, and in 1959 was made a Knight of St. Gregory by Pope John XXIII as a result of his service to the poor. After his retirement, Rea launched a ministry in Florida for Haitian field workers. But it is Rea's wartime career, when he served in a senior position at what is now the Oak Ridge National Laboratory, Tennessee that is of most interest and relevance.[12]

Spreading out along broad valleys cut by the Clinch River and framed by the foothills of the Appalachian Mountains, Oak Ridge seems an unlikely setting for events that changed the course of history. In early 1942, the Army Corps of Engineers designated a 59,000-acre swatch of land between Black Oak Ridge to the north and the Clinch River to the south as a federal reserve to serve as one of three sites nationwide for the development of the atomic bomb.

No less than 3,000 residents received court orders to vacate - within a matter of weeks - the homes that their families had occupied for generations. Thousands of scientists, engineers, and workers swarmed into Oak Ridge to build and operate three huge facilities that would change the history of the region and the world forever. On the reservation's western edge rose K-25, or the gaseous diffusion plant, a warehouse-like building covering more area than any structure ever built.

Completed at a cost of $500 million and operated by 12,000 workers, the K-25 Plant separated uranium-235 from uranium-238. On its northern edge grew the workers' city, named Oak Ridge; south of the city rose the Y-12 Plant, where an electromagnetic method was used to separate uranium-235. Built for $427 million, the Y-12 Plant employed 22,000 workers; and near the reservation's southwest corner, about 10 miles from Y-12, was the third plant, X-10.

During the war, X-10 was called Clinton Laboratories, named after the nearby county seat of rural Anderson County; and in 1948, Clinton Laboratories became Oak Ridge National Laboratory. Today, the Laboratory, which celebrated its 50th anniversary in 1993, has evolved from a war emergency pilot plant operated under an overwhelming cloak of secrecy into one of the nation's outstanding centers for energy, environmental, and basic scientific research and technology development. Laboratory endeavors range from studies of nuclear chemistry and physics to inquiries into global warming, energy conservation, high-temperature superconductivity, and new materials. Its institutional roots, however, lie with the awesome power released by the splitting of the atom.[13]

A memorandum dated August 10, 1943 from Colonel K. D. Nichols of the Corps of Engineers, Deputy District Engineer, at Oak Ridge outlines the background to Rea's employment at Oak Ridge: "The organization of the Medical Section and the personnel assignment's are noted. The Section itself will be administered by: Dr. Stafford L. Warren, Chief, Medical Section [and] Dr. H. L. Friedell, Executive Officer, Medical Section. The assignment of Captain John Ferry to the Medical Section, Special Products, has been approved in a communication dated 8 August 1943. The assignments of Dr. Charles Rea as Clinical Supervisor, Clinton Engineer Works, and Dr. William B. Holt as Chief, Hospital Services, Clinton Engineer Works, are hereby approved."[14]

A second Oak Ridge document of 1943, titled *Officer Personnel – The Medical Section of the Manhattan District*, provides further background data on Rea "The first medical officer attached to the District was Lt. Colonel, (then Captain) Hymer L. Friedell who was assigned as liaison officer to the Metallurgical Laboratory of the University of Chicago in August 1942. With the appointment of Dr.

Warren as consultant to the District Engineer, Lt. Colonel Friedell became his executive officer. In May 1943, Major (then Captain) John L. Ferry was added to the staff and was given the responsibility of supervising the industrial medical programs of District contractors and of acting as liaison officer to the research at the University of Rochester. During the summer of 1943, Charles E. Rea, M. D. (now Lt. Col.), Harry Fitluck, D. D. S., and the late William B. Holt, M. D., were procured from civil life to provide care for the community at Oak Ridge. Dr. Rea was appointed Chief of Clinical Services for the area. On 5 November 1943, Dr. Warren was commissioned a Colonel in the Army Medical Corps...and designated Chief of the Medical Section."[15]

The collective references contained within the two, above pieces of documentation to Dr. Stafford L. Warren are intriguing, as will now become apparent. Born in 1896, Warren attended the University of California, Johns Hopkins University, and Harvard University. A Professor of Radiology at the University of Rochester School of Medicine and Dentistry from 1926 to 1946, Warren later served as Dean of the Medical School from 1962 to 1963; and was appointed, by President Kennedy, as the Special Assistant to the President for Mental Retardation, where he was responsible for developing and coordinating programs for the mentally retarded. Warren held this position until June 1965.

Other government service included work on the Manhattan Project (from 1943 to 1946), directorship of the Atomic Energy Project (from 1947 to 1958) and work with the Department of Health Education and Welfare, along with membership in many local, state and federal health and medical committees and agencies. Throughout his lifetime, Warren also authored over 300 reports on subjects such as cancer, arthritis and radioactive isotopes. He died in 1981.[16]

Interestingly, in July 1964, Warren corresponded with none other than Joshua Lederberg (whose longstanding concerns about alien-originated viruses were detailed in the *Prologue* to this book).[17]

On April 12, 1944, Warren wrote the following to Rea:

"There are special hazards in each of the operations conducted at Oak Ridge which cause or may cause in the body of the patient a certain series of changes which are not commonly understood by physicians. Some changes may be produced also, which are unknown at present.

"Physicians specially trained in these matters and with a specially assigned responsibility for safe-guarding personnel from these hazards have been appointed to the dispensary facilities of the operating companies of each area. These dispensary physicians are hereby appointed as consultants to the Oak Ridge Hospital Staff, and their function shall be as follows:

"When personnel have been exposed to some special hazard, and it is deemed necessary by the Dispensary physicians to hospitalize such a person or persons for observation and possible treatment, the patient shall be referred for hospitalization to the Oak Ridge Hospital in the usual manner, but special arrangements shall be made at the same time by the Chief of the referring dispensary with the Clinical Director of the Oak Ridge Hospital for the specialized care of the patient by the Chief of the hospital service concerned.

"The Chief of the accepting service in the Oak Ridge Hospital shall utilize to the full extent any pertinent special information and suggestions from the Chief of the referring dispensary or his designated assistant who shall act as Consultant throughout the period of hospitalization.

"The Consultant should participate as much as the situation warrants in the treatment of the case during the hospital stay, but the final responsibility for the treatment and care of the patient lies with the officer in charge of the service on which the patient has been admitted.

"On discharge of the patient, full or abstracted data on the progress and treatment of the patient shall be sent promptly to the Chief of the referring dispensary."[18]

On the same day, Stafford L. Warren wrote the following to a Dr. Stone at the Clinton Labs, Knoxville, Tennessee: "Dear Dr. Stone, Reference is made to the inclosure, 12 April 1944, regarding the appointment of Dispensary physicians as Consultants on the Oak Ridge Hospital Staff. It is recommended that you submit a list of those members of your staff who will be in this category to Major Rea, with a copy to this office. The responsibility for this appointment lies with the Chief of the Dispensary, and will be in force on receipt of such notification by Major Rea. Subsequent changes in these appointments will be made as circumstances require, by arrangement between the Chief of the Dispensary and the Chief of the Medical Staff of the Hospital, Major Rea."[19]

An Oak Ridge originated document of 1944 titled *Procurement of Medical Personnel*, refers to Charles Rea, and his line of thinking with respect to the work undertaken at Oak Ridge. It states: "Medical Corps officers were used as far as possible in the secret sites at Oak Ridge, Hanford, and Los Alamos, for two reasons. The first was that it was impossible to find civilian physicians with the required quality of training in large enough numbers to staff the hospitals and clinics at these sites. The second reason was that medical (military) officers were more desirable, for security reasons, in locations in which accidents with radiation exposure might occur. On the advice of Maj. Charles E. Rea, MC., as many officers as possible who were to serve in a given site were secured from the same medical school residency programs, so that they would already know each other and would be used to working together. The policy was very effective, one reason being that since the families were already acquainted with each other, there was less loneliness and a better spirit de corps is [sic] these isolated assignments."[20]

In addition, Rea's unpublished memoirs reveal that he was well acquainted with General Leslie R. Groves, Director of the Manhattan Project that gave birth to the atomic age. As evidence of this, in a chapter from his memoirs titled *Oak Ridge Story*, Rea states that: "...the general and I got along well because I had a great respect for his ability."[21]

As all of the above demonstrates, Rea held a position of keen note at Oak Ridge, and he mixed with prestigious and senior sources in the medical and military communities, and would have been an ideal candidate to participate in an alien autopsy. Plus, the fact that Rea had been briefed by Stafford L. Warren on the issue of certain "special hazards" at Oak Ridge that could "cause or may cause in the body of the patient a certain series of changes which are not commonly understood by physicians," may be an indication that Warren had an awareness of pre-1947 references to fatal encounters with an alien virus. Indeed, all the evidence currently available does suggest that the alien virus *was* a hazard, and *did* cause cataclysmic changes within the human body that were not fully understood.

* * *

Chapter 4 Notes:

1. *Majestic Documents Dated Prior To 1948*, Ryan Wood. See: www. majesticdocuments.com/documents/pre1948.php

2. Interplanetary Phenomenon Unit Summary, July 22, 1947. Available at www.majesticdocuments.com by downloading: http://209.132.68.98/pdf/ipu_report.pdf

3. Letter from Colonel William B. Guild, Director of Counterintelligence, Department of the Army, to Richard Hall, September 25, 1980.

4. Letter from Lieutenant Colonel Lance R. Cornine, Department of the Army, to William Steinman, May 16, 1984.

5. *FOI/Privacy Act Standard Operating Procedure (SOP, UFOs and the Interplanetary Phenomenon Unit*. See: www.cufon.org

6. Ibid.

7. Ibid.

8. *Interplanetary Phenomenon Unit Summary*, July 22, 1947. Available at www.majesticdocuments.com by downloading: http://209.132.68.98/pdf/ipu_report.pdf

9. Letter from Thomas Cantwheel to Timothy Cooper, February 22, 1996.

10. Ibid.

11. *Johns Hopkins University Past Presidents*: http://webapps.jhu.edu/jhuniverse/information_about_hopkins/about_jhu/past_presidents/

12. *Physician Charles Rea, 87*, St Paul Pioneer Press, September 26, 1995. *In Memoriam: A Tribute To Two Former Faculty Members, The Cutting Edge*, January 1997.

13. *History of Oak Ridge National Laboratory*: www.ornl.gov/ornlhome/history.shtml

14. Memorandum, Colonel K.D. Nichols, Corps of Engineers, Deputy District Commander, Oak Ridge National Laboratory, August 10, 1943.

15. *Officer Personnel – The Medical Section of the Manhattan District*, Oak Ridge National Laboratory, (undated) 1943.

16. *The Papers of John F. Kennedy, Presidential Papers, White House Staff Files (# 8.27) of Stafford L. Warren, 1896-1981*. See: www.jfklibrary.org/fa_warren_wh.html#bio

17. Letter from Joshua Lederberg to Stafford L. Warren, July 7, 1964.

18. Letter from Dr. Stafford L. Warren to Charles E. Rea, April 12, 1944.

19. Letter from Dr. Stafford L. Warren to Dr. Stone, Clinton Laboratories, Knoxville, TN, April 12, 1944.

20. Memorandum, *Procurement of Medical Personnel*, Oak Ridge National Laboratory (undated), 1944.

21. Chapter titled *Oak Ridge Story*, extracted from Charles E. Rea's unpublished memoirs.

Chapter 5
Analyzing the 1st Annual Report
1947-51

The one MJ-12-related document that, more than any other, has provoked intense controversy is a 17-page document titled *MAJESTIC TWELVE PROJECT: 1st Annual Report*. Provided to Timothy Cooper by Thomas Cantwheel, it purports to be a "review of the President's Special Panel to investigate the capture of unidentified planform space vehicles by U.S. Armed Forces and Agencies."[1]

There can be no doubt that the 1st *Annual Report* contains some provocative data that has a direct bearing upon the subject matter of this book. It must be said, too, that the *Report* also contains some glaring inconsistencies that need to be addressed. However, some (if, indeed, not *all*) of those inconsistencies might easily be explained by Thomas Cantwheel's admission to Cooper that a number of the documents that he, Cantwheel, provided Cooper with were neither photocopies of real papers nor straightforward hoaxes, but were something in between: namely, faked documents containing genuine data, that had been carefully prepared in such a way as to (a) ensure that Cooper was not prosecuted for being in possession of, and utilizing, classified, official files; and (b) provide Cooper with legitimate data (if not legitimate documents) to aid him in his quest for the truth about MJ-12.[2]

One of the most problematic areas of the *Report* relates to the date on which it was written. An initial assumption might be that a 1st *Annual Report* would be written twelve months after the creation of the relevant group – in this case, MJ-12. However, the document internally references events that occurred as late as May 1951, suggesting that the earliest date upon which it could possibly have been written was during the summer of 1951.[3]

The date upon which the *Report* was prepared is made even more problematic by virtue of the little-known, and seldom-discussed, fact that Timothy Cooper received the document from Cantwheel in no less than three, separate installments that spanned a period of more than twelve months: the *Cover* page was provided to Cooper on January 19, 1994; the *Table of Contents* on December 30, 1994; and the main body of the *Report* itself on February 22, 1995. And although all three sections of the overall *Report seem* to be written on the same typewriter, and all three parts *seem* to originate with the same document, we cannot state that for certain.[4]

However, given the fact that we know Cantwheel had provided Cooper with data that he claimed was legitimate, it is perhaps wise for us to focus for the most part on the *information* that is contained within the *1ˢᵗ Annual Report*.

The *Cover* page would seem to suggest that the team that prepared the *1ˢᵗ Annual Report* was not the MJ-12 committee itself, but a "Special Panel" that was linked to MJ-12. Its membership reportedly included some illustrious figures, who are identified in the *Report* as: Dr. Vannevar Bush; General Hoyt S. Vandenberg, USAF; Brigadier General George F. Schulgen, USAF; Dr. J. Robert Oppenheimer; Detlev Bronk, of the National Research Council; Jerome Hunsaker, of the National Academy of Sciences; James Doolittle; Lieutenant General Lewis H. Brereton; Rear Admiral Paul F. Lee, Office of Naval Research; Major General George C. McDonald, USAF; Dr. Hugh L. Dryden; Admiral John Gingrich; Major General George C. McDonald, USAF; and Major General Luther D. Miller, U.S. Army.[5]

In the *Report*, General J. Lawton Collins is described as Deputy Chief of Staff, United States Army. In reality, Collins was Deputy Chief only from 1947 to mid-August 1949. He attained the rank of Chief of Staff on August 16, 1949 and held that position until August 15, 1953.[6] Likewise, Major General Luther D. Miller is listed in the *Report* as Chief of Chaplains with the Army. He was: but only from 1945 to 1949.[7] Similarly, the reference to Lieutenant General Lewis H. Brereton being Chairman of the Military Liaison Committee to the Atomic Energy Committee is incorrect: he was attached to the Liaison Committee of the AEC in 1947 and through early 1948, but by June 1948 he was Secretary General of the Air Force.[8] Hoyt S. Vandenberg is listed in the *Report* as Vice Chief of Staff with the U.S. Air Force; yet, in reality, he had attained the rank of Chief of Staff by April 30, 1948.[9] George C. McDonald's name appears in the *Report* as the Director of Intelligence with the Air Force. McDonald was indeed appointed to that position – in October 1947. However, in June 1948, he became Chief of the Air Section of the United

States' Military Commission at Rio de Janeiro, Brazil, and did not even return to the United States until June 1950, at which point he was assigned to the Office of the Department of the Deputy Chief of Staff for Personnel.[10]

Quite clearly, there is a very recognizable trend here: whoever wrote the *1ˢᵗ Annual Report* specifically described the ranks held by the alleged members of the *Special Panel* in 1947 and into the early part of 1948 *only*. The ranks that practically *all* of the members held in 1947 and 1948 were *utterly* redundant by 1951, which is the earliest possible year in which the *Report* could have been prepared, *if* it is a single entity, that is. And we know that the *Report*, as a *single* entity at least, could not have been written any earlier than mid-1951 by virtue of the fact that it references events and activities in its pages that occurred in May of that year. There may be a logical explanation for this conundrum, however.

It is possible that the *Cover Page* of the document *does* date from 1948 (which *would* explain the discrepancies regarding the post-1950 ranks held by the alleged members), but that the main body of the *Report* post-dates 1948 by a number of years. As has been noted, Timothy Cooper received the document in three, separate installments spread across a period of more than twelve months. And it is only *presumption* that the three segments are all a part of the same document. It is not beyond the bounds of possibility that the *Cover Page* relates to MJ-12's *1ˢᵗ Annual Report* generated in 1948, as its title *does* suggest; but that the *body* of the *Report* (that describes events dating from the early 1950s) is extracted from a *4ᵗʰ* or *5ᵗʰ Annual Report*. Few have considered this possibility, but it is one that should be given serious attention.

Of course, the skeptic would argue that these unanswered issues are merely the fall-out of the sloppy actions of a hoaxer that had not bothered to fully research the available historical background data on those listed as *Panel* members. However, *if* Thomas Cantwheel's claims that some of the MJ-12 documentation at issue that he provided to Timothy Cooper were merely "constructs" designed to act as guidelines and pointers to assist Cooper in his search for the truth and are *not* genuine, leaked papers, then this may go some way towards resolving this issue. Let us now turn our attention to the content of the *1ˢᵗ Annual Report*.

The purpose of the *Report* is described concisely: "The aforementioned panel under the direct presidential directive signed on 26 September 1947, has been tasked with responsibility of providing answers to a most troubling and disturbing phenomenon, that of other-world visitation and what it portends for the human family. It is in this vein that the panel has addressed the problem and in providing possible answers."[11]

The document continues that: "In consonance with your instructions, advisors from State, Treasury, War and Navy Departments assisted me on a two month exploratory mission concerning the reality of other-world visitation. The principle investigators and storage areas were visited. Successful efforts were made to reach scientists of all levels as measured by their work in classified defense projects. Approximately 1,200 memoranda and intelligence reports were considered. The report presents this situation against a global background, my estimates, current and projected, in both the U.S., and allied countries, and recommendations deemed to be sound courses of action for formulating plans and policies in light of recent developments."[12]

It is made abundantly clear that the secret world of MJ-12 had come to the conclusion that UFOs were almost certainly a manifestation of alien technology: "All efforts have been made to identify the country or private concern which could have the technical and financial resources necessary to produce such a long-range flight. So far, no country on this earth has the means and the security of its resources to produce such. A consensus reached by members of the panel, that until positive proof that the Russians did not attempt a series of reconnaissance flights over our most secure installations—the sightings and recovered objects are interplanetary in nature. The occupants of these planform vehicles are, in most respects, human or human-like. Autopsies, so far indicate, that these beings share the same biological needs as humans."[13]

It becomes very clear that the Panel's main concern and area of research was in determining how the military might best take advantage of the incredible technology that had, quite literally, fallen into its lap: areas covered in the *Report* specifically with respect to the utilization of alien materials include: "Technology;" "Nuclear Weapons Development;" "New Materials Development;" "Planned Future Rocket Development;" "Nuclear Propulsion Development;" "Intelligence Gathering and Analysis;" "Foreign

Policy and National Security;" "Domestic and Constitutional Issues;" "Social, Religious and Scientific Reaction;" "Cold War Development;" "Genetic and Pharmaceutical Development Programs;" and "Government Policy of Control and Denial." The Panel also addressed one other area that is of critical importance and relevance to this book: "Biological Warfare Programs."[14]

Before discussing this issue in depth, however, it is worth noting that a historical summary of the background to the U.S. Government's secret UFO program is outlined in a series of three *Annexes* (*A* to *C*) contained within the document. As with other MJ-12 documents supplied to Timothy Cooper, *Annex A* of the 1st *Annual Report* reinforces the scenario of: (1) several UFO crashes within the State of New Mexico in the summer of 1947 that may have been the result of mid-air collisions; (2) the recovery of a number of alien bodies that had ejected from one of the vehicles in an "escape cylinder," and that had "suffered from sudden decompression and heat suffocation, as a result of damage sustained from unknown causes;" and (3) the establishment of the super-secret MJ-12 group in the wake of these startling discoveries.[15]

Annex B details the background to the creation of MJ-12 in 1947, as well as its work for the next four years, much of which was focused upon highlighting and determining how the recovered technology might be best utilized and exploited for military gain.[16]

Annex C is a concise, four-page history of what MJ-12 had learned about the UFO presence on the Earth, and that highlights some of the more disturbing aspects of the alien issue, including: unexplained disappearances of soldiers on the battlefield; "missing aircraft, pilots and crews;" unresolved aircraft crashes and related pilot deaths; "aerial interference with military aircraft;" and close encounters with UFOs in the vicinity of sensitive military, intelligence, and defense establishments.[17]

But what of the issue most relative to the subject of this book: biological warfare and alien viruses? According to the 1st *Annual Report*: "BW programs in U.S. and U.K. are in field test stages. Discovery of new virus and bacteria agents so lethal, that serums derived by genetic research, can launch medical science into unheard of fields of biology. The samples extracted from bodies found in New Mexico, have yielded new strains of a retro-virus not totally understood, but, give promise of the ultimate BW weapon.

The danger lies in the spread of airborne and bloodborne outbreaks of diseases in large populations, with no medical cures available."[18]

The document continues: "The Panel was concerned over the contamination of several SED personnel upon coming in contact with debris near the power plant. One technician was overcome and collapsed when he attempted the removal of a body. Another medical technician went into a coma four hours after placing a body in a rubber body-bag. All four were rushed to Los Alamos for observation. All four later died of seizures and profuse bleeding. All four were wearing protective suits when they came into contact with body fluids from the occupants."[19]

Further data is elaborated upon: "Autopsies on the four dead SED technicians are not conclusive. It is believed that the four may have suffered from some form of toxin or a highly contagious disease. Tissue samples are currently being kept at Fort Detrick, Md."[20]

And most disturbing of all: "In the opinion of the senior AEC medical officer, current medical equipment and supplies are wholly inadequate in dealing with a large scale outbreak of the alien virus." There are two aspects of these specific extracts that have provoked extreme controversy within the tightly knit UFO research arena: namely, the allegation that tissue samples had been forwarded to Fort Detrick, and the reference to a poorly defined "retro-virus."[21]

With respect to Fort Detrick: in 1929, Frederick County purchased ninety acres of farmland for use as a municipal airport. In 1930, this tract of land was leased to the Maryland National Guard for use as a summer training camp for the 104th Observation Squadron, the first military presence at this site.

Detrick Field, as Fort Detrick was originally designated, was used as a summer training camp until 1940, when, by joint agreement of Frederick County and the Maryland National Guard, the field was leased to the U.S. Civil Aeronautics Administration (CAA). The CAA used the field as a pilot training center until the outbreak of World War II.

In 1941, President Roosevelt ordered the establishment of the U.S. Biological Warfare program. As a result, in 1943, the newly-named Camp Detrick was assigned to the Army Chemical Warfare Service for the development of a Biological Warfare Research Center. The original ninety-acre tract plus an adjoining fifty-three acres were purchased in 1944. By that time, Camp Detrick was well established as an installation for the research and development of offensive and defensive biological warfare techniques and agents.

Camp Detrick was designated a permanent installation shortly after the end of the Second World War. A seven-acre and a five-acre tract were acquired in 1944 and were respectively developed for use as water and sewer treatment plants. Collectively, these two tracts are now referred to as Area C. In 1946, 399 acres, now designated as Area B, was acquired to provide an outdoor test area, commonly called the "grid test area." An additional 153 acres adjoining Area A were acquired during 1946 and 1947. The Army acquired an additional 503 acres of land adjacent to the Post in 1952. This land was used primarily for plant science research.

The Flair U.S. Army Reserve Center was constructed in 1955 and 1956 as a separate entity in the northeast corner of Area B. In 1956, the name of the installation was changed from Camp Detrick to Fort Detrick. Subsequently, the land transfer reverted to Fort Detrick, and the facility became an on-post tenant in 1958. Permanent technical and installation support facilities were constructed during subsequent years, including major development projects such as the East Coast Telecommunications Center (now the 1110th Signal Battalion) and the U.S. Army Medical Research Institute of Infectious Diseases (USAMRIID).

After the discontinuance of official biological warfare activities, on April 1, 1972, the control of Fort Detrick was transferred from the U.S. Army Material Command to the Office of the Surgeon General, Department of the Army, and further assigned as a subordinate installation of the U.S. Army Medical Department. In 1973, Fort Detrick was reassigned from the U.S. Army Surgeon General to the newly created U.S. Army Health Services Command (HSC). In 1995, HSC was itself reorganized into the U.S. Army Medical Command (MEDCOM).[22]

The reader will have noted that Fort Detrick did not receive that title until 1956: from 1943 until 1955 the installation was designated Camp Detrick, having previously been known as Detrick Field. Moreover, a detailed analysis, undertaken by Nick Redfern, of available documentation housed at the National Archives, Maryland, and also that which has been declassified by Fort Detrick itself under the terms of the Freedom of Information Act, demonstrates that on *no* occasion was the term Fort Detrick *ever* utilized in documentation prior to the name change in 1956. Moreover, the *only* documentation to *ever* make a reference to Fort Detrick prior to 1956 is the *1ˢᵗ Annual Report*.

This has led some commentators to suggest that, even though the *1ˢᵗ Annual Report* does not refer to events that post-date 1951, the document *must*, therefore, be of 1956, or post-1956, vintage. However, this scenario falls apart for one, specific reason: of those listed as a member of the MJ-12 Special Panel, one is General Hoyt S. Vandenberg. Unfortunately, Vandenberg died in 1954. Therefore, he could not possibly have been a member of such a Panel in 1956, two years after his death. This discrepancy is further evidence that the *Report* was probably one of Cantwheel's "constructs."[23]

It is intriguing to note and important to stress, however, that there *are* official documents available that *do* have a highly positive bearing upon this aspect of the *1ˢᵗ Annual Report*. For example, recall the concerns expressed within the *1ˢᵗ Annual Report* regarding: "the spread of airborne and bloodborne outbreaks of diseases in large populations, with no medical cures available."[24]

It transpires that in the crucial year of 1947, Theodor Rosebury, of the Society of American Bacteriologists, wrote a paper titled *Experimental Air-Borne Infection* that focused upon "equipment and methods for the quantitative study of highly infective agents." Interestingly, in his paper, Rosebury noted that he had received a great deal of assistance in the preparation of his paper from "the Technical Staff of Camp Detrick," as well as from its British equivalent, Porton Down, of which more will be discussed in a later chapter. So, in other words, personnel at Camp Detrick/Fort Detrick *were* concerned specifically about "airborne" outbreaks of serious diseases in the *exact* year that the New Mexico UFO crash-retrievals occurred.[25]

And what of the reference to an apparently lethal "retro-virus" present at one of the New Mexico crash sites of July 1947?

Essentially, retroviruses are RNA-containing viruses that use the enzyme reverse transcriptase to copy their RNA into the DNA of a host cell. Retroviruses have been isolated from a variety of vertebrate species, including humans, other mammals, reptiles, and fish. The family Retroviridae includes such important human pathogens as human immunodeficiency virus (HIV) and human T lymphotropic virus (HTLV), which are the causes of AIDS and adult T-cell leukemia respectively.[26]

The retrovirus has an intriguing history: as far back as 1904, Ellerman and Bang, searching for an infectious cause for leukemia, studied the disease in chickens and successfully transferred it via cell-free tissue filtrates. Seven years later, Peyton Rous transmitted solid tumors from chickens by transplanting tissue, but also isolated the infectious agent. This discovery was followed by many other examples of acutely transforming retroviruses, together with the structural characterization of the viruses involved. Filtrates that led to the inducement of tumors would become known variously as filterable agents, filterable viruses, Rous agents, and Rous viruses.[27]

In 1928, A.E. Boycott, the President of the Royal Society of Medicine, Section of Pathology, in his Presidential Address entitled *The Transition from Live to Dead: the Nature of Filterable Viruses*, said: "If we believe that all malignant tumors contain more or less of a carcinogenic agent akin to the Rous virus, it follows that we can with a considerable degree of certainty stimulate normal tissues to produce virus."[28]

During the 1940s, following the development of the electron microscope, particles observed in malignant tissues could be isolated and separated. Because these particles were seen in malignant tissues, it was determined that the particles constituted the aetiological agent of the disease; and by the 1950s Rous's filterable agents became known as oncoviruses. During this same period, retro-virologist J.W. Beard recognized that cells including uninfected cells, under various conditions, were responsible for the generation of a heterogeneous array of particles, some of which take on the appearance of oncoviruses.[29]

By the 1960s, Howard Temin had determined that retrovirus genomes were composed of RNA, and observed that replication was inhibited by actinomycin D, which inhibits DNA synthesis, and led to the proposal of the concept of reverse transcription.[30]

In 1969, Huebner and Todaro proposed the viral oncogene hypothesis – namely, the transmission of viral and oncogenic information as genetic elements, rather than as a pathogenic response to a virus. David Baltimore at MIT independently replicated Temin's work, and the pair published a joint article in *Nature* on June 27, 1970 that described their discoveries. And in 1981, the Human T-cell leukemia virus was discovered, and became the first universally acknowledged pathogenic human retrovirus.[31]

There is, however, one issue that must be addressed. While none of the above data that concerns the history of retroviruses is in dispute, it becomes highly problematic when trying to validate the *1ˢᵗ Annual Report* to note that although a great deal of research was undertaken into retroviruses throughout much of the 20ᵗʰ Century, the actual usage of the specific word, retrovirus, appears not to have entered the English language until the 1970s.

For example, *Medline*, the computerized database on biomedical research that has access to all medical related journals dating back to 1965, confirms that the first modern usage of the term retrovirus did not surface until the 1970s; and it was in the September 8, 1977 issue of *Nature* that we see the term first used in its now well-defined format.[32] Similarly, the term retrovirus is actually derived from the first two letters of Reverse Transcriptase. Eleni Papadopolous-Eleopulos, a bio-physicist engaged in AIDS research in Western Australian states in her paper, *A brief history of Retroviruses*: "Reverse transcriptase is an enzyme first discovered in Oncoviruses in 1970 hence their present name, retroviruses." As Papadopolous-Eleopulos' statement makes clear, the term retrovirus was an outgrowth of terminology applied to an enzyme that was *not even discovered* until around thirty years after the *1ˢᵗ Annual Report* was allegedly written.[33]

On a similar path, Ryan Wood has stated that: "a noted virologist, Dr. Jay Levy of UCSF Medical Center wrote in an email to me that the term 'retrovirus,' all one word, was first used around 1970."[34] This, too, accords well with the words of Papadopolous-Eleopulos as it relates to the timeframe in which the term entered into the English language.

There are, however, fragments of data that suggest the issue just *might* not be so clear cut: Robert and Ryan Wood also note that in the January 28, 1949 issue of *Science*, there appears an *In Memoriam* obituary for one Robert Gladding Green. Born in Wadena, Minnesota in 1895, Green was both Professor and Chairman of the Department of Bacteriology and Immunology at the University of Minnesota. He had served in the Students' Army Training Corps during the First World War, was a captain and medical officer with the Air Corps in the Second World War, and was a member of the Society of American Bacteriologists, as well as a member of the Society for Experimental Biology and Medicine. He died on September 6, 1947, at the young age of fifty-two, from the effects of heart disease. Notably, according to *Science*, Green had "put the case for viruses being *retrograde* organisms."[35] Green had also authored a paper on November 8, 1935 titled *On the Nature of Filterable Viruses* that posited viruses stemmed from the "retrograde evolution" of free-living cells.[36]

Of equal interest, is the fact that Green was a close colleague and acquaintance of none other than Major Charles Ethan Rea, listed in the *Interplanetary Phenomenon Unit Summary* of July 22, 1947, as having conducted the autopsy of an alien body retrieved from the wreckage of a crashed UFO found in New Mexico earlier that same month.[37]

In summary, as we have seen, the data contained within the *1ˢᵗ Annual Report* is *highly* provocative and *very* relevant to the subject matter of this book. And, quite clearly, Thomas Cantwheel had a keen and personal desire to reinforce to Timothy Cooper the idea that crash-recovered alien bodies represented a serious biological threat to humankind. Cantwheel may have also provided Cooper with the real names and places implicated in this disturbing aspect of the larger UFO puzzle. But, ironically, Cantwheel's decision to provide Cooper with such data via carefully distorted "constructs" of real documents, and with historically inaccurate data on the people and places in the story, has unfortunately resulted in many people within the UFO research community dismissing the *1ˢᵗ Annual Report* as nothing more than a mere hoax.

As will now become apparent, however, there are countless, further examples of precisely the type of data that Cantwheel provided to Cooper – and, importantly, these additional examples appear to have no direct connection to either Cooper or Cantwheel.

* * *

Chapter 5 Notes:

1. *Majestic 12, 1ˢᵗ Annual Report*. Available at www.majesticdocuments.com by downloading: http://209.132.68.98/pdf/MJ-12_annualreportcover.pdf and http://209.132.68.96/pdf/MJ-12_toc.pdf and http://209.132.68.98/pdf/MJ-12_fifthannualreport.pdf

2. Ibid.

3. Ibid.

4. Ibid.

5. *Majestic 12, 1ˢᵗ Annual Report, Cover Page.* Available at www.majesticdocuments.com by downloading: http://209.132.68.98/pdf/MJ-12_ annualreportcover.pdf

6. www.arlingtoncemetery.net/josephla.htm

7. www.arlingtoncemetery.net/ldmiller.htm

8. www.arlingtoncemetery.net/brereton.htm

9. www.arlingtoncemetery.net/hsvanden.htm

10. *Major General George C. McDonald, Biography.* See: www.af.mil/bios/ bio.asp?bioID=6384

11. *Majestic 12, 1ˢᵗ Annual Report.* Available at www.majesticdocuments.com by downloading: http://209.132.68.98/pdf/MJ-12_annualreportcover.pdf and http:// 209.132.68.96/pdf/MJ-12_toc.pdf and http://209.132.68.98/pdf/MJ-12_ fifthannualreport.pdf

12. Ibid.

13. Ibid.

14. Ibid.

15. Ibid.

16. Ibid.

17. Ibid.

18. Ibid.

19. Ibid.

20. Ibid.

21. Ibid.

22. *Fort Detrick, Installation Description*: http://www.detrick.army.mil/rab/ index.cfm?page=6&part=3

23. www.arlingtoncemetery.net/hsvanden.htm

24. *Majestic 12, 1ˢᵗ Annual Report.* Available at www.majesticdocuments.com by downloading: http://209.132.68.98/pdf/MJ-12_annualreportcover.pdf and http://209. 132.68.96/pdf/MJ-12_toc.pdf and http://209.132.68.98/pdf/MJ-12_ fifthannualreport.pdf

25. *Experimental Air-Borne Infection*, Theodor Rosebury, The Society of American Bacteriologists, Williams & Wilkins Company, 1947.

26. *A Brief History of Retroviruses*, Eleni Papadopolous-Eleopulos, Valendar F. Turner, John M. Papadimitriou, Barry A. Page & David Causer, *Continuum Magazine*, Vol. 5, No. 2. See also: http://www.garynull.com/cms/index.php/plain/documents/ a_brief_history_of_retroviruses

27. *Retroviruses.* See: http://www.mcb.uct.ac.za/cann/335/Retroviruses.html

28. A.E. Boycott, President of the Royal Society of Medicine, Section of Pathology, *The Transition from Live to Dead: the Nature of Filtrable Viruses*, 1928.

29. *Retroviruses.* See: http://www.mcb.uct.ac.za/cann/335/Retroviruses.html

30. *Howard Temin, Autobiography.* See: http://nobelprize.org/medicine/laureats/1975/ temin-autobio.html

31. *Nature*, June 27, 1970.

32. *Nature*, September 8, 1977.

33. *A Brief History of Retroviruses*, Eleni Papadopolous-Eleopulos, Valendar F. Turner, John M. Papadimitriou, Barry A. Page & David Causer, *Continuum Magazine*, Vol. 5, No. 2. See also: http://www.garynull.com/cms/index.php/plain/documents/a_ brief_history_of_retroviruses

34. E-mail from Ryan Wood to Robert Wood, December 5, 1998.

35. *Science*, Vol. 109, January 28, 1949.

36. *On the Nature of Filterable Viruses*, Robert G. Green, November 8, 1935.

37. *Interplanetary Phenomenon Unit Summary*, July 22, 1947. Available at www.majesticdocuments.com by downloading: http://209.132.68.98/pdf/ipu_ report.pdf

Chapter 6
Psychological Warfare and Forgery
1941-1951

One of the questions that inevitably surfaced after the MJ-12 documentation made available via Timothy Cooper appeared in the public domain was: Did Cooper himself fake the documents? If that *was* the case, and there was *no* Cantwheel, and there was *no* Salina, then that would have cast grave doubt on much of the history of MJ-12. Both Robert and Ryan Wood are as certain as they can be, however, that Cooper is himself *not* problematic with respect to this specific question.

As Robert Wood has stated:

"The newcomer to Ufology often thinks that that it is extremely unlikely that we have actually been visited by E.T.s and that their vehicles have crashed and we have retrieved them. They inadvertently establish a standard of 'proof' that is exceptionally high, recalling Carl Sagan's widely quoted remark that, 'Extraordinary claims demand extraordinary proof. Where is the evidence?'

"Anyone familiar with the thousands of high quality reports and very believable crash retrieval testimony knows there is fair degree of agreement that an alien craft crashed in New Mexico; and maybe other places, too; that they have been seen at close range; that they leave marks on the ground; and they appear to have occupants. If this *is* true, it is inconceivable that we, the United States, would not have initiated a project to find out everything we can, and do so in great secrecy.

"It is a virtual certainty that such a project would have had some written records over the years. It is also widely believed that documents 'leak' and that 'people cannot keep secrets.' If this *is* so, we would be expecting to have some documents surface. And we have some. The only question is: Are they genuine, or are they a fake?

"Most would agree that if there was a classified project, it would have had excellent security both back then and now, so doesn't that suggest that the documents are likely to be fake? The answer is: Not at all. Questioned document examiners try to avoid making a priori assumptions before they do their work. It has been established that the U.S. has been involved in psychological warfare for many years. Even the documents we are examining allude to this. It is certainly reasonable to consider that under certain circumstances that Psy-War could have been used on our foreign enemies over the years, somehow using UFOs as part of the process.

"If it is known that UFOs have crashed and been retrieved, and if it is also known that people fake documents sometimes, it thus turns out to be equally likely that any randomly selected document is just as likely to be real as to be fake. Thus, one can add up all of the points that argue for genuineness, and all of the points that suggest fakery, and see how the balance comes out. One possible anachronism suggesting fakery does not counteract five or ten features suggesting authenticity.

"Since many of the documents have been around for several years, those people suggesting fakery have had a lot of opportunity to ask questions. Because nobody wants to be caught claiming that they have the 'proof' only to be shown later that it was a fake, document researchers like to be careful and consider all challenges or concerns. We therefore use of the techniques of questioned document examination.

"Before continuing, it is worth a sidebar to comment that we believe that the public evaluation of these documents is not against the law, since we did not steal them, bribe someone to, or coerce anyone. Furthermore, the General Accounting Office, the FBI, and the Air Force have all taken public positions that questioned documents involving Majestic, MAJIC, or MJ-12 are *all* fake (even though, of course, they are in error.) However, if the documents are genuine, it is conceded that someone violated a security oath at some time to keep them personally and then decided to share them with the recipients. This is an obvious reason for not wishing to be identified publicly, since they could be prosecuted.

"We go through an orderly process of document evaluation, looking for clues that would suggest fakery: anachronisms in paper, ink, typewriters, format, stamp impressions, or content. For the most part, we do not possess original documents, with the exception of the *Burned Memo*, the *Bowen Manuscript*, the *Cutler-Twining* memo (which is not in our possession) and a new version of the *Eisenhower-Briefing Document*."[1]

On the specific issue of Timothy Cooper and fakery, Robert Wood explained his position:

"Tim Cooper has signed affidavits to the effect that he *did* get these materials from his mailbox and that he has *never* fabricated any documents. He took a lie detector test that showed deception in some of his answers, which surprised us, but I have concluded it was because of his continuing desire to protect the identity of two sources that he refuses to identify.

"A recent article in *Science* magazine notes that the probability of truthful answers being declared deceptive is seven times more likely than deceptive answers being called truthful. My partner and I have spent many hours with Tim Cooper, and have found him consistently truthful over the years, with a great tendency to protect confidences, a quality that has merit.

"Much has been made of a similarity of raised letters in the typewriting used by him to write a letter to Tim Good and the type in the *Interplanetary Phenomenon Unit (IPU) Report*. My own questioned document examiner, James Black, concluded that the typewriter used was a *Royal* in both cases, but that one could not say much more than each could be any one thousands of typewriters, and that fast typists typically do not hit the capitalization bar uniformly.

"Furthermore, we are in physical possession of several of the original mailing envelopes from the sources, and have used them to track down the meter or zip code in detail. There is just no question that Tim has been getting these packages in the mail from sources who are happy to see the data spread further. We feel it is important to apply our document authentication expertise before releasing everything to everyone, and so we have temporarily withheld some documents about which there are questions we cannot yet answer.

"After we publicized more of the documents, offering them for sale to defray costs, a number of concerns were posed about their authenticity, ranging from logical valid questioned document issues to ad-hominem attacks."

As Robert Wood noted, this included two specific criticisms:

"Concern 1: Evidence exists that the documents are fraudulent.

"Response: No such evidence exists. The ability to discriminate the real from the fake is the correct way to view the issue.

"Concern 2: The presence of numerous grammatical, punctua-

tion and spelling errors strongly suggests fakery. This extrapo-
lates to 'the more errors, the more genuine it is.'

"Response: Most of the pages we are seeing are unsigned,
unfinished *draft* material. Technical people are not well known for
their writing ability. It is incredible that a faker would permit so
many errors. It is reasonable that one of the reasons we have them
is that they were drafts, less well controlled by security than the final
copies. Errors need to be placed in the context of the author and the
typist, who may or may not be the same person."[2]

Similarly, on the issue of whether or not the collective body of
MJ-12-related documents that surfaced via Timothy Cooper
represents deception and forgery by Cooper himself, Ryan Wood has
made critically important comments and observations. In a paper
titled *Ten Reasons Why Tim Cooper is NOT a Provenance Problem*,
Wood notes the following, specifically with regard to Cooper:

"He did not seek out publicity for himself. In fact, he gave away
documents and publicity to Tim Good with the 'Hillenkoetter to
Military Assessment of the Joint Intelligence Committee memo of
19 September 1947.'

"If Bob and Ryan Wood did not visit him, talk with him, become
his friend and ask for documents they would still be in Cooper's attic
gathering dust. This shows that Cooper is not seeking recognition
for his alleged forgery, which is a characteristic action of forgery
criminals.

"Tim Cooper has a skeptical attitude. He did not openly embrace
the documents nor did he have the time to verify the details that
have been partially checked by Wood and Wood and others.

"Despite claims of forgery by Tim Good [that some of the MJ-12
documents supplied by Tim Cooper were prepared on the same
typewriter that Cooper utilized to write letters to Good), Dr. James
Black (a forensic typewriter specialist) was unable to conclude that
the documents in question were typed with the same typewriter,
only that the make and model are the same. Any of the tens of
thousands of typewriters are suspect.

"Tim Cooper is just one of many sources of the Majestic documents that mutually reinforce the content of the Cooper originated
documents. Cooper is NOT the linchpin to dismissing the government paper trail of UFO and ET complicity.

"There is clear evidence in the form of postage meters, original envelopes, and postmarks showing that many of the documents Cooper received did in fact travel through the mail. Furthermore, two were postmarked "Langley, Virginia" (CIA headquarters postage meter) and Ft. Meade, FOIA office.

"Several researchers have commented to Wood and Wood that Cooper's writing style is inconsistent with the leaked documents. Forensic linguistics are being applied and support the conclusion that Tim did not write the documents in question.

"Cooper's failed lie detector test is consistent with him protecting his in-person documents sources – the CIA archivist, the legion-naire, and Thomas (Cy) Cantwheel.

"No one has admitted, or come forward claiming, authorship.

"Although of speculative value, high quality remote viewing (psychic) assets have targeted Tim Cooper and the documents and concluded the documents are predominantly real and Cooper is not a forger. In fact, there seem to be multiple origins of documents feeding to Cooper."[3]

Collectively, Ryan Wood's observations strongly suggest that Cooper had no motivation for forging such material, and did not, and still does not, fit the profile of someone seeking either personal fame or financial gain.

But what of the possibility that the documents are examples of *official* deception: psychological warfare and disinformation designed to mislead either the UFO research community, or, at the height of the Cold War, the Soviets specifically? Again, Ryan Wood's observations, extracted from his paper titled *Psychological Warfare and the Majestic Documents: Little Evidence of Deception*, are of vital relevance to unraveling the truth behind the MJ-12 documents.

As Wood states: "Be it modern day covert planning and leaking, or old psychological warfare documents that have leaked out of the garage into mailboxes and via personal meetings; this paper seeks to examine these theories and other relevant probabilities along with expert testimony as they relate to psychological warfare and propaganda operations. Let's begin with a couple of modern definitions of psychological warfare and psychological operations both from the *Joint Chief's of Staff Publication 1*, 1987:

> *PSYWAR:* The planned use of propaganda and other psyche logical actions having the primary purpose of influencing the opinions, emotions, attitudes and behavior of hostile foreign groups in such a

way as to support achievement of national objectives.

PSYOP: Planned operations to convey selected information and indicators to foreign audiences to influence their emotions, motives, objective reasoning and ultimately the behavior of foreign government, organizations, groups, and individuals. The purpose of psychological operations is to induce or reinforce foreign attitudes and behavior favorable to the originator's objectives."

Wood continues, and makes a noteworthy observation: "Most experienced corporate citizens will recognize the above basic principles of marketing, 'spin,' and salesmanship. What is different is the focus on national objectives and foreign audiences. The reader should feel comfortable that these are not exotic, exclusive, expert-only skills: it is really just standard marketing practices, except the stakes may be higher and the tools to deliver the message may be forged documents delivered by covert means."

Indeed, Wood was careful to make note of the following, extracted from the *Psychological Warfare Casebook*, prepared by Operations Research at John Hopkins University of 1958: "If you give a man the correct information for seven years, he may believe the incorrect information on the first day of the eighth year when it is necessary, from your point of view, that he should do so. Your first job is to build credibility and the authenticity of your propaganda, and persuade the enemy to trust you although you are his enemy."

But he also asks: "Do the Majestic documents show any evidence of a history of building credibility, let alone a long one, with potential targets of deception, such as the Soviet Union or China?" Let us examine Ryan Wood's findings on this matter:

"The goal of this paper is answer these questions and determine the extent to which there is any real and hard evidence that covert psychological warfare techniques were used in conjunction with the Majestic documents. It is generally conceded that only a foreign or domestic intelligence agency has the resources, intelligence and sophistication to deliver an alleged psychological warfare deception using the comprehensive, often sophisticated, intertwined Majestic documents. Such an undertaking, if true, would have started at least as early as 1981 (Air Force Office of Special Investigations Telex) and used six different sources, physically planted documents in government archives as well as mailboxes. They would have had numerous trained psychological war experts thoughtfully creating an expensive, clever deception targeted at a foreign power for the past 19 years. Does that sound credible?"

Wood does concede that: "It is certainly not beyond modern intelligence service capabilities to have fabricated some or all these documents, and it is not beyond thinking they would mount such an effort for marginal or even illogical reasons. Even that a psywar team would intentionally or carelessly include some anachronistic 'ringers' is believable."

Notwithstanding the above, there is the following from Wood:

"However, there are severe disconnects between the wide scope, possible purpose(s), presumed target(s), likely risks, and extended duration of this alleged psywar operation. The real question is how do we test for the use of psychological warfare and propaganda?

"Ask yourself the following questions:

Is there a low risk of attracting foreign intelligence organizations to the targeted topic? What is the extent of the risk involved with such a deception? Is it worth the tradeoffs?

Has there been a long, multi-year history of a credible relation-ship between the target of deception and the authors of the decep-tion?

Is the reaction of the target predicable? Will they swallow the bait and move in the desired direction for some length of time?

Is there a specific purpose, goal, objective or intent of the deception? Can it be clearly stated?

Does the phrase, sentence or document establish believability in the eye of the target of deception?

Is there any direct evidence that the documents were ever launched at the target?

Are there a credible number of unique language words to draw suspicion about authorship?

Do the historically competent experts in Psychological Warfare agree with the answers to these questions?"

In a section of his paper titled *How Does Reason Stand Up To These Questions?* Wood notes the following:

"First, if we are intellectually honest, we cannot discard the possibility that the documents are genuine and represent the intent of the authors at the time they were written, even with their misspellings, currently unresolved 'anachronisms,' and occasional errors. It is important not to think that discrepancies are not evidence of psychological warfare. To date there is not a single anachronism or other error that has been raised and then thoroughly researched that *clearly* shows the documents to be false. An error may be misleading, or it may be incomplete, but the examples are not outside the scope of reasonable error in human bureaucracies."

Wood expands further, with a valuable question: "Now who might be the authors and who might be their target? We know, by analysis, that SOM 1-01 is on *original 1954 paper* and that other documents are on original paper with watermarks from the proper period. Thus, if there were a psychological warfare operation, it could have been created and launched on its target during the cold war of the 50s by someone with access to such materials. Using the law of *Occam's Razor*, the simplest source for such materials is the United States. Targeted against whom? Naturally, the only believable target is the Soviet Union: they had nuclear capability and so did we. The alleged deception foisted on them via the documents could be: 'Don't mess with the United States — we have extraterrestrials and their technology and amazing advanced weaponry.' Is creating an elaborate series of mutually reinforcing, incredible documents over nearly two decades necessary to accomplish credible deterrence?" Wood's succinct response to this question: "Hardly."

He elaborates further:

"Is North Korea a viable target of deception for the Majestic documents dated before 1951? No, not really. It defies most military historians to believe that any leaked UFO document, even something as intriguing as *SOM 1-01: Extraterrestrial Entities and Technology Recovery and Disposal* would have changed any tactical or strategic objective, troop movement or anti-aircraft battery. Psychological Warfare *was* certainly used during the Korean conflict—with typical operations involving dropping leaflets out of airplanes urging surrender. 'Genuine' UFO reports from soldiers during military action seemed to have had no impact on the course of battles.

"Again, how do these documents serve a valid, officially authorized Cold War purpose, assuming they were U.S.-produced? Would they desensitize Soviet air defenses to the meaning of sudden unexplained radar returns? If so, how does that square with the Robertson Panel's public report available to the Soviets, which debunked UFO reports as a valid input to air defense calculations? Would they conceal experimental aircraft development — as if anyone would doubt that we were proceeding in this direction anyway? Would they mask some other terrestrial, but overwhelming, American super-technology? This would stimulate greater espionage to acquire it, clearly undesirable."

Wood then focuses his attention upon an area that few of those with an interest in the MJ-12 controversy have even considered:

"Or do the documents create a 'fire break' against learning an even deeper secret? Suppose that any one of the explicit and controversial sentences, let alone entire documents, of the MJ-12 material are genuine, in the sense that it was produced by a real psychological warfare organization. It is conceivable to concoct a very *closely similar*, but *intentionally different*, project as a smokescreen against a deeper secret. Is the secret being concealed one of those truths so precious that a 'bodyguard of lies' must protect it? What would warrant such an effort? Is the current Majestic discussion of crashed extraterrestrial discs and technology a smokescreen for *live* E.T.s and fully functional lines of communication and technology transfer? This argument leads deeper than the debunkers can dare imagine." Indeed, it does. Wood continues:

"If the Majestic documents are mere fabrications, how far must we go to rationalize the creation of such documents? Is it credible that a crack psychological warfare disinformation team — whether operating out of the bowels of the NSA, the underground Groom Lake mine, or elsewhere — would decide to be 'really clever' and try to hide some super secret, or divert the enemy's attention by taking an existing highly secure project (MJ-12), use its actual name, subject matter, along with identifying scores of living personnel, then change presumably key details, and then reveal this alleged deception to a target, and potentially to the public? As one fellow researcher said to me, it's 'like doing the dance of the seven veils with wet Kleenex.'"

A "logical conclusion," states Wood, "might be that one of the most highly protected super secrets of our time was intentionally revealed, whether to a wider public, or to foreign intelligence, it does not matter. The initial disclosure would be *very* risky, as it would draw attention to the general nature of the UFO and ET matter, irrespective of clouding the details, and would certainly prompt more intensive and sophisticated intelligence targeting by foreign intelligence assets. In short, if it is a psychological warfare operation, revealing the MJ-12 documents is inept because it will attract, and *has* attracted, much new attention.

"Alternatively," Wood asks, "did the Soviets or Chinese create these materials, insert some in the files of the National Archives and Records Administration, then release most of them in the 1990s after the fall of the Berlin Wall, in order to bring the capitalist enemy to its knees? America, your government is hiding UFOs: throw off your chains and embrace the glorious socialist future. Judge for yourself."

Wood then reveals the words of a "senior government official" who has commented specifically on the MJ-12 documents: "My gut says they're real; contain the usual inconsistencies, mistakes and anomalies that derive from government work every day (even at the highest levels, especially where there is no effort to make things 'credible' for outside view, since they were never intended for outside view); and correspond to a set of phenomena that have been too consistently reported, for too long, by too many sane people. What otherwise do we do with apparently authentic letters like that from Sarbacher? Tools of the same disinformation campaign? Or if from the Soviets (who else?), is it to promote distrust and cynicism toward our 'government conspiracy' and foster social unrest? If so, they spent a lot of time and money and incredibly detailed research to little effect, since the vast majority of Americans have no knowledge of these documents, and the few who do are in conflict over them."

"Do the Majestic Documents Specifically Mention Psychological Warfare? What is the internal evidence of the documents themselves? What posture do they assume?" asks Wood. As he notes, the 19-page *White Hot Technical Report* discusses Psychological Warfare in the following way.

"There is a good chance that the Russians may try to make use of the flying saucer scare by public news media and diplomatic means [sic] of a technological breakthrough in aircraft and missile development. We feel that such a disclosure would most certainly cause great embarrassment to our elected officials and to the military, not to mention the panic felt by the citizenry. To counter such a threat, it is recommended that a counterintelligence program be drawn up and held in abeyance if at such time the situation should present itself. It might be suggested that we should make a preemptive use of these objects for the purpose of psychological warfare once the true nature of these objects are known and understood. ...It would be advisable for the respective Secretaries of the Armed Forces to devise a security policy of plausible denial, if and when the public becomes aware of the reality of these objects and the interest of the military in such incidents. In conclusion, for reasons of national security and the public well being, the US must be perceived as being the top of the heap, and every effort must be made to insure that there is [sic], and never has been, a threat to the country."

Wood notes that the implications of the wording of the above-document are vitally important to the question of whether or not the MJ-12 documents are verifiably real, or are some form of deception: "In September of 1947, top military leaders were recommending to the President that the U.S. consider using our existing crashed hardware and absolute proof of the reality of UFOs as a tool to deceive the Soviets once we figured out the technology. Then if this document is psychological warfare propaganda, why include this paragraph? It just attracts attention to the topic and makes alleged foreign intelligence analysts analyzing such a document more suspicious." Indeed, it does. And Wood elaborates further:

"There is another brief explicit discussion of psychological warfare, from the *1st Annual Report*: 'MAJESTIC SS&P are currently focused on Psy-op development for Cold War CI activities.' So what does this mean? We know that the National Security Council authorized an interdisciplinary Special Studies group consisting of Army, Navy, Air Force and CIA with their May 5, 1948 directive. We also know that President Truman made the decision to establish the Psychological Strategy Board (PSB) on April 4, 1951. This further relates to UFOs when you consider who was on the PSB:

- Secretary of the Army, the Honorable Kenneth Royall;
- Secretary of War, the Honorable Robert Patterson;
- Assistant Secretary of the Army, the Honorable Gordon Gray;
- Chief of Staff & General of the Army, Dwight D. Eisenhower;
- Lt. General Albert C. Wedemeyer;
- Brigadier General Robert McClure;
- Lt. General J. Lawton Collins;

- Major General Charles Bolte;
- Undersecretary of War, the Honorable William Draper;
- Major General Stephen Chamberlain, USA (G-2)."

As Wood makes clear: "Many of these people are deeply involved with MAJESTIC-12 according to other documents. Note the similarity of panel personnel between the November 1952 *Eisenhower Briefing Document* and the *1st Annual Report*; the team distribution has the same interagency structure. Is this a coincidence, standard procedure or is it the same MAJESTIC committee just six years later? What is the mission of 'Cold War CI activities' as it relates to UFOs? Who is the target and what are the objectives?

"The second explicit mention of psychological warfare is from the 'Annual Report' on Majestic, page 10, Annex B, point 10: 'MAJCOM-1 with the assistance of the Panel persuades the President to establish a Psychological Strategy Board on 4 April 1951.'

"This is an obscure fact that the Psychological Strategy Board was authorized on April 4, 1951. To discover this would take intense digging nowadays and would be known to only a few insiders in 1951. This is powerful evidence in favor of Majestic document authenticity. However, following the disinformation theory, why attract attention to the fact (verifiable and known today) that you had established a very secret board with staff, plans, and very likely operational capabilities to mislead the enemy?

"Is it logical to believe that if the *1st Annual Report* document was a part of psychological warfare deception that it would highlight that fact to the target of such a deception? I don't think so. In addition to the examples above, here is more evidence that such a deception is not a factor. Why would the following paragraph be included if the goal were to deceive? 'Based on what is known of the technology and intelligence of the visitors, it is fairly certain there will be other sightings and encounters of a spectacular nature.'"

As Wood reasonably asks: "Wouldn't it be more logical to change phrases to leave the impression that the July 1947 events were a random miracle that will likely *never* happen again? That way the Soviets would pay less attention to the event. Another example is the Majestic mention of the Nuclear Energy for the Propulsion of Aircraft (NEPA) project. The highly classified NEPA project, an actual initiative and logical extension of the Manhattan project, was to provide the U.S. with an atomic-powered aircraft. Why specifically mention it in these documents, if they were designed to be 'leaked,' and encourage, and accelerate, spy activities and intelligence collection around atomic airplanes? This could be viewed as a far more important secret to keep than telling the Soviets about crashed flying saucers; yet, the statements in the documents are not deceptive (the NEPA initiative was real) and would *encourage* espionage."

Wood then turns his attention to one of the most critical questions of all: "Is there any evidence of official governmental falsification in relation to UFOs?" His answer to this question follows:

"Speculation about UFOs could offer a powerful tool to the military and intelligence communities. Early on, as evidenced from official declassified documents NASA was ordered by President Kennedy to communicate clearly to the Soviets about known and 'unknown' (UFO) aircraft and spacecraft. Some have made the obvious suggestion that we could build military or intelligence craft that 'look like' UFOs and will thus be ignored, since it is understood that modern defense systems are looking for specific anticipated targets with established 'signatures,' not 'erratic' UFOs. There is a recently declassified top-secret technical report called Snowbird that describes a Mach 3 single seat UFO that was written in 1955. It would be logical to assume that other more modern craft have been made. In relation to documents in Ufology, to date, there has not been a single, clear, classified psychological warfare product. The Majestic documents fail the basic tests as a psychological warfare activity."

But what of Wood's next question: "Have The Skeptics Raised Any Valid Objections Or Evidence?" He reveals: "A paper, from an anonymous author with unknown and unverified credentials, and titled *Deceptive UFO Documents: Doubt Debate and Daunting Questions* states the obvious concerning the polarizing debate in Ufology and provides no detailed evidence of deception in the Majestic documents. Take this statement for example: 'Ongoing research indicates that many, possibly all, of the so called MJ-12 UFO documents were officially fabricated as instruments of U.S. covert psychological warfare, perhaps beginning in 1950 during the most threatening period of the Korean War.' Whose research? What specifics are being alluded to? Without clear answers, this statement is simply an argument-by-assertion and is just pontificating by an unknown author.

"Or the critical assertion is made: 'Document examination and authentication is a science of expert opinion, and are, as other sciences, generally probabilistic; however, it is an empirical and not a statistical science.' To the contrary: document examination and authentication is not a matter of expert opinion according to Dr. James Black, 30-year practitioner in document forensics and past president of the questioned documents professional organization but is a matter of applying key straightforward tests and presenting a logical set of evidence.

"Or the critical assertion is made: 'If one notices and accepts irregularities and alterations of all the MJ-12 documents as indicative of covert psychological warfare operation, then the deception cannot be adjusted, explained away, trivialized, excused or denied....' This concept is very weak and unsubstantiated, just because there are irregularities does not mean they are psychological warfare. Furthermore, if a crack psychological warfare team had created these documents, would there not be far fewer mistakes? Don't we want the enemy to believe these documents? What's the objective? Why attract attention? The psychological warfare theory fails before it even gets to the starting gate. Don't take my opinion about it; see what an identified, accountable expert has to say."

But perhaps the most important question asked by Wood is: "What does a *real* Psychological Operations Officer say about the Majestic documents?" From Dr. Michael Aquino, Colonel, U.S. Army, Ret., who spent his entire 24-year career both creating and managing enemy deception in psychological operations and propaganda, comes a firm, and authoritative, answer to that question:

"I don't see the MJ-12 documents as comprising an effective psyop campaign of any sort. What would be the purpose? If MJ-12 existed and the docs were supposed to be believable, they would just draw more attention to the Majestic program that the government wanted under wraps. If the docs' occasional format errors were supposed to be deliberate, what would be the point of creating & disseminating such docs? All they would do would be to attract presumably unwanted amateur interest in MJ-12, which again the government would presumably not want.

"PSYOP, despite the *ooga-booga* mythology around it, is not a very complicated process. A target audience is thinking about a subject one way, and you want to get them to think about it another way. So an audience analysis is performed to find out how to talk to them, how to gain credibility with them, and how to appeal to their needs and interests. Then phrase your objective accordingly and communicate it. If you do all this correctly, their minds change and they think/act the way you want them to. That's it.

"If MJ-12 were in fact a real, top-secret government operation, which the government intended to keep secret, then anything using its name or orbiting around its business (such as the MJ-12 docs or SOM 1-01 manual) would not be remotely appropriate for any advertisement or publicity whatever.

"The only situation in which I could see PSYOP resources playing a part would be one in which the cat were out of the bag about MJ-12's existence, and the government then acted to trivialize or minimize it. When I saw *Dark Skies* on television, it occurred to me that this could be one way of turning the entire topic into a 'science fiction cartoon', in much the same way that the movie Philadelphia Experiment and its even zanier sequel did for that topic."

And Wood is careful to note that: "Dr. Aquino further added in a conversation that he would be very surprised if there was not a blue ribbon panel such as the membership of MJ-12 to investigate UFOs. After all there are high-ranking panels on all sorts of threats to national security, such as domestic biological weapons and terrorism."

In the concluding summary-section of his paper, titled *Top Reasons Why PSYWAR Theory Is Not Credible*, Wood states: "Is it a stretch to believe that a program of systematic desensitization of the world public through a variety of media outlets, with movies such as *Independence Day*, TV programs, print articles and adverts all lead to the inescapable conclusion - psychological warfare and propaganda are at play in the public's mind. Yet, clear evidence of document operations is lacking.

"Evidence of psychological warfare and the Majestic documents does *not* exist according to expert opinions. Moreover, fundamentally the basic discriminants for determining the chance of an official government psychological warfare and propaganda all fail. Is credibility established? No: there are too many errors in the documents. Is there a low risk of attracting foreign intelligence assets? No: the documents are rich in detail. Is there a clear deception objective? No: the content is too varied and there are a multitude of objectives present. Is there a reasonable timetable? No: the duration is more than two decades."

Ryan Wood's conclusion is unshakeable: the MJ-12 documents are *not* examples of bogus material created out of the imagination of Tim Cooper, and they are *not* the work of ingenious psychological warfare planners in the Pentagon. They are unique, fascinating, and sensational examples of genuine, and highly classified, official documents describing visitations to our planet by extraterrestrials, and the establishment of an ultra-secret committee – the MJ-12 – that oversees this extraordinary secret.[4]

* * *

Chapter 6 Notes:

1. *Mounting Evidence for Authenticity of MJ-12 Documents*, Robert M. Wood, *Mutual UFO Network Symposium Proceedings*, 2001.

2. Ibid.

3. *10 Reasons why Tim Cooper is not a Provenance Problem*, Ryan S. Wood. Available at www.majesticdocuments.com by downloading: http://209.132.68.98/pdf/10reasons.pdf

4. *Psychological Warfare and the Majestic Documents: Little Evidence of Deception*, Ryan S. Wood. Available at www.majesticdocuments.com by downloading: http://209.132.68.98/pdf/psywar.pdf See also: *Validating the New Majestic Documents*, Robert M. Wood, *Mutual UFO Network Proceedings*, Robert M. Wood, 2000.

Chapter 7
Animals and Biological Warfare
1947-1948

According to the *Interplanetary Phenomenon Unit Summary* document:

"...The most disturbing aspect of this investigation was there were other bodies found not far from LZ-1 that looked as if they had been dissected as you would a frog. It is not known if army field surgeons had performed exploratory surgery on these bodies. Animal parts were reportedly discovered inside the craft at LZ-2 but this cannot be confirmed. The team has reserved judgement on this issue..."[1]

For at least four decades, rural North America has played host to an uninvited, and most definitely unwelcome, guest. With remarkable stealth, it prowls the length and breadth of the country by night and day, committing atrocious acts of mutilation on innocent cattle. Blood, bodily organs, fluids and glands are removed with disturbing speed and precision, giving every impression that a superior technology is at work.

In many instances of mutilation, strange aerial lights are reported in the same area suggesting that the two phenomena, whatever their ultimate nature, have a common point of origin. Military and unmarked helicopters are also seen in the direct vicinity, and stories abound of witnesses to the mutilations being threatened into silence by dark and shadowy forces. Who or what is responsible for committing these grisly acts is a subject that has provoked intense debate: predators, satanic cults, UFOs and covert biological warfare operations have all been suggested and the mystery continues to rage.[2]

However, the *1ˢᵗ Annual Report* would seem to suggest that such animal mutilations can be traced back as far back as the New Mexico crashes of the summer of 1947. The exact means and motivations behind the mutilations (as well as their possible relationship to alien viruses) are discussed comprehensively in a later chapter. However, it is intriguing to note that formerly Top Secret papers have surfaced under the terms of the Freedom of Information Act showing that, in the critical period of the summer of 1947, American authorities became highly concerned that the United States' cattle-herd was about to be ravaged by biological warfare.

Prepared by the Committee on Biological Warfare at the request of the American Government's elite Research and Development Board, the 50-page file in question dates from March 1947 through to the latter part of 1948 and makes for disturbing reading.

In a Top Secret paper of March 28, 1947 it was stated that: "A memorandum from the Secretaries of War and Navy dated February 21, 1947, Subject: International Aspects of Biological Warfare, regarding biological warfare in relation to United Nations negotiations for regulation of armaments was referred by the Board to Committee 'X' for consideration and recommendations."[3]

Seven months later, the Research and Development Board prepared an in-depth report (also classified Top Secret) that outlined its concerns with respect to biological warfare. As the Board stated: "Preparations for biological warfare can be hidden under a variety of guises. The agents of biological warfare are being studied in every country of the world because they are also the agents of diseases of man, domestic animals and crop plants. The techniques used in developing biological warfare agents are essentially similar to the techniques used in routine bacteriological studies and in the production of vaccines, toxoids and other beneficial materials."[4]

In its report, the Board continued: "...the Committee feels that although it may be possible to control atomic research and insure that it be devoted to peaceful purposes, it is impracticable to control research on biological agents because of the close similarity between such research and legitimate investigations of a medical, agricultural or veterinary nature."[5]

What of the possibility that biological warfare could have been utilized as a weapon of mass destruction and the cause of extreme devastation? In March 1947, the Board had its doubts that biological warfare could be considered to be a tool of destruction on a par with atomic weapons; however, seven months later (during which time-period the New Mexico crashes had occurred), that view had changed radically.

With respect to this matter, in October 1947, the Board wrote that: "On the basis of present knowledge the Committee feels that biological weapons cannot be compared in their effect with such so-called weapons of mass destruction as, for example, the atomic bomb. It is doubtless true that if a self-sustaining epidemic of a fatal disease could be established in a human population, indiscriminate destruction of life on a great scale might result. However, as has been pointed out earlier in this discussion, the Committee knows of no epidemic agent that could presently be used with confidence in its significant epidemic-producing property. The spread of epidemics depends upon a number of complex inter-related factors, many of which are poorly understood or perhaps even unknown. Furthermore, it is believed that the chances of discovering an unusually virulent epidemic-producing biological agent is highly improbable and cannot be anticipated at any time in the predictable future."[6]

So much for the Committee's beliefs with respect to biological warfare and the Human Race. On the issue of the animal kingdom, however, the Committee added that: "The statements made in the preceding paragraph do not apply equally well to epizootic agents. Within this group are highly infectious agents that the Committee believes could be used to cause widespread epizootics in domestic animal populations. However, these agents could not be considered as a means of indiscriminate destruction of life in terms of human beings."[7]

The Committee continued in its 1947 document collection: "As far as non-epidemic producing agents are concerned, the Committee feels that the use of these as weapons would cause no more indiscriminate destruction of life than would, for example, use of incendiary munitions. Also destruction of property would be practically nil with biological agents, whereas it is considerable with conventional incendiary or explosive munitions. While it is granted that innocent civilians would be affected by all biological agents, the same can be said for any type of explosive munitions. Furthermore, since non-epidemic agents do not spread rapidly from one individual to another, an attack with these agents would be as indiscriminate and probably as localised as would an attack with incendiary bombs or high explosive munitions."

In conclusion, it was stated that: "As a matter of fact, predictions of effectiveness of biological agents against a human population must be taken with reservations. No experimental animal is available that can be used to measure the effectiveness of these weapons against man. For these reasons the Committee feels that at present biological warfare cannot be correctly classed as a means of mass destruction of human beings. The use of most biological agents might be more humane and less objectionable than the use of conventional weapons, for two reasons. In the first place, property is not destroyed in biological warfare and production facilities of a defeated nation may recover more quickly than if large amounts of property were destroyed. In the second place, destruction of life may be less with biological warfare if debilitating but non-fatal agents are used. For example, the use of the agent causing undulant fever as an offensive weapon might be expected to cause large numbers of casualties and thus greatly aid the war effort of the attacking nation, but most of the casualties would recover after a period of illness and could resume active lives."[8]

With that, the Committee chairman (and alleged head of Majestic 12), Vannevar Bush, prepared a Confidential memorandum for the Joint Chiefs of Staff that summarised the Committee's findings and recommendations with respect to biological warfare from a defensive perspective.[9]

By the latter part of 1948, as will now become apparent, biological warfare was seen as a major threat to the United States by the Research and Development Board. Moreover, the fear that a hostile nation would attempt to ravage the American food-supply by deliberately infecting its cattle herd with diseases and viruses was running high in official circles.

According to the 1948 documents at issue: "Biological warfare lends itself especially well to undercover operations, particularly because of the difficulty in detecting such operations and because of the versatility possible by the proper selection of biological warfare agents."

The Committee continued: "Within the *last few years* there have been several outbreaks of *exotic diseases* (author italics) and insect pests which are believed to have been introduced accidentally but which could have been introduced intentionally had someone wished to do so. The use of epizootic agents against our animal population by sabotage methods is a very real and immediate danger. Foot-and-mouth disease and rinderpest are among those which would spread rapidly, and unless effective counter-measures were immediately applied, would seriously affect the food supply of animal origin."

Grimmer still is the following extract: " Since foot-and-mouth is now present in Mexico, it would be relatively easy for saboteurs to introduce the disease into the United States and have this introduction appear as natural spread from Mexico. Since rinderpest and foot-and-mouth disease are not present in the United States, our animal population is extremely vulnerable to these diseases."

Alarmingly, the papers reveal the United States was (and logic dictates, *still is*) in no position to prevent a large-scale biological attack on the animal population had it indeed occurred: "The United States is particularly vulnerable to this type of attack. It is believed generally that espionage agents of foreign countries which are potential enemies of the United States are present already in this country. There appears to be no great barrier to prevent additional espionage agents from becoming established here and there is no control over the movements of people within the United States."

The document continues: "North America is an isolated land mass and hence specific areas therein present feasible biological warfare targets for an extra-continental enemy since fear of backfiring is minimized."

Most disturbing, however, was the potential outlook for the United States in the event of a country-wide biological warfare on the nation's cattle herd: "The food supply of the nation could be depleted to an extent which materially would reduce the nation's capacity to defend itself and to wage war. Serious outbreaks of disease of man, animals or plants also would result in profound psychological disturbances."

But how would a covert introduction of foot-and-mouth disease into the United States' food chain be undertaken? The Committee had a number of ideas: via "water contamination;" "fodder and food;" "infected bait;" "contamination of soil;" "Biological Warfare aerosols;" and deliberate "contamination of veterinary pharmaceuticals and equipment."

Realizing the potentially grave implications that such a scenario presented, the Government carefully and quietly began to initiate a number of plans to try and combat any possible attack on the continental United States that might have occurred. Recommending that a special unit should be established to deal with the situation, the Committee asserted that ventilation shafts, subway systems and

water supplies throughout the country should be carefully monitored. Similarly, the Committee stated, steps should be taken to
determine "the extent to which contamination of stamps, envelopes,
money, cosmetics, food and beverages as a means of subversively
disseminating biological agents is possible."

In addition to preparing for the worst from a defensive perspective, however, authorities were not above planning their own
biological warfare operations from an offensive perspective. "Major
goals and objectives of a research and development program in the
field of offensive special biological warfare operations include: (1)
development of new agents suitable for special operations; (2)
development of methods of dissemination for special BW operations; (3) determination of effectiveness and feasibility of methods
of dissemination; and (4) estimation of approximate dosages
required for specific special BW operations."

But it was in the conclusions of the Committee's report on the use
of foot-and-mouth disease and other diseases as a biological weapon
that the utter lack of defense against such an attack was spelled out:
"It is concluded that: (1) biological agents would appear to be well
adapted to subversive use. (2) the United States is particularly
susceptible to attack by special BW operations. (3) the subversive
use of biological agents by a potential enemy prior to a declaration
of war presents a grave danger to the United States. (4) the biological warfare research and development program is not now authorized to meet the requirements necessary to prepare defensive
measures against special BW operations."[10]

Indeed, such was the concern shown that even the FBI got in on
the act. A Confidential memorandum to FBI Director, J. Edgar
Hoover on May 9, 1950 from Raymond P. Whearty, Chairman,
Interdepartmental Committee on Internal Security and titled
Alerting of Public Health Agencies re Biological Warfare, states:

"The Public Health Services has a long-established relationship
(direct or through regional offices) with official State—and through
them to local—health agencies. Accordingly, the Public Health
Service should be the chief agency on which NSRB [Note from the
authors: The National Security Resources Board] will rely as a
source of advice to these agencies on biological warfare matters in
so far as they are a part of civil defense of people. NSRB will rely on
the Bureau of Animal Industry in the same manner for defense of

animals against BW. The National Security Resources Board has kept the Public Health Service fully informed as to biological warfare plans. In developing these plans the NSRB created an Interdepartmental Committee on Defense Against Biological Warfare. The Public Health Service and BAI are, of course, represented on this committee. Definite plans are being made in this field, as shown by the two attached "Restricted" documents. The Public Health Services and Bureau of Animal Industry are planning the training course for civil defense against biological warfare and will conduct such courses if and when appropriations are available. Approximately fifty Public Health Service top administrative officers recently spent one week at Camp Detrick for orientation in BW as part of the training, for Public Health Service officers in this particular field."[11]

And while it could be argued that this document could solely apply to the activities of hostile nations of a terrestrial nature, it is a proven fact that at some point between March and October 1947, an event occurred that caused the Committee on Biological Warfare to become highly disturbed by the possibility that someone – or *something*, perhaps – was planning a large-scale assault on North America's cattle-herd. That this concern was prompted by the apparent discovery of "animal parts" at the site of a UFO crash in the summer of 1947 is something that should be considered highly plausible.

* * *

Chapter 7 Notes

1. *Interplanetary Phenomenon Unit Summary*, July 22, 1947. Available at: www.majesticdocuments.com by downloading: http://209.132.68.98/pdf/ipu_report.pdf.

2. For an in-depth examination of the cattle mutilation mystery, see: *An Alien Harvest* by Linda Moulton Howe, Linda Moulton Howe Productions, 1989. See also: *Brain Trust*, Colm Kelleher, Paraview-Pocket Books, 2005.

3. Committee on Biological Warfare, Top Secret memorandum, March 28, 1947.

4. Committee on Biological Warfare, Top Secret memorandum, October 16, 1947.

5. Ibid.

6. Ibid.

7. Committee on Biological Warfare, Secret memorandum, October 19, 1947.

8. Committee on Biological Warfare, Restricted memorandum, October 22, 1947.

9. Vannevar Bush to the Joint Chiefs of Staff, November 16, 1947.

10. Committee on Biological Warfare, Top Secret memorandum, September 14, 1948.

11. *Alerting of Public Health Agencies re Biological Warfare*, Letter from Raymond P. Whearty, Chairman, Interdepartmental Committee on Internal Security to J. Edgar Hoover, Federal Bureau of Investigation, May 9, 1950.

Chapter 8
UFOs, Germ Bombs, and Bio-War
1947-1949

During the summer of 1947, the FBI received a letter of some significance from one Edwin M. Bailey of Stamford, Connecticut. According to a Bureau memorandum-to-Headquarters on the letter:

"Bailey prefaced his remarks by stating that he is a scientist by occupation and is currently employed at the American Cyanamid Research Laboratories on West Main Street in Stamford, Connecticut, in the Physics Division. Bailey further indicated that during the war he was employed at MIT, Cambridge, Massachusetts, in the Radiation Laboratory which Laboratory is connected with the Manhattan Project. Bailey advised that he is thirty years of age and is a graduate of the University of Arizona."

The FBI continued: "Bailey stated that the topic of 'flying saucers' had caused considerable comment and concern to the present day scientists and indicated that he himself had a personal theory concerning the 'flying saucers.' Prior to advancing his own theory, Bailey remarked that immediately after the conclusion of World War II, a friend of his, [Deleted], allegedly observed the 'flying saucers' from an observatory in Milan and Bologna, Italy. He stated that apparently at the time the 'flying saucers' had caused a little comment in Italy but that after some little publicity they immediately died out as public interest. Bailey stated that it is quite possible that actually the 'flying saucers' could be radio controlled germ bombs or atom bombs which are circling the orbit of the earth and which could be controlled by radio and directed to land on any designated target at the specific desire of the agency or country operating the bombs."

How illuminating that in the crucial period of the summer of 1947 when, according to the 1st *Annual Report* the elite of the military, intelligence and scientific communities was beginning to recognize that alien creatures potentially posed a grave biological threat to the human race, a source with an illustrious background at MIT was suggesting that UFOs might actually be "germ bombs." Was perhaps the dark and classified truth about the biological threat posed by the strange bodies found in New Mexico already starting to leak out? And, if so, was the concern of Bailey as expressed to the FBI about Flying Saucers and "germ bombs" prompted by those same leaks? The fact that Bailey certainly had a notable background, and may perhaps have been exposed to such leaks, is something that cannot be dismissed out of hand.[1]

Six decades ago, a doctor from Indiana was certain that he had uncovered the shocking truth about the UFO presence on Earth, and was determined to warn the American Military and Government of the potentially cataclysmic plans that alien beings had for us. Notably, the doctor's theories focused upon nothing less than a stealthy attack on the Human Race by the non-human intelligences. Interestingly, that attack, the doctor had concluded, was not going to come by fantastic and futuristic weaponry. Rather, the aliens were going to wipe us out via biological warfare.

That the doctor's theory surfaced only two years after the alleged recovery of strange corpses at Roswell that exhibited signs of an unknown – and lethal - virus is intriguing. But more intriguing is the extraordinary fact the doctor himself had made a correlation between his bio-war research and crashed UFO reports, too.

Officially-declassified documentation reveals that the controversy was addressed very closely by a number of agencies, including: the Federal Bureau of Investigation; the Aero Medical Laboratory at Wright-Patterson Air Force Base, Ohio; the Atomic Energy Commission; and the Air Force's Office of Special Investigations. Indeed, the AFOSI even made a specific and secret visit to the home of the doctor to interview him about his theories.

Essentially, the story began on July 1, 1949 when, along with his wife, the doctor (whose name is completely excised from released memoranda on the case) had a close encounter of a very strange kind while vacationing in Canada. Special Investigations Agent Elbert W. Farris from Scott Air Force Base, Illinois, prepared a report dated September 6, 1949 that was marked for the attention of HQ AFOSI and the Director of Technical Intelligence at Wright-Patterson Air Force Base. It began:

"Dr. and Mrs. [Deleted] of Decatur, Indiana, were interviewed on August 15, 1949, and stated that they had seen an unidentified aerial object which they thought to be a flying saucer. The sighting took place July 1, 1949 on Highway 70 about 50–70 miles north of Ft. Francis, Ontario, Canada, and near the east side of Lake of the Woods, Canada."

Farris's report continued that, based upon an interview conducted with the doctor by Special Agent Clarence A. Trumble of the AFOSI at Offutt Air Force Base: "The object was described as silvery gray in color, flying in a westerly direction and was in sight for about 5 seconds. No vapor trails or protruding objects were noted...The object pursued a straight path of flight with an erratic motion comparable to that of an oblong object being thrown through the air. The aerial anomaly appeared to be faster than an airplane. It did not hover...and was likened to a small aircraft at two thousand feet. Dr. [Deleted] observed no fins, no vapor trail and heard no sound. After passing across his line of vision, the object was lost from view behind the trees. The day was bright and sunny, and Dr. [Deleted] emphasized that he had definitely observed an object in the air unlike any other known to him. Mrs. [Deleted] corroborated her husband's statements."[2]

On the same day that the Air Force became deeply involved in the events at issue, the FBI Special-Agent-in-Charge (SAC) at the Bureau's Indianapolis office advised J. Edgar Hoover of the same, adding that the FBI was going to keep a close watch on the doctor, too, and primarily because: "...he found himself in the midst of a polio epidemic and that as a result he had read as much literature as possible with respect to polio, its symptoms, diagnosis, etc. Dr. [Deleted] told that in his opinion, the cases which were thought to be polio in the vicinity of Decatur, Indiana, were not polio, but possibly the result of uranium poisoning and that he felt the presence of flying saucers had direct bearing on the polio epidemic."[3]

The Special-Agent-in-Charge at Indianapolis informed Hoover of Dr. [Deleted]'s unique line of thinking: "[He] pointed out that flying saucers were observed in the Carolinas in 1948 and there was a polio epidemic in the vicinity at that time. Dr. [Deleted] stated he had consulted one of the physicians at the Benjamin Harrison Air Base and had also checked the records with reference to allegations concerning the sighting of flying saucers and had done a little research with respect to correlating the presence of flying saucers and any polio epidemic."[4]

It was also recorded by the FBI that —according to its investigations— the doctor was reporting his conclusions to "the proper Air Force authorities" and had also spoken with staff at the Indiana University Medical School, "where doctors treated the entire matter as a big joke." J. Edgar Hoover was further advised, however: "Dr. [Deleted] had heard while in Canada that there had been some rather strange events somewhere in the interior with respect to finding what might have been remains of flying saucers."[5]

The "remains of flying saucers," escalations of the polio epidemic when UFO sightings were prevalent: what was going on? The Air Force wanted answers. Indeed, despite the unusual and unique nature of the doctor's theories, the Air Force did not dismiss him as a fool or as a deluded soul. Instead, Air Force Agent Elbert W. Farris elected to undertake some highly detailed background investigations himself: "Tabulation of flying saucer sightings from the available sources of the *Indianapolis Star* and the *Indianapolis News*, reveals that the majority of sightings took place in July and August for the years 1947, 1948 and 1949," Farris recorded.

More notable is Farris's next statement: "A responsible medical authority, confidential informant, CI-1, advised that the theory is 'interesting' and worthy of further research." In other words, the Air Force appeared to take the idea that aliens were possibly engaged in a covert operation to poison the human species with biological or radiological warfare seriously. One might ask, what on Earth, or indeed off it, would prompt the Air Force to pursue this particularly novel (and, if true, highly disturbing) theory? The background of the doctor was a key and contributing factor, and was something that the official world took very careful note of.

According to Air Force Agent Farris: "Dr. X produced membership cards which show him to be a member of the Masons, Scottish Rite, Knights of Pythias, Loyal Order of Moose and the Eagles. He served as a Naval officer for 14 months and also held a commission in the United States Public Health Service...he is an associate member of the Association of Medicine, Bloomington, Indiana, and he is an associate member of the Association of Military Surgeons. He is a physician and surgeon." Without doubt, the doctor was no fool.[6]

Agent Farris further advised his superiors that, as a part of its mission to gather additional background data on the doctor, he had visited the Chief of Police at Decatur, James Border, who had personally vouched for the integrity and character of the doctor, stressing strongly that he was "reliable," "responsible," and "enjoys an excellent reputation in the community."[7] And Agent Farris was still not finished. Indeed, he was by now a man on a mission.

On August 17, 1949 Farris carefully perused the available UFO reports collected by the Air Force from the period July 4, 1947 to July 26, 1949 and prepared an official report that detailed the sightings and their exact locations. Farris's next step was to contact a person he described as a "reliable medical authority at Benjamin Harrison Air Force Base, Indiana," in an effort to "determine whether the possibility of uranium poisoning, as expounded by Dr. [Deleted] had any basis in fact."

According to Farris's report, "The authority, who preferred to remain anonymous, is hereinafter known as Confidential Informant CI-1. Informant CI-1 advised the writer that the polio period extends from April to October, with the peak months of the disease being reached in July and August. Informant CI-1 was doubtful if the answer to the question of uranium poisoning could be readily answered, and he was of the opinion that the possibility and its connection with the polio epidemic prevalent throughout the United States had never been explored."[8]

As a result of this, plans were initiated to approach the Aero Medical Laboratory Research Department at Wright-Patterson Air Force Base for comment. "Does [the] uranium element produce any physiological reaction in human beings corresponding to symptoms applicable to many of the so-called polio clinical and sub-clinical conditions?" asked Agent Farris, continuing, "Are topographical areas where so-called Flying Disc are predominantly seen (or known uranium deposits) pin points of endemic areas of clinical symptoms resembling polio?"[9]

In addition to forwarding these questions, inquiries were also made with a source at the Indiana University School of Medicine who was described as "an authority on poison" and who was subsequently interviewed on August 25, 1949. The source advised that in his opinion, the "Flying-Saucers-are-poisoning-us-with-uranium" idea espoused by the doctor was "negligible." The source added that while he did recall the doctor as a student who had graduated from the Indiana University School of Medicine in 1941 and considered him to be a "good boy," he was also of the opinion that the doctor was "not the best student Indiana University ever turned out," and was somewhat "imaginative."

Yet the same source recommended bringing the Atomic Energy Commission (AEC) into the controversy. Indeed, he was of the opinion that the AEC was "the only Agency in the United States capable of answering this question once and for all." As a result—and in what was certainly a highly unusual and unique scenario—the FBI, the Aero Medical Laboratory at Wright-Patterson Air Force Base, the Atomic Energy Commission, and the Air Force's Office of Special Investigations all became deeply embroiled in the intriguing theories of the doctor, his background, and questions concerning his motivations for digging into this strange aspect of the UFO mystery.[10]

On October 6, 1949 an answer was forthcoming to the mystery. In a one-page document titled *PROJECT GRUDGE—Incident at Lake of the Woods, Ontario, Canada—1 July 1949*, Major D. Lynch, Acting District Commander of the AFOSI, revealed the results of an investigation prepared by Wright-Patterson's Aero Medical Laboratory. Signed off by Lieutenant Colonel A.P. Cagge of Wright-Patterson, the report read thus:

"While it is true that some of the clinical symptoms of poliomyelitis may be similar to uranium poisoning, the over-all clinical syndrome is quite different. Progress in the case of uranium poisoning is very dismal, with recovery unlikely. Besides the heavy metal poisoning effect of uranium poisoning, there is also the prolonged and continuous radiation effect of uranium which can be detected in the broad picture."

The report continued, "This is quite a distinctive clinical feature of uranium poisoning which any physician should readily be able to recognize. It is also a feature which does not diminish with time and, hence, the patient does not recover. This results because the uranium is a long-lived radioactive isotope, which becomes fixed in the body and cannot be eliminated to any appreciable extent. Because of the above considerations, it is the opinion of this office that there is little, if any, ground for the theory that the annual poliomyelitis epidemics are related to radioactivity in any way.

"It is also to be noted that the annual outbreak of poliomyelitis during the summer months has been prevalent for many years prior to flying saucers and the widespread use of radioactive isotopes."[11]

This would seem to suggest that as ingenious as the doctor's theories certainly were, they were somewhat off-target when it came to providing a definitive answer as to what was motivating the apparent UFO presence on our world. Nevertheless, the initial response of the military, the intelligence world, and the Atomic Energy Commission to the theories espoused by the doctor was one of immediate interest and even concern.

Could it be that this concern and interest surfaced as a direct result of the secret knowledge gleaned from Roswell (and known only to a select and elite group of individuals), suggesting that there *was* a link between alien activity, strange viruses and biological warfare? It is reasonable to assume that if such data had to be closely guarded, that anyone – such as the doctor – investigating similar theories would be watched closely. And the significant fact that the doctor's theories also tied in with "some rather strange events somewhere in the interior with respect to finding what might have been remains of flying saucers," is immensely important, and highly relevant to the subject matter of this book, too.

* * *

Chapter 8 Notes

1. Federal Bureau of Investigation memorandum, July 18 1947.

2. Air Force Office of Special Investigations, September 6, 1949, Scott Air Force Base.

3. Federal Bureau of Investigation, *Flying Saucers: Security Matter*, September 6, 1949.

4. Ibid.

5. Ibid.

6. Air Force Office of Special Investigations, September 6, 1949, Scott Air Force Base.

7. Ibid.

8. Ibid.

9. Ibid.

10. Ibid.

11. Air Force Office of Special Investigations, *PROJECT GRUDGE—Incident at Lake of the Woods, Ontario, Canada—1 July 1949*, Major D. Lynch, Acting District Commander, AFOSI.

Chapter 9
Unconventional Aircraft
1948-1950

U ntil relatively recently, it has been believed that, aside from a few sporadic UFO investigations, the British Government did not become seriously concerned by the UFO mystery until September 1952, when multiple encounters were reported over the North Sea, and the British mainland, during the course of a NATO exercise code-named *Mainbrace*. Records available at both the National Archive at Kew, England, and at the National Archives, Maryland in the United States, reveal that numerous UFO reports were filed by Royal Air Force and USAF personnel who had seen unusual, circular-shaped vehicles maneuvering over strategic airfields and over the *USS Franklin D. Roosevelt* aircraft carrier during the *Mainbrace* exercise. Notably, as has been previously discussed, the *USS Franklin D. Roosevelt* encounters were cited within the pages of the *1st Annual Report* document. As a result of the *Mainbrace* events, in the months that followed, at least one division of the British Air Ministry established a project to try and determine the truth that lay behind the *Mainbrace*, and similar, events.[1]

This scenario was bolstered further by the words of the late Ralph Noyes, who was involved in UFO investigations while working with the British Ministry of Defense in the 1960s and 1970s. Noyes wrote: "I reached a fairly senior grade in the MoD and had access to whatever documents were necessary to my responsibilities. These included TOP SECRET material generally, as well as many other papers of a still-restricted character. The Air Staff, in 1950 to 1952, were taking only the most perfunctory (and embarrassed) cogni-zance of 'saucer stories.'"[2]

Moreover, commenting on the UFO encounters reported during *Mainbrace* in September 1952, Noyes asserted that: "No folder, still less an official file, had yet been opened by the Operations staff on flying saucers. Whether or not that was a dereliction of duty I leave to others."[3]

While Noyes *did* prove to be a valuable source of data on matters pertaining to official British Government policy on the UFO subject, it can now be firmly demonstrated that he was not in possession of the full facts. It was in 1999 that researcher and author Nick Redfern was able to secure from the British National Archive at Kew, a copy of a lengthy file, titled *Unorthodox Aircraft* that provides an illuminating insight into previously unknown government involvement in the UFO subject.[4]

The file itself is of interest and significance for a number of reasons. First, much of the material contained within it was classified at *Secret* level (with a considerable number of papers stamped *Top Secret*). Second, the file makes it very clear that the Air Ministry was not the only department involved in the UFO subject during the late 1940s. And third, there is evidence to show that, at the time, the British Government was monitoring the UFO subject on what was quite literally a global scale.

It should be noted that much of the file centers upon the analysis of radical and new (for the time, of course) secret aircraft designs perfected by the-then Soviet Union. Given the fact that, in the late 1940s, the Soviets were becoming a major world threat, this is perfectly understandable. And, as the file also makes clear, detailed studies were undertaken by British Air Intelligence in an attempt to determine the extent to which the Soviets had made advances in both rocket and jet propulsion. Interestingly, the file shows that Air Intelligence conducted a large number of interviews in the period 1948-50 with former wartime prisoners of war, who were held on military camps in Russia, and who might have viewed the results of secret, radical aircraft trials undertaken by the Soviets in the immediate post-war era.

Moreover, the results of Air Intelligence's investigations were forwarded for analysis to a veritable host of departments and agencies within the British Government and military. This routinely included:

- The head of the Joint Intelligence Bureau at Bryanston Square, London;
- The director of the Air Ministry's Scientific and Technical Intelligence Branch (STIB);
- Several key intelligence divisions in the Royal Air Force; and
- MI 10 at the War Office.

Most notable of all: also contained within the *Unconventional Aircraft* file are a host of papers all directly pertaining to UFOs – all of which were circulated to the aforementioned departments. With respect to unidentified flying objects, what, precisely, does the relevant paperwork tell us? In the period 1948-1949, sources within the British Government were extremely interested in determining the extent to which the Nazis had succeeded in constructing flying saucer-like aircraft during the Second World War. And furthermore, those same sources were expressing concern regarding the extent to which the Soviets might have capitalized upon this technology in the post-war era. This may, of course, be due to the fact that there was a belief in some official quarters that the Nazis were responsible for elements, at least, of the UFO mystery.

This official British interest can be amply shown by virtue of the fact that as far back as September 1949, the Air Ministry's Scientific and Technical Intelligence Branch was regularly receiving clippings culled from all manner of publications on both Nazi-designed saucers and various other UFO reports. To illustrate this, on September 14, 1949, the STIB received from the Press Information Room of the Air Ministry's Intelligence Division, a selection of newspaper reports concerning UFO activity over Vienna, Austria. *Now it's Flaming Saucers*, proclaimed one such clipping from the *Daily Herald* on September 12, 1949.[5]

Similarly, only months later, the STIB received from the Press Information Room, a large batch of magazine articles photocopied from German newspapers and science periodicals on both highly-advanced flying saucer designs postulated by the Nazis during the Second World War, as well as post-War designs on the drawing-boards of the Soviets and the Americans. But there is more.

Those sources within the JIB, the Air Ministry, STIB and MI 10 who were regularly receiving such material from at least 1949 onwards, also took note of two matters that, historically speaking, are now an established part of UFO lore. Of those who in the 1950s, 60s and 70s openly accused the American Government of conspiring to hide the truth surrounding the UFO problem from the general public, perhaps the most vocal was Major Donald Keyhoe. A graduate of the Naval Academy and a former pilot with the Marine Corps, Keyhoe went on to write five highly controversial books that chronicled his UFO investigations – the first, titled *The Flying*

Saucers Are Real was published in 1950. In 1949, however, Keyhoe had written a now-historic article for *True* magazine that detailed his findings and thoughts on the UFO subject. According to a *True* write-up of Keyhoe's article: "This is the most interesting and important true story we have ever published. It is utterly true. We can document every occurrence reported here. It is our sober, considered conviction that the conclusion arrived at in this story is a fact, that...The Flying Saucers Are Real."[6]

In his 1950 book, *The Flying Saucers Are Real*, Keyhoe recalled the effect that the publication of the *True* article had in official circles: "The publicity was far more than I had expected. I phoned up a reporter in Washington whose beat includes the Pentagon. 'The Air Force is running around in circles,' he told me. "They knew your story was due, but nobody thought it would raise such a fuss. I think they're scared of hysteria. They're getting a barrage of wires and telephone calls. They're going to deny the whole thing. But I heard one Press Branch guy say it might not be enough – they're trying to figure some way to knock it down fast.'"[7]

In other words, Keyhoe's article, that concluded UFOs were very possibly "interplanetary spacecraft," was causing major repercussions on the part of the Government. It is, therefore, highly illuminating to note that a copy of Keyhoe's article features prominently in the British Government's *Unorthodox Aircraft* file, too. Moreover, a copy found its way to *all* of the aforementioned British government and military departments. Evidently, therefore, it was not just the Americans who were concerned by Keyhoe's disclosures.

In addition to the Keyhoe article, the Air Ministry's Scientific and Technical Intelligence Branch also took a keen interest in the now famous series of photographs taken by a farmer named Paul Trent at McMinnville, Oregon, on May 11, 1950. And again, the data received a wide distribution throughout the British Government's intelligence community. Of all the many and varied photographs of UFOs that have been taken since 1947, it is notable that the Air Ministry should have been so intrigued by the Trent pictures. Consider the following extract from an official report on Trent's experience. "This is one of the few UFO reports in which all factors investigated, geometric, psychological and physical, appear to be consistent with the assertion that an extraordinary flying object, silvery, metallic, disk-shaped, tens of meters in diameter, and evidently artificial, flew within sight of the two witnesses."[8]

It is also worth noting that in a newspaper clipping contained within one of the *Unorthodox Aircraft* file entries, Air Chief Marshal Sir Philip Joubert commented that: "The object pictured is very odd, and it is impossible even to guess what it is. It is clearly not a meteorite. Therefore, it is either a machined or cast structure. It shows no sign of any method of propulsion. It looks like a 'skimming dish' – except for that little stump at the top, which in both pictures is at the same angle."

Perhaps most eye opening is Joubert's comment that: "*We have had at least thirty instances of this sort of object being seen.*" Note also that Joubert, a British Air Chief Marshal, very clearly stated "*we*" as opposed to the Americans.[9]

Also contained within the *Unorthodox Aircraft* file is a series of enclosures that may have a bearing on an altogether far more serious and controversial matter: namely the Timothy Cooper MJ-12 files. And specifically the *1st Annual Report* document and the links between UFOs and bacteriological warfare operations, in which it is stated:

"*BIOLOGICAL WARFARE PROGRAMS*: BW programs in U.S. and U.K. are in field test stages. Discovery of new virus and bacteria agents so lethal, that serums derived by genetic research, can launch medical science into unheard of fields of biology. The samples extracted from bodies found in New Mexico, have yielded new strains of a retro-virus not totally understood, but give promise of the ultimate BW weapon. The danger lies in the spread of airborne and blood borne outbreaks of diseases in large populations, with no medical cures available."[10]

Of course, if the governments of both the United States and Britain *have* succeeded in creating the ultimate biological warfare weapon from alien-derived DNA, then this would be a matter of profound significance. However, the problem is that absolutely nothing has surfaced officially to link together the two issues of UFOs and biological warfare. Or has it?

When Nick Redfern received the *Unorthodox Aircraft* papers from the National Archive, he discovered that in precisely the same time frame referenced in the *1st Annual Report*, the Air Ministry's Intelligence Division was regularly forwarding classified data to the Directorate of Scientific Intelligence at the Metropole Buildings,

London on two subjects: UFOs and bacteriological warfare. Moreover, those documents were declassified officially in the United Kingdom only months after Timothy Cooper received (in an unofficial capacity) the allegedly leaked *1st Annual Report.*

A quote from one of the entries (picked entirely at random) from the National Archive-originated material reads: "Subject: Bacteriological Warfare Article. Forwarded herewith is a further installment of a series of articles at present appearing in the publication *Kristall* by Dr. Stubenbauer. Your attention is also drawn to the article on 'Flying Saucers' appearing in the same publication."[11]

Although only brief in nature, this uniquely important paper (that, recall, has been declassified officially by the British Government – it is *not* a leaked paper of unknown provenance) links both "bacteriological warfare" and "flying saucers." Moreover, the department that received the report (of which the above is simply one of many) was none other than the Directorate of Scientific Intelligence (DSI) at the Metropole Buildings.

This is of profound interest for two reasons. First, in 1990, the National Archive had informed Nick Redfern of the astonishing fact that a number of DSI files were, at that time, classified for one hundred years. And second, according to the late intelligence officer and *Flying Saucer Review* editor, Gordon Creighton, who himself worked at the Metropole Buildings at the time in question: "I was on the next floor to the department that dealt with UFOs...There weren't any other departments on that floor. But I and one or two other people in my department used to have fun when we were going up or down in the lift with a bunch of these chaps, talking about UFOs!"[12]

It may not be entirely coincidental that only three months after the *Unorthodox Aircraft* files surfaced, Nick Redfern was given an original edition of a NASA paper titled *Concepts for Detection of Extraterrestrial Life.* NASA had sent the document to the A.V. Roe aircraft company at Manchester, England - and specifically to its Weapons Research Division. Here, then, is yet another example of official files making a link between the biological aspects of extraterrestrial life and weapons-research.[13]

With the essence of the *Unorthodox Aircraft* documentation now largely detailed, let us try and come to a few conclusions. The file highlights graphically the fact that certain elements of the Air

Ministry were interested in the issue of secret UFO-like technology developed by Nazi Germany and the Soviet Union. That same material was circulated amongst a host of departments, including the Joint Intelligence Bureau, MI 10 and the Directorate of Scientific Intelligence. And finally, senior and key figures within the DSI were, as far back as 1950, receiving classified briefings on both UFOs and bacteriological weapons research, and under cover of the same memoranda, no less.

This, of course, raises important questions. Is it merely down to chance that in precisely the same time frame that unofficial papers surfaced in the United States linking the exploitation of the bodies allegedly recovered at Roswell in 1947 with biological and bacterio-logical warfare operations, officially released papers referencing both UFOs and bacteriological warfare were declassified by the British Government? Is this, perhaps, an indication of a drip-feed operation on the part of sources within both the American and British intelligence services?

Whatever the ultimate answers to those questions, in April 2000, the British National Archive released a second volume of documen-tation, also titled *Unorthodox Aircraft* that covered the period 1950-1952. Again, the contents of the file centered upon UFOs, newspaper and magazine articles on unidentified aerial phenomena, and so-called Nazi Flying Saucers. What set this latest release of files apart from any other UFO-related documents declassified into the public domain by officialdom was its cover page.

Classified *Top Secret*, at the top of the page the following words appeared: *THE TITLE OF THIS FILE MUST NOT APPEAR ON THE OUTER COVER*. And at the foot of the document, this is followed by: *TO BE KEPT UNDER LOCK AND KEY*.[14]

As Nick Redfern stated after examining the document at issue: "I have had the opportunity to examine literally thousands of pages of formerly classified files on UFOs. Never before, however, have I come across a UFO-related file that was deemed so sensitive by officialdom that its contents were to be kept under lock and key at all times."[15]

Perhaps this is an indication of the high-degree of secrecy that surrounds the issue of UFOs and bacteriological warfare. And links between UFOs and what may be deaths by an alien virus do not end there.

In August 1980, *Playboy Press Paperbacks* published a book titled *The Ogden Enigma*. A fictional title written by novelist Gene Snyder, the book tells the story of an unidentified object that crashes in the vicinity of Ogden, Utah, in 1950, and that is promptly spirited away by the military to a "sealed airplane hangar" for 30 years.

Is the object, as some believe it to be, a Russian secret weapon or, incredibly, is it the remains of a vehicle from another world? These, and other, questions are asked and ultimately answered in what is a highly entertaining piece of fiction. However, according to the author, *The Ogden Enigma* is based upon fact. Snyder states that, in 1977, he had occasion to meet a man that he referred to as "Charlie," who related a remarkable account:

"He told me of something secreted in the Utah desert for nearly three decades," said Snyder. "He said the secret was housed in an airplane hangar at a U.S. Army supply base, near Ogden, Utah. He claimed that on a June night in 1950, five air force personnel had driven a flatbed truck onto the base in the middle of the night. The truck's cargo was covered with a tarpaulin that had been carefully lashed down. He went on to say that after driving the truck into the hangar, the five men hurriedly closed the doors and bent the bolt locks. In the days that followed, a huge security screen was erected around the hangar. It included electrified fences, guard dogs, and a restricted air traffic space above the building. An Air Force Security Service detachment, he maintained, still guarded the hangar, despite the fact that such a detachment would be unusual on an Army base."

The strangest part of the story, according to Snyder, was to come, however. "Charlie" asserted that within twelve months, all five of the men involved in the delivery of the unknown object to the base were dead. How the men died is unknown; however, the possibility that their deaths were due to an encounter with a virus of unknown origins as described in the *1st Annual Report* cannot be discounted.

"On this note," recalled Snyder, "he left, with a vague half commitment to return and tell me more. He never did. I tried to reach him in the wake of the story. I never succeeded. I have not seen 'Charlie' since."

While it should be stressed that *The Ogden Enigma* is a work of fiction, it may indeed be based upon a genuine event of the type described by to Snyder by the elusive Charlie and expanded upon in the pages of his book.[16]

* * *

Chapter 9 Notes

1. *A Covert Agenda: The British Government's UFO Top Secrets Exposed*, Nick Redfern, Simon & Schuster, 1997.

2. *Magonia*, No. 29, 1988.

3. *UFO Brigantia*, May 1991.

4. National Archive, Kew, England, file number: DEFE 41/117. Crown copyright exists.

5. "Now it's Flaming Saucers," *Daily Herald*, September 12, 1949.

6. *The Flying Saucers Are Real*, Donald Keyhoe, Fawcett Publications, 1950.

7. Ibid.

8. *The Hynek UFO Report*, Dr. J. Allen Hynek, Sphere Books, 1978.

9. *UFO Magazine*, May/June 1999.

10. *Majestic 12, 1st Annual Report*. Available at: www.majesticdocuments.com by downloading: http://209.132.68.98/pdf/MJ-12_fifthannualreport.pdf.

11. National Archive, Kew, England, file number: DEFE 41/117. Crown copyright exists.

12. *Above Top Secret: The Worldwide UFO Cover-Up*, Timothy Good, Sidgwick & Jackson, 1987.

13. *Concepts for Detection of ET Life*, NASA, 1965. Available at www.majesticdocuments.com by downloading: http://209.132.68.98/pdf/nasa-etlife.pdf.

14. National Archive, Kew, England, file number: DEFE 41/118. Crown copyright exists.

15. Statement from Nick Redfern, February 4, 2006.

16. *The Ogden Enigma,* Gene Snyder, Playboy Press, 1980.

Chapter 10
The Kingman UFO Crash
1953

The story of the reported recovery of a UFO near Kingman, Arizona in May 1953 has circulated within the UFO research community for decades. When placed into a collective context, separate strands of data secured across four decades by a variety of sources, do strongly suggest that an event of unusual proportions did indeed occur and does merit our close attention. More significantly, within the last few years, new, and potentially important, data on the case has surfaced that suggests the retrieval team present at the Kingman crash site may have been exposed to a virus very similar, if not identical, to that which was present at some of the New Mexican crash sites of the summer of 1947.

The genesis of the Kingman, Arizona, UFO crash can be traced back to February 3, 1971, the date that two young men with an interest in UFOs – Jeff Young and Paul Chetham - conducted an interview with a man that investigator Ray Fowler would later refer to as "Fritz Werner," and who claimed personal knowledge of a crashed UFO and alien body recovery near Kingman, Arizona, specifically on May 21, 1953. Chetham and Young were the first people within the UFO research community to speak with the source; and very brief aspects of the story and interview were published in the Framingham, Massachusetts Edition of the *Middlesex News* on April 23, 1973. According to the newspaper, Jeff Young had interviewed a man who asserted that he had worked with Project Blue Book and had made, "contact with an alien craft."[1]

The Young-Chetham interview revealed that their source had been at the site of a UFO crash at Kingman, Arizona, approximately twenty years previously. The source identified himself as a graduate engineer with degrees in mathematics and physics and a master's degree in engineering. During the course of the interview, the man *initially* advised that he had only seen a UFO flying near the site of an atomic test in Nevada that was part of a larger series of tests known as *Operation Upshot-Knothole*, which was the ninth series of atmospheric nuclear weapons tests and which were conducted by the Atomic Energy Commission (AEC) at the Nevada Proving Ground from March 17, 1953, to June 4, 1953.[2]

The series consisted of eleven nuclear tests in total. One detonation was an atomic artillery projectile fired from a 280mm cannon, three were airdrops, and seven were detonated on towers, ranging from 100 to 300 feet in height. The operation involved an estimated 21,000 Department of Defense personnel, who participated in observer programs, tactical maneuvers, scientific studies, and support activities. *Operation Upshot-Knothole* was intended to test nuclear devices for possible inclusion in the United States' arsenal, to improve military tactics, equipment, and training, and to study civil defense needs.[3]

The man stated to Young and Chetham that he and a colleague had been drinking beer when they heard a noise described as a cross between a hum and a whistle. The object was difficult to describe, said the source, due to the fact that it was nighttime, which made an accurate visual observation of the object difficult. He also stated that he worked for Project Blue Book and offered the theory that the project was created because the Air Force was "getting too much publicity and there were too many people, other than official people seeing these things and reporting them."[4]

In the specific part of the interview with Young and Chetham that dealt with the Kingman crash, the source stated: "The object was not built by anything, obviously, that we know about on Earth. At that time I was out of the atomic testing, but I was still with the Air Force and this was the time I was on Blue Book. There was a report that there was a crash of an unexplained vehicle in the west and they organized a team of about forty of us. I was one of those forty." He went on to inform Young and Chetham that he had been alerted, "through official channels and on a private phone line from the base commander at Wright Field saying that: 'You're a member of Blue Book and we would like for you tomorrow to get on a plane, go to Chicago and from there to Phoenix.'"[5]

Young and Chetham were further informed that the object was "more like a teardrop-shaped cigar. It was like a streamlined cigar." With respect to a body or bodies found at the scene, the source added: "I saw the creature [that] you're talking about. It was real and I would guess about four feet tall." He stated that the body was dark brown in color; and offered the theory that perhaps the creature's skin had darkened due to "atmospheric exposure." The initial Cheatham-Young interview does not provide anything more of real significance. That situation changed radically, however, when Ray Fowler began digging into the case in 1973.[6]

The UFO researcher Ray Fowler learned of the Kingman case from the Framingham, Massachusetts, edition of the *Middlesex News* of April 23, 1973, and tracked down the witness himself, in a determined effort to uncover the truth. In his book, *Casebook of a UFO Investigator*, Fowler stated: "In 1973 I came even closer to documenting the reality of crashed UFOs, with a signed affidavit from an alleged member of the USAF investigating team! He must remain anonymous; I've dubbed him Fritz Werner."[7]

Fowler had concerns about the witness, since it became clear to Fowler that the story that Werner had told Fowler was somewhat different to that which he had imparted to Chetham and Young. Werner explained this by saying that he had confused dates, and that he was also under the influence of "four Martinis" when the pair interviewed him in 1971, and was prone to exaggeration when drinking. Despite the fact that this raised suspicions, the Werner account is a valuable one that needs to be addressed and not discarded. Werner's signed affidavit to Fowler states:

"I, Fritz Werner, do solemnly swear that during a special assignment with the U.S. Air Force, on May 21, 1953, I assisted in the investigation of a crashed unknown object in the vicinity of Kingman, Arizona. The object was constructed of an unfamiliar metal which resembled brushed aluminum. It had impacted twenty inches into the sand without any sign of structural damage. It was oval and about 30 feet in diameter. An entranceway hatch had been vertically lowered and opened. It was about 3-1/2 feet high and 1-1/2 feet wide. I was able to talk briefly with someone on the team who did look inside only briefly. He saw two swivel seats, an oval cabin, and a lot of instruments and displays. A tent pitched near the object sheltered the dead remains of the only occupant of the craft. It was about 4 feet tall, dark brown complexion and had 2 eyes, 2 nostrils, 2 ears, and a small round mouth. It was clothed in a silvery, metallic suit and wore a skullcap of the same type material. It wore no face covering or helmet. I certify that the above statement is true by affixing my signature to this document this day of June 7, 1973."[8]

In his book *Casebook of a UFO Investigator*, Ray Fowler stated with respect to his informant Fritz Werner that: "Between June 1949 and January 1960 Fritz held several engineering and management positions at Wright-Patterson AFB near Dayton, Ohio. During the period in which the incident took place, he worked within what was known as the Air Material Command Installations Division, within the Office of Special Studies headed by Dr. Eric Wang. His special ties at that particular time included the engineering design of Air Force engine test cells, development techniques for determining blast effects on buildings and structures, and the designing of aircraft landing gear. Fritz worked his way up to become chief of alighting devices within the aircraft laboratory, Wright Air Development Center; which position led him up to management positions at Wright-Patterson, and later at a variety of civilian companies involved with defense contracts. At the time of his reported experience, he was on special assignment to the AEC at the atomic proving ground in Nevada."[9]

The source interviewed in 1971 by Jeff Young and Paul Chetham, and interviewed in 1973 and given the pseudonym of Fritz Werner by Ray Fowler, is known to have graduated from Ohio University in 1949 and was first employed by Air Material Command at Wright-Patterson Air Force Base in Dayton, Ohio as a mechanical engineer on testing Air Force aircraft engines. He is also known to have worked for Raytheon in Sudbury, Massachusetts, in the early Seventies on avionics systems. Dr. Eric Wang, who has been linked with classified UFO investigations, headed the Installations Division within the Office of Special Studies where Werner worked. Dr. Wang was an Austrian-born graduate of the Vienna Technical Institute. Wang taught structural and metallurgical engineering at the University of Cincinnati from 1943 to 1952. In 1949, Wang became Director of the Department of Special Studies at Wright-Patterson where he worked with scientists from the Office of Naval Research and with Dr. Vannevar Bush and others from the Research and Development Board. Dr. Wang relocated his research from Wright-Patterson to Kirtland AFB in Albuquerque, New Mexico. Wang died on December 4, 1960.[10]

In addition to the testimony of Fritz Werner himself, there are other accounts that may have a direct bearing on this particular case. In his 1978 paper, *Retrievals of the Third Kind*, presented at the annual Mutual UFO Network (MUFON) Symposium of that year, Leonard Stringfield related the account of researcher Charles Wilhelm, whose father had been told an account by a "Major Daly" of his (Daly's) flight to the site of a UFO crash in April 1953. Daly was then blindfolded and driven out to a desert location that was hot and sandy. Inside a tent the blindfold was removed and he was taken to another location where he saw a "metallic ship," twenty-five to thirty feet in diameter, and that was undamaged.

According to Stringfield and Wilhelm, Major Daly spent two days analyzing the UFO and stated that it was not made on earth. Daly stated that at no time was he allowed to enter the UFO; however, it did have a hatch or opening that was four-to-five feet in height and two-to-three feet wide and which was open. After concluding his analysis, Daly was taken from the area by escort. Given the closeness of the date to the Kingman crash, it is not inconceivable that Daly was mistaken in his recollection of the date by just one month – May 1953 and not April 1953.[11]

Interestingly, in the wake of the publicity given to the Kingman case in Leonard Stringfield's 1977 book, *Situation Red: The UFO Siege* (which summarized the data acquired by Ray Fowler – including the Fritz Werner affidavit), other accounts of crashed UFOs and alien bodies from the crucial year of 1953 surfaced. In a letter dated March 23, 1979, Richard Hall, then-editor of the *MUFON UFO Journal*, wrote to Leonard Stringfield thus:

"...Don Berliner (aviation writer) just returned from visiting an aviation historian friend in Illinois, Truman Weaver. While there, Weaver showed him a copy of a letter dated March 1978 from a good friend of Weaver's in the aviation business...who worked as a technician at Wright-Patterson, retiring in 1954. This gentleman said that he worked 'across the alley' from where they kept the bodies, and that in 1953 they had 13 of them in a room on the third floor. A strong odor used to waft across the way, and upon inquiring they were told it was embalming fluid. The bodies he said, are now stored at a small Air Force Base (Langley) at Hampton Roads, Virginia..."[12]

Stringfield stated that he phoned Truman Weaver – who was himself a retired Air Force Major, who had a UFO encounter while flying in Korea in 1952, in which he and his crew saw a 12-foot diameter disc "off his wingtip."[13]

Stringfield continued that: "Without hesitation, Weaver gave me the phone number of his friend, Robert Thompson, whom he knew through mutual aviation interests. On the same day I phoned Thompson. He confirmed the data Berliner had related to Hall about his work at Wright-Patterson. He added...'Suddenly, the building nearby became very busy; trucks drove up and right into the building. This was before air-conditioning was installed and with windows open I could smell the strong odor of formaldehyde. It was sickening.'"[14]

Stringfield elaborated further: "Thompson said he never saw a flying saucer or a little body personally, but he did claim to see what he called an 'interim' report. His boss, named McAdams, showed it to him and fellow workers, which he said confirmed the rumors that alien craft and bodies were on the base. The next day he said the paper was snatched from McAdams and officials denied it even existed. Thompson couldn't remember if the report was on official stationary or marked Secret, or if it was mimeographed. Curious, I called Weaver about such a document. He was not aware of such a report for general circulation unless it was a document that leaked out without authorization. On April 5, Thompson sent me a note which stated briefly: 'The building was number 18F, 3rd Floor. The 13 bodies and 2 saucers are at a small air base at Hampton Roads, Virginia, if they have not been moved again.'" According to Stringfield, Thompson said that he had heard about the transfer to Hampton Roads from "a source" in Canada.[15]

In his paper *The UFO Crash/Retrieval Syndrome* published in 1980 by the Mutual UFO Network, Leonard Stringfield referenced a case that *very* closely matched the story of the Kingman crash. Described in his paper as Case A-1 (and which is itself a more comprehensive version of Abstract 6 contained in Stringfield's paper presented at the annual MUFON Conference in 1978, and titled *Retrievals of the Third Kind*), the following is Stringfield's account of an interview he conducted in 1977 with a pilot who had knowledge of a UFO crash in Arizona in 1953 – significantly, both the year and location of the Kingman crash:

"During the summer of 1977 I was asked by a local business executive, a former Naval Intelligence Officer, to speak on the UFO at the September 1st meeting of the Cincinnati Chapter of the World Wings held in the Administration Building at Lunken Airport. During the Question and Answer period, following my talk, one member of a group of 25 pilots arose and brought up the legendary subject of recovered alien UFOs and occupants. His comment, I thought, indicated that he was unusually well informed on the matter, so I asked that he standby for a chat later. When the crowd finally disassembled he led me to the privacy of a back room which was dominated by a huge topographical map of the United States.

"Staring at the map he said bluntly, 'I have seen the bodies.' Still looking at the map and noting my protracted silence, he pointed vaguely to an area inside the State of Arizona. 'There's approximately where the saucer crashed,' he said. 'It was in a desert area, but I don't know the exact location. I'm almost positive it happened in 1953.'

"The pilot was my first encounter with a firsthand witness. As he stood at the map with a straight-on glance, he impressed me as a person who is sincere and forthright, possessing a no-nonsense character. 'I saw the bodies at Wright-Patterson,' he said. 'I was in the right place at the right time when the crates arrived at night by DC-7.'

"As we lingered at the map he recalled that he had stood inside a hangar at a distance of about 12 feet, peering at five crates on a forklift. In his judgment, the crates appeared to be hastily constructed and were made of wood. In three of these, little humanoids appearing to be 4 feet tall, were lying unshrouded [sic] on a fabric, which he explained prevented freeze burn from the dry ice packed beneath. As a number of Air Police stood silent guard near the crates, he managed to get a reasonably good but brief glimpse of the humanoid features. He recalls that their heads were hairless and narrow, and by human standards were disproportionately large, with skin that looked brown under the hangar lights above. The eyes seemed to be open, the mouth small, and nose, if any, was indistinct. My informant also heard from the crewmember that one of the entities was still alive aboard the craft when the U.S. military team arrived. Attempts were made to save its life with oxygen, but they were unsuccessful."[16]

In his February 1994 paper, *UFO Crash/Retrievals: Search For Proof In A Hall Of Mirrors*, Leonard Stringfield provided yet further data in support of the 1953 UFO crash at Kingman, Arizona. Stated Stringfield: "My new source, JLD, a resident of Ohio, north of Cincinnati, in a surprising disclosure claimed that a close relative, the late Mr. Holly, who had served in the top command (in a defense department capacity) at Wright-Patterson in 1953, told him about one of two crashes in Arizona. He also told him three bodies, one severely burned, and parts of the wrecked craft, were delivered to the base. On July 16, 1993, when JLD and his wife visited me in Cincinnati, he told me that Holly had seen the bodies, maintained in an off-limits building – and it was not the legendary Hangar 18. Of note, he also learned that the aliens were free of harmful bacteria and suffered no teeth decay. In trust, JLD gave me his relative's name, title of his position at Wright Patterson and, that having the highest security clearance, was informed with 'eyes only' details of the Arizona incident. Said JLD, as a young teenager, when he was told about the crash, his interest was airplanes, making models of World War II aircraft and admitted that he had a curiosity about flying saucers. However, in later years when he asked for more details, his relative did not wish to discuss the subject."[17]

While conducting research into alien abductions, the investigator Don Schmitt spoke with a woman named Judy Woolcott, who had an intriguing tale to tell concerning the Kingman crash and that centered on a strange letter that Woolcott had received in 1965 from her husband, who was serving in Vietnam at the time. Ominously, Woolcott's husband felt that he would not be returning home – at least not alive. According to Woolcott's memory, her husband told her that he had seen "something strange" twelve years previously. Woolcott *thought* that the incident dated from August 1953. And while she could not be certain of the month, she was certain that the location was Kingman, Arizona. Her husband was a military officer and was on duty in an air base control tower when something strange was picked up on radar. It began to lose altitude and disappeared from the screen.

Woolcott informed Schmitt that her husband had said that various MPs began talking about something "being down," and both her husband and a number of military personnel left the base in jeeps and headed for the location where the object was believed crashed. Finally, they located a "domed disc" that had evidently hit the ground with some force, embedding itself in the sand. There was no external damage to the object at all and no sign of debris on the ground. Before they had chance to close in on the object, however, Woolcott's husband and his colleagues were escorted from the area and told never to discuss the incident with anyone. There was no indication as to what had caused the crash and Woolcott's husband did not see any bodies; however, he did advise his wife that some of the military police had said there were casualties and that they were "not human." He further advised his wife that, with regard to the bodies angle, he had only "heard the talk." Schmitt stated that the letter to Judy Woolcott from her husband indicated that he knew more which he did not want to put onto paper. A week later he was killed.[18]

One of the most intriguing figures to surface with regard to the Kingman affair was Bill Uhouse, a retired "mechanical engineer" from Las Vegas who claimed to have worked on classified projects at certain locations in Nevada that focused upon the reverse-engineering of crashed-and-recovered UFO technology. Uhouse's story is a strange one and much of it is beyond the scope of the Kingman story. With specific regard to the Kingman crash and Bill Uhouse, however, the researcher Bill Hamilton has provided good background and commentary:

"Engineer Bill Uhouse claims there was a crash of an Eben aerial craft near Kingman, Arizona in 1953 and that four entities survived. That would have been six years after the more famous Roswell crashes and retrievals of 'interplanetary craft of unknown origin.' In Kingman, according to Uhouse, two disabled Ebens, and two more that were in good condition, were retrieved by US Government units, specially trained for retrieval missions. The two non-humans in good condition were allowed to re-enter the craft and the disabled entities were taken to an unspecified medical facility.

"He also states that a recovery crew that entered the craft to inspect it came down with a mysterious sickness. The craft was then loaded aboard a trailer and hauled off to the Nevada Test Site north of Las Vegas. Bill Uhouse claims that the events at Kingman eventually resulted in the project which employed him to design and construct a flight simulator that our airmen could use to learn how to fly a saucer."[19]

That, in essence, was the story of the Kingman affair, as it was known until 2005, at least. However in early 2006, new and provocative data surfaced on the crash that eerily parallels the events at New Mexico in 1947 when personnel present at the crash site began to exhibit alarming signs of sickness. The source of the new data is an individual who claims a background within the United States' Intelligence community and whose story can be found at the website, www.serpo.org. While some researchers believe the data to be Government-generated disinformation, the fact that some of the material dovetails with that contained in the pages of this book is reason enough to scrutinize it closely.

According to the *Serpo* website: "The information began to be released on 2 November 2005 by a retired senior official within the US Defense Intelligence Agency (DIA) who calls himself 'Anonymous.' Until he chooses to make his name known, this is the way he will be represented here. Anonymous reports that he is not acting individually and is part of a group of six DIA personnel working together as an alliance: three current and three former employees. He is their chief spokesman."

Furthermore *Serpo* state that on December 24, 2005, two-pages of a "classified document" were provided to the site by an unnamed researcher that, "appear to be transcripts of a prepared briefing or lecture – or perhaps a single memo – dated 24 March 1995, of the experiences of a number of military personnel when entering a downed craft (Kingman, Arizona, 1953)."

According to the document (which, it must be stressed, reads like a preliminary, rough draft, rather than a finely-tuned, finished report):

"The background as told to my group had a very interesting twist regarding craft retrieval, and the visitor confrontation. Little did the Government know that retrieval operations were monitored by the visitors. They the visitors were well aware of the mishap of one of their vessels[;] however, the military got to the crash site first. 'Note' vessel is the term used by the visitors rather than disc or craft, and this was not known until the initial meeting in the fall of 1953. One other point was that the 'Alien/EBE' phraseology was not used in any later discussions. They also had names mostly unusual. But when translated to English the names were easily pronounced. No details were provided on how contact was made to set up the initial meeting. The reason for contact after almost 6 years was recalled as follows: the vessel that fell in Arizona contained 4 entities, 2 were disabled and 2 were reasonably well, but somewhat confused. The visitors monitoring the retrieval activities noted with much pleasure the humane treatment provided to those involved. All entities were later taken to Facility X for medical treatment and tests; whatever they were for? Additionally before leaving the scene the 2 which were standing upright were allowed to re-enter the vessel. The hatch was left open to monitor their activity and disappeared inside the craft. Some time had passed before exiting. It was latter [sic] assumed that they were communicating with the monitoring craft. (Explained later on)."

With respect to the issue of adverse effects on the part of the human recovery team, the document continues:

"A bizarre situation was encountered at the retrieval site. With the entities removed from the area[,] work proceeded clean up and loading of the vessel on a tank trailer used to haul Sherman tanks. While these preparations were being made a [sic] entry crew was formed. They were dressed in clean room clothing with medical surgical masks. The size of the crew was not mentioned. Communications between the crew and the team outside was set up prior to entry. What happened with the entry crew while inside of the vessel was noted as follows: [1] Communications failed; the crew after one hour inside emerged from the craft confused, with upset stomachs, removed their masks and threw up. What was astonishing they could not remember any of the inside details of the craft. The craft was sealed[,] camouflaged[,] loaded and shipped to an undisclosed Nevada test facility. The entry crew was sent to Facility X to undergo medical examinations. Results of tests were not explained to us."[20]

If this final (thus far, at least) revelation in the Kingman controversy of May 1953 is true, then it offers yet further evidence of the potentially life threatening hazards that face UFO crash/retrieval units.

* * *

Chapter 10 Notes:

1. *Middlesex News*, April 23, 1973.

2. Ibid.

3. *Operation Upshot/Knothole, Nevada Test Site, 1953*. See: http://www.aracnet.com/ ~pdxavets/upshot.htm.

4. *Middlesex News*, April 23, 1973.

5. Ibid.

6. Ibid.

7. *Casebook of a UFO Investigator: A Personal Memoir*, Raymond Fowler, Prentice-Hall Trade, 1981.

8. Affidavit, June 7, 1973. For further details of the Affidavit, see: *Situation Red: The UFO Siege*, Leonard Stringfield, Sphere Books, Ltd., 1977.

9. *Casebook of a UFO Investigator: A Personal Memoir*, Raymond Fowler, Prentice-Hall Trade, 1981.

10. *Kingman, Arizona UFO Crash Retrieval*, Nick Redfern, *3rd Annual UFO Crash Retrieval Conference Proceedings, November 4-6, 2005*, Wood & Wood Enterprises, 2005.

11. *Retrievals of the Third Kind*, Leonard Stringfield, *Mutual UFO Network Symposium Proceedings*, Mutual UFO Network, 1978.

12. Letter from Richard Hall to Leonard Stringfield, March 23, 1979.

13. *The UFO Crash/Retrieval Syndrome, Status Report II: New Sources, New Data*, Leonard Stringfield, Mutual UFO Network, 1980.

14. Ibid.

15. Ibid.

16. Ibid. See also: *UFO Crash/Retrievals: Search for Proof in a Hall of Mirrors: Status Report VII*, Leonard Stringfield. Published privately, 1994.

17. *UFO Crash/Retrievals: Search For Proof In A Hall Of Mirrors: Status Report VII*, Leonard Stringfield. Published privately, 1994. For a definitive look at the life and work of Leonard Stringfield, see: *Correlating Leonard Stringfield's Crash-Retrieval Reports*, Dr. Robert M. Wood, *2nd Annual UFO Crash Retrieval Conference Proceedings*, November 12-14, 2004, Wood & Wood Enterprises.

18. *A History of UFO Crashes: Documented Proof of UFO Visits to Earth*, Kevin D. Randle, Avon Books, 1995.

19. *The Strange Story of J-Rod, An EBE*, Bill Hamilton, 1999. See: www.worldofthestrange.com/modules.php?name=Newsletters&op=ViewItems&vid=405.

20. *Documents newly disclosed, reporting confusion, sickness and disorientation when entering a disk at the Kingman crash site*, www.serpo.org/consistencies.html.

Chapter 11
Flying Triangles, SOM 1-01, and
Human Injuries, 1954-1966

O ne of the most intriguing of the many unofficially released documents on Majestic 12 that have surfaced over the course of the last two decades is a lengthy document that has come to be known as the *Special Operations Manual*. As will become abundantly clear shortly, there is one particular entry contained within the file that has a major bearing on the subject matter of this book. First, however, some vital information on the story of the Manual from Robert Wood:

"The *Special Operations Manual SOM 1-01* was mailed from Quillin's Drug Store to Don Berliner, an author and UFO researcher, in 1994 in the form of undeveloped 35 mm film. Upon development it turned out to be a manual titled '*Extraterrestrial Entities and Technologies – Recovery and Disposal*,' dated April 1954. Clearly the purpose was to provide instruction to recovery units about the background of this program and how to handle the parts, while deceiving the public into believing that nothing important had crashed.

"Immediately skeptics came forward and offered numerous claims of fakery, ranging from *ad hominem* attacks to the typical position that if it didn't follow the security procedures in detail, it must be phony. Three of the critics claimed to have been involved in classified work and expected that they would have known about it. Leaving aside these largely non-constructive charges, and some erroneous claims such as the use of the War department logo being an anachronism, there were still several authentication issues raised that warranted attention. Overall, about twenty objections were raised, of which five have some logical merit, as summarized below:

1. There was no document control page, a missing piece for a top secret document.
2. Personnel were encouraged to tell onlookers that it might have been a 'downed satellite,' but the first satellite was not launched until 1957.
3. It alludes to 'Area 51,' which is claimed not to exist in 1954.

4. The document reports on shape and size measured by radar, and the old dish radars could not have accurately measured shape and size.

5. There is a classification 'restricted' along with 'Top Secret,' which is incompatible.

"Where is the document control? Actually as Don Berliner and Robert Wood were making copies of the negative, there was one that was so hard to read that Don had not run a copy. When a copy was made and studied, there was the document control page! It showed eight entries over nearly three years, replacing or removing pages from the document. Each of these actions was accompanied with a time and date typed in, and the authority of either MJ/04 or MJ/01, and the initials either EWL or JRT. In addition, facing the control page is the back of the cover page without a security caveat, but it does have the equivalent of a control, in that it is identified 'Unit KB 88, Bldg. 21 from Kirtland AFB, N. MEX.' This is also significant in that the present abbreviation of New Mexico as NM for address did not occur until much later. In 1954, 'N. Mex.' was common."

With respect to the comment concerning the entry within the document about utilizing the scenario of a "crashed satellite" to hide a crashed UFO behind, Robert Wood stated: "In the first place, the entire strategy is that of deception – it is even the title of the paragraph in question! Deceptive statements are not usually true. Furthermore, it was just one of five choices offered to keep nosy people away. The big argument, though, comes from those who say, 'Why would anyone be impressed by a known false statement?' Actually, most people were aware of our plans for satellites in April of 1954, as a result of enormous coverage of this new space thinking. There are prominent public references to satellites before this date, including a *Time Magazine* article just the previous month speculating on whether a satellite had already been covertly launched. So, satellites were on the public's mind and 'downed satellites' were a very credible concept."

Wood continued:

"The third objection that warrants discussion is the claim that Area 51 did not exist in 1954, and therefore the Manual must be a fake. Interestingly, early responses to the *SOM 101* by the Air Force that claimed it to be a fake had the paragraph discussing this issue blacked out, as if it was so sensitive they didn't want to touch the topic. Actually, there is evidence that this facility was started in 1951, probably for the express purpose of having a good place to send the EBEs recovered. We have a copy of the *Las Vegas Review-Journal* for January 5, 1951, describing a massive construction project near Indian Springs of $300 million 1951 dollars. This is easily enough money to build this kind of a complex. Furthermore, accompanying the article was the testimony of a local witness of the time who described the large number of construction actions going on at the time.

"The fourth challenge was that the description of the vehicles include details on the shapes and lengths with precision not possible with the 1950s kind of dish radars. Two of the shapes (cigars, triangles) specifically referred to radar as the source of the size and shape data. Although dish radar puts out a rather wide-angle beam, the returns from the target are quite precise in time (and thus, distance), although angles are poorly estimated. The return from the nose of the object provides the mark at one end, and the last return before the signal drops is the end of the vehicle. Therefore, if you have several measurements, especially if you do not ignore the obvious visual information, one can make quite good estimates of size. Furthermore, the critics assume that these measurements are using ground-based radar. Aircraft had radar, too, and could have measured lengths with great accuracy. There is no reason to doubt the sizes and shapes reported in the Manual.

"The final challenge was that the 'Restricted' caveat on the cover page is not consistent with the use of Top Secret. Although the classification of Restricted at one time existed and was lower than Confidential, it was eliminated in about 1953. The word 'restricted' can have a generic meaning, too – access to this information is restricted to those who have both the clearance and the need to know. While this is officially true, the publisher of the Manual clearly thought about making it very clear that this Manual was to have extremely limited distribution. Examples of the use of re-stricted together with Top Secret exist. One great example is a July 14, 1954 memo from Cutler to Twining, changing the arrangements for an MJ-12 Special Studies Project meeting of the National Security Council. This memo came from the National Archives and is one of the few archival confirmations of the existence of MJ-12. Its classification is 'Top Secret Restricted Security Information.'"

Having addressed the main criticisms of the *Manual,* Wood continued: "Other critics have shot at the authenticity early and often, but hardly a single critic has ever asked for a high quality copy of the *Manual.* Critics claims that if the evidence is not available in the archives, this suggests that it does not exist. It is well known that the archives have a declassification procedure that is charged with not releasing information that would be unfavorable to National Security. It should be evident to anyone that if the Government really wants to keep a secret, they would have no compunction about lying about the existence (or non-existence) of documents. Even 'making them disappear' would clearly be expected.

"In the history of questioned documents, one can only establish a trail of evidence pointing to fakery. One cannot prove they are genuine, but one can prove they are fake, using the techniques outlined earlier. Therefore, the onus is him who claims 'fake' to find the evidence for fakery, rather than to say, 'You haven't proved them to be authentic.' Failing all the tests for fakery is about as close as you can come to proving authenticity. All the claims for fakery fail the tests for the *SOM 1-01.*

"All these exposures to claims of fakery have led me to create a summary list of phony claims of fakery:
- 'Government says they are fake'
- 'There is no provenance'
- 'Archives cannot locate them'
- 'Anything can be faked today'
- 'Content is the theme of science fiction'
- 'Such secrets would have leaked out'
- 'Why would governments keep ET life secret?'"

Wood concluded: "There are two major clinchers, however, for the fact that the *SOM 1-01 Manual* was printed in 1954. The first is the etymology or word usage for that decade that does not apply later on. Kraft (tape) was capitalized. Screw driver was two words, and First Aid was capitalized. Now they are kraft tape, screwdriver and first aid. This use of the proper language for the time period is extremely powerful. The second clincher is the fact that a careful inspection of the text shows that the lower case text font was Monotype Modern, used on hot lead printing presses. Sometimes some of the 'z's would not seat properly because they were so seldom used, and the 'z' would be raised in the text. Our copy has three raised 'z's, telltale evidence of the use of a hot lead printing press. Knowing to fake such an anomaly then actually faking it with software available before 1994 are virtually impossible. These clinchers are called 'zingers' and essentially make the *SOM 1-01* a rock solid production of circa 1954."[1]

There is another aspect of the *SOM 1-01 Manual* that has provoked controversy, too: namely, the inclusion of references to a type of UFO that, in recent years, has become known as the Flying Triangle. Many people with an interest in the UFO mystery will have heard of the Flying Triangle puzzle. For two decades, sightings of large triangular-shaped UFOs, often black in color, usually with rounded corners, and that make a low humming noise, have been reported throughout the world. These reports are in stark contrast to the classic saucer-shaped UFOs, and have led some commentators to suspect that the Triangles are military aircraft developed relatively recently, and are perhaps along the lines of a next-generation Stealth-type vehicle.

This argument has, in turn, led to assertions that since the Triangles have only been seen in the last twenty years or so, the *SOM 1-01* must be fake because it describes encounters with such craft as far back as the mid-1950s, and long before the Triangles were being seen. However, evidence can now be demonstrated that the Triangles *were* indeed being seen as far back as the late 1940s, throughout the period in which the *SOM 1-01* was reportedly written, and into the 1960s. Moreover, one particular case from the 1960s seems to have a connection with the prime issue addressed in this book: namely, alien-originated viruses.

An extract from the *SOM 1-01 Manual* that describes the Flying Triangles states thus: "This craft is believed to be new technology due to the rarity and recency [sic] of the observations. Radar indicates an isosceles triangle profile, the longest side being nearly 300 feet in length. Little is known about the performance of these craft due to the rarity of good sightings, but they are believed capable of high speeds and abrupt maneuvers..."[2]

Notably, an investigation of a Flying Triangle is described in officially declassified Air Force documents of May 26, 1949 that originated with the Air Force Office of Special Investigations at Barksdale Air Force Base, La. According to Special Agent Bernard A. Price: "Investigation at Vicksburg, Mississippi regarding an unidentified aerial phenomena described as being a flying triangle failed to verify definitely just what type of object was sighted." In this case the object, seen on the night of April 22, 1949, was small – only in the region of four feet in overall length, but was described by the witness to SA Price as moving "faster than mail planes, or National Guard planes, but slower than a jet type aircraft." Also, the object did not exhibit "any kind of propulsion," nor "stabilizers or antenna."[3]

But for a case that sounds far more like the classic Flying Triangle as described within the pages of the *SOM 1-01*, we have to turn to Britain and the previously mentioned *Operation Mainbrace*.[4]

Barely one day into the exercise, a UFO report was filed with authorities by naval personnel on board ships in the Atlantic between Ireland and Iceland. The encounter in question involved what was described as a "blue/green triangle" that was observed flying over the sea at a speed of 1,500 miles per hour – which accords very well with the data contained in the *SOM 1-01 Manual*.[5]

For the most convincing evidence that exists to support the notion that the Flying Triangles were being seen far earlier than many students of the mystery believe, we have to turn our attention to, once again, the British Isles – but this time of early 1965. And it is this case that may have direct relevance to the "alien virus" angle of the UFO puzzle that apparently so alarmed the Majestic 12. While digging through a whole host of formerly classified UFO files at the National Archive at Kew, England in 1996, Nick Redfern found a one-page document that revealed some startling data.

According to the Ministry of Defense paperwork, on the night in question, March 28, 1965, at approximately 9:30 p.m. over moorland near Richmond, North Yorkshire, a man saw, "Nine or ten objects—in close triangular formation each about 100ft long—orange illumination below—each triangular in shape with rounded corners, making low humming noise."[6] Interestingly, the "rounded corners" and "low humming noise" are precisely what many witnesses to Flying Triangle-style UFO encounters are reporting today—in a worldwide capacity, no less. Moreover, the SOM 1-01 Manual contains a picture of a Flying Triangle that also displays these exact rounded corners. Recognizing the significance of this, Redfern began a search to locate the witness.

On finding the man, named Jeffrey Brown, Redfern introduced

himself, and explained that he had located at the National Archive a copy of the original report that dealt with his sighting all those years ago. It is fair to say that Brown was shocked, to say the least, to find that details of his long-gone encounter had been kept on file by the Ministry of Defense for decades.

"Yes, I did send in a report all those years ago, but I didn't think they would have kept it all this time," Brown said. As he explained, he had been driving through the North Yorkshire moors of England, when, on approaching the village of Skeeby, near Richmond, the engine of his car began to splutter and die.

"It was a 1951 Ford," he stated, adding with some humor, "and it was a good car but a bit unpredictable at times. I didn't want to break down on the moor because it was icy cold. I got out of the car to have a look at the engine and that's when I saw this light."

Brown continued: "At first, because it was so dark, I wondered if it might be a weather balloon. But then I had a good look at it over the hedge and realized how big it was and how low down it was. It was about one hundred feet from end-to-end, about one hundred feet above the moors and shaped like a huge triangle and white, milky-white in color. It kept coming towards me and then stopped about two hundred yards from me over the moors. It hovered for a while—nothing came out of it, but there was a light below it that just pulsated like a light bulb. There could have been quite a few lights on it but from a distance the light just looked like a glow. Then without a warning, it just took off at a speed that isn't recognized. Good gracious, I thought, it must be a UFO.

"As it shot up, not vertically but at an angle, it joined a group of others that were identical and that were in a triangular or V-formation. The others were very, very high; a whole fleet of them. They all then headed south, I think, at a tremendous speed and disappeared over the horizon. I saw the main one for no more than a couple of minutes, but after they had gone I was still and stood by the moor watching this fleet disappear. I waited in case something else exciting happened, but of course it didn't."

Shortly after the encounter and after reporting the incident to the Ministry of Defense at Whitehall, Brown began to notice, "awful red marks on my skin which were like a stretch mark, but they were like a deep salmon red and they kept coming and going. But I didn't have them before."

The most bizarre angle of the entire episode was still to come as the man graphically illustrated: "For about eighteen months after the sighting, I would get strange telephone calls from people. These would be every two or three months. They just phoned out of the blue but didn't introduce themselves. They just said they were from some bureau or other. They didn't mention the name of the bureau but kept mentioning 'sightings' and asked whether I had seen anything else strange. Had any men come to interview me?"

Brown was never visited by anyone with regard to his Flying Triangle encounter, nor did the MoD ever offer an explanation as to what it was that he saw on that fateful night in March 1965. To this day, that series of strange and unnerving telephone calls continues to mystify him, primarily because aside from informing the MoD of what had occurred, he made no other report to anyone—either official or unofficial as he is at pains to point out: "The only report I ever made was the one I sent to the MoD. It was so exciting that I had to tell someone."

Brown's important testimony raises a number of vital questions: Why was someone so determined to find out if he had received any strange visits with regard to his encounter? Why the interest in knowing if he had had any other unusual encounters of a UFO nature? Who were his mysterious callers? Was he subjected to such lengthy questioning because he inadvertently caught sight of a classified military project that the authorities wanted to keep under wraps? Or perhaps he had viewed something that was truly out of this world?

To this day, Jeffrey Brown remains mystified by his extraordinary encounter over the Yorkshire moors in 1965. Of one thing we can now be certain: the Flying Triangles are not a new phenomenon. It is truly ironic that confirmation of this fact should come via the previously withheld files of the British Ministry of Defense.

And consider again what Brown had to say about the movements of the Flying Triangle: "It hovered for a while...then without a warning it just took off at a speed that isn't recognized." Now, consider, again, also the following extract from the *SOM 1-01 Manual* on the Flying Triangles: "...they are believed capable of high speeds and abrupt maneuvers..."

Note too the fact that the witness received some form of skin affliction from being in proximity to the Flying Triangle. This may not be dissimilar to the 1947 deaths of Sandia technicians as described in the *Interplanetary Phenomenon Unit Summary*. That the witness in the 1965 event in England was much further away from the object than the unfortunate technicians, however, may very well have been what saved him from a grisly death by a lethal bacteriological agent. It may also have been what prompted the series of on-going telephone calls made to him from an unidentified agency.[7]

* * *

Chapter 11 Notes:

1. Statement from Dr. Robert Wood, August 2005.

2. *SOM1-01 Majestic-12 Group Special Operations Manual: Extraterrestrial Entities and Technology, Recovery and Disposal*, April 1954. Available at: www.majesticdocuments.com by downloading: http://209.132.68.98/pdf/som101_part1.pdf and: http://209.132.68.98/pdf/som101_part2.pdf.

3. *Project Sign, Subversive Activity*, May 26, 1949. Prepared by Special Agent Bernard A. Price, Air Force Office of Special Investigations.

4. Records pertaining to the history of Mainbrace made available to Nick Redfern in 1990 by Bernard F. Cavalcante, Head, Operational Archives Branch, Naval Historical Center, Washington, D.C., 20374-0571.

5. Letters to Nick Redfern from UFO researcher Victor Kean, March 27 and April 7, 1995. Project Blue Book Report 2087.

6. The document in question is contained within file reference: AIR 2/17527.

7. Interview with Jeffrey Brown, September 11, 1999.

Chapter 12
Crashed UFOs, Bio-War, and the
JFK Assassination, 1961-1963

O ne of the areas of controversy surrounding both MJ-12 and
crashed UFOs that is seldom discussed in a serious forum is
that which posits a link between those same issues and the assassination of United States President John. F. Kennedy on November
22, 1963 at Dealey Plaza, Dallas, Texas. As fantastic as it may
appear, there is a demonstrable body of evidence available that links
numerous people to the JFK saga who were also allied to the UFO
subject. More notably, *all* of those people with connections to the
JFK story were specifically linked with crashed-saucer accounts,
rather than just the UFO subject in general.

It must be stressed that not all of the individuals in questions had
personal and direct connections to the assassination – some were
merely acquainted with the President, or had an awareness of his
UFO links and interests. However, a central core of characters in the
story also had links to a number of the issues contained within the
pages of this book, such as biological warfare; bacteriological
warfare and the United States' cattle-herd; and the secret work of
Fort Detrick, the rumored home of secret research into alien viruses
in the 1950s.

A variety of documents that have surfaced into the public domain
via researcher Timothy Cooper suggest that between 1961 and his
death in November 1963, President Kennedy was trying, somewhat
unsuccessfully, to determine the full story behind the Intelligence
community's involvement in the subject of UFOs. Most disturbing
to that same community, however, is the claim that Kennedy wanted
to completely open up the secrecy surrounding UFOs and share it
with the public, with the media, and possibly even with the higher
echelons of the Government of the former Soviet Union.

A Top Secret document obtained by Timothy Cooper, and dated
June 28, 1961 from Kennedy to the Director of the Central Intelligence Agency demands a, "review of MJ-12 Intelligence Operations
as they relate to Cold War Psychological Warfare Plans," and adds,
"I would like a brief summary from you at your earliest conve-

nience."[1]

According to Allen Dulles, in a Top Secret document dated November 5, 1961, and titled *The MJ-12 Project*, the United States' Intelligence world was particularly concerned about the way in which Soviet air defenses perceived UFOs, or perhaps *didn't* perceive them. As Dulles noted: "The overall effectiveness about the actual Soviet response and alert status is not documented to the point where U.S. intelligence can provide a true picture of how Soviet air defense perceive unidentified flying objects."[2]

As a result of this worrying revelation, the United States had been launching "decoy" devices to test Soviet radar, and was planning on building and flying "more sophisticated vehicles whose characteristics come very close to phenomena collected by Air Force and NSA elements."[3]

In other words, the United States Government was concerned that Soviet air defenses were unable to firmly differentiate between what may have been a true UFO and an American spy-plane, or worse still, an incoming Inter-Continental Ballistic Missile. Indeed, the nightmarish scenario that hung over the heads of the CIA and MJ-12 was that the Soviets would mistakenly interpret a UFO over its airspace as an American missile and initiate a nuclear strike that would, inevitably, lead to Armageddon and the end of civilization.

Of course, American Intelligence was gambling recklessly by flying "decoy" devices and advanced aerial platforms over the Soviet Union. On the one hand, the United States needed data on how accurately, or not, the Soviets were able to track fast-moving, incoming vehicles of unconventional design, in the event that a Third World War broke out between the two super-powers. And flying devices that mimicked the movements of true UFOs offered the United States convenient camouflage and plausible deniability of involvement if the Russians protested. But, there was also the ever-present danger that initiating such actions might have led the Soviets to panic and launch a strike against the West.

Kennedy, realizing that this was a highly reckless way of trying to establish the extent to which Soviet air defenses could correctly track fast-moving objects in its airspace, privately began to formulate a plan to share "real" UFO data with the Soviets, in an attempt to ensure that the Russians were fully able to interpret the difference between a UFO and an American ICBM, and therefore avoid triggering an accidental war.

Ten days before his death, according to a document secured by researcher Timothy Cooper, JFK wrote to the Director of the CIA stating that he had instructed NASA's Director, James Webb, to "develop a program with the Soviet Union in joint space and lunar exploration." In that document, too, Kennedy made it clear that the Soviets needed to be aware of the differences between "bona fide" UFOs and "classified CIA and USAF sources." Or as Kennedy succinctly put it: "...the knowns [sic] and the unknowns."[4]

Interestingly, a hand-written note at the foot of this document states: "Angleton has MJ directive."[5]

Equally controversial is an alleged National Security Agency intercept of a telephone conversation that Kennedy had on the same day with Soviet Premier Nikita Khrushchev that Timothy Cooper secured. Titled *UFO Working Groups*, the document reads as follows:

Kennedy: Mr. Premiere a situation has developed that affects both our countries and the world and I feel it necessary to convey to you a problem that we share in common.

Khrushchev: Mr. President, I agree.

Kennedy: As you must appreciate the tension between our two great nations has often brought us to the brink of showmanship with all the tapestry of a Greek comedy and our impasse last year [Note from the authors: a reference to the Cuban Missile Crisis of 1962] was foolish and deadly. The division that separates us is through misunderstanding, politics, and cultural differences. But we have one thing in common which I would like to address to your working group on the UFO problem.

Khrushchev: Yes, yes, I agree with your assessment. We nearly tied the knot that divides us permanently. Our working group believes the same way as yours. The UFO problem presents grave dangers.

Kennedy: Then you agree, Mr. Premiere that we should cooperate together on this issue?

Khrushchev: Yes, Mr. President.

Kennedy: Mr. Premiere, I have begun an initiative with our NASA to exchange information with your Academy of Sciences in which I hope will foster mutual concern over this problem and hopefully find some resolution. I have also instructed our CIA to provide me with full disclosure on the phantom aspects and classified programs in which I can better assess the situation. Can you persuade your KGB to do likewise?

Khrushchev: Mr. President, I cannot guarantee full cooperation in this area but I owe it to future history and the security of our planet to try. As you must know I have been somewhat limited in my official capacity as Party Chairman to order such cooperation in this area. We too feel that the UFO is a matter of highest importance to our collective security. If I can arrange for a secret meeting between our working groups at a secret location and at a time designated by you. I feel that this much on my part can happen.

Kennedy: Mr. Premiere, if a meeting at this level can convene it will be an important first step. It will lead to more dialog and trust between our countries and reduce the ever present threat of nuclear war.

Khrushchev: Yes, Mr. President, it will.

Kennedy: Then we are in agreement.

Khrushchev: Yes.

Kennedy: Yes. Until we talk again.[6]

As the above transcript demonstrates, Kennedy's desire to inform the Soviets of "the phantom aspects and classified programs," strongly suggests that the worry that UFOs would be misinterpreted as secret U.S. Air Force and CIA reconnaissance aircraft and could result in an all-out war was *still* on Kennedy's mind, hence his wish to provide Khrushchev with the facts. And JFK's comment that the sharing of data would, "lead to more dialog and trust between our countries and reduce the ever present threat of nuclear war," only reinforces that fact.

Of course, this was all completely unacceptable to MJ-12 and the CIA, and the inevitable countdown to Kennedy's assassination at Dallas on November 22, 1963 began. And the fact that, as will now become apparent, many of the alleged players in the assassination had links to the crashed UFO controversy, suggests strongly that there was a pressing desire on the part of this small cabal to not only terminate the president, but to protect themselves from public exposure by Kennedy, and to maintain the secrecy surrounding MJ-12's crashed UFO program.

Guy Banister

A character that turns up in most of the books on the JFK assassination is Guy Banister, a former FBI agent, who, at the time of the killing, was running his own detective agency – Guy Banister Associates – in New Orleans. Banister had been the subject of an investigation by the Warren Commission that investigated Kennedy's death, but he was the subject of a much deeper investigation by New Orleans District Attorney, Jim Garrison (portrayed in the movie, *JFK*, by Kevin Costner).

Banister's detective agency was based at 531 Lafayette. However, the building had a second entrance at 544 Camp Street, which was the location of an anti-Castro organization (the Cuban Revolutionary Council) created by E. Howard Hunt and Bernard Barker, of Watergate infamy. It was determined by the Warren Commission that investigated the assassination of JFK, that Lee Harvey Oswald, used the 544 Camp Street address for the pro-Castro Fair Play for Cuba Committee.

After Banister died, his widow found Fair Play for Cuba Committee papers at Banister's office. Similarly, Banister's secretary confirmed that Banister and Oswald were acquainted. Banister employed as an investigator a man named David Ferrie (about whom more later), and his other acquaintances included the World Anti-Communist League. During his FBI years at Chicago, Banister worked with Robert Maheu, a consultant to Howard Hughes, who planned various assassination plots against Fidel Castro. Banister also worked as the Louisiana coordinator for a group known as the Minutemen – a militia-style organization that was looking for Communist infiltrators and supporters in the United States. In March 1957, Banister had testified before the Louisiana Joint Legislative Committee and confirmed that during the time of his work with the FBI, he had worked in the fields of counter-espionage, counter-sabotage and "counter-subversive activity work."

Only a few hours after JFK was shot, Banister drunkenly beat one of his investigators, Jack Martin, with a gun, concerned that Martin was going to reveal David Ferrie's role as getaway pilot for the real assassins of Kennedy.[7]

As far as UFOs are concerned, Banister was one of the first FBI agents that investigated crashed UFO events for J. Edgar Hoover, when Hoover instructed his agents, in the summer of 1947, to assist the Army Air Force in its UFO inquiries and studies. The most notorious UFO event that Banister investigated occurred in Twin Falls, Idaho in July 1947 and ties Banister in directly with the crashed UFO controversy.

The following is extracted from the *Tacoma News Tribune* of July 12, 1947:

"Butte, Montana. July 11 – AP – FBI agent W. G. Banister said an object which appeared to be a 'flying disk' was found early today at Twin Falls, Ida., and turned over to federal authorities there. Banister, Special Agent in Charge of the FBI in Montana and Idaho, said the bureau had reported the discovery to the army at Fort Douglas, Utah. An FBI agent in Twin Falls, inspected the 'saucer' and described it as similar to the 'cymbals used by a drummer in a band, placed face to face.' The object measured 30 ½ inches in diameter, with a metal dome about 14 inches high on the opposite side, anchored in place by what appeared to be stove bolts. The gadget is gold plated on one side and silver (either stainless steel, aluminum or tin) on the other. It appeared to have been turned out by machine, reports from Twin Falls said. The FBI declined to elaborate further."

This case was almost certainly nothing more than a hoax. However, there is a point worth noting: Banister had behind-closed-doors meetings with the Army at Fort Douglas, Utah, to discuss the nature of the object. As this alleged crash and subsequent meeting occurred during the time of the New Mexico UFO recoveries, it is not implausible that Banister (being the original custodian of the object) may have been exposed to the truth about the genuine crashed saucers, particularly if there had been initial confusion about the real nature of the object – as indeed there was.[8]

Fred Crisman

One reviewer of Kenn Thomas' authoritative book on the events of June 21, 1947 at Maury Island (titled *Maury Island UFO*) wrote that it contained "information rich to the point of saturation." True; however, there can be little doubt that Thomas's research has provided what is certainly the clearest picture of the curious events at issue. As Thomas has revealed, the Maury Island story began on June 21, 1947, three days before what is widely regarded as the first modern UFO event – pilot Kenneth Arnold's sighting of a number of elliptical shaped objects over Mt. Rainier, Washington State.

So the story goes, on the morning in question, a lumber salvager named Harold Dahl, his son, and two still-unidentified individuals witnessed six, disc-shaped aircraft – one in the middle, wobbling in a strange fashion while the remaining objects surrounded it – flying in formation over Puget Sound, Tacoma at a height of around 2,000 feet.

Dahl described the objects as being "shaped like doughnuts," and with "five portholes on their sides." Suddenly, the central disk began to wobble even more and dropped to a height of no more than 700 feet. The remaining discs then broke formation, with one of them descending to the same height as the apparently malfunctioning disc and then proceeded to "touch it."

Without warning, the malfunctioning disc then began to "spew forth" what appeared to be two different substances: a white-colored material that Dahl described as a thin, white "newspaper-like" metal that floated down to the bay; and a black substance, that also hit the water, and that was reportedly hot enough to "cause steam to rise." Indeed, sections of the black substance allegedly hit both Dahl's son and his pet dog that were also on the boat, and reportedly killed the animal outright.

According to the story, Dahl reported the events in question to a man described as his superior: Fred Crisman, a man with a long and complicated life story, and suspected ties to the murky world of American Intelligence. Since Dahl had supposedly retained samples of the recovered debris, he convinced Crisman to go to the Maury Island shore and take a look for himself. Crisman would later claim that he saw on the shore an "enormous amount" of both the black and the white material, and recovered some of it for his own safekeeping.

Crisman duly reported his experience to the publisher Ray Palmer (of *Amazing Stories* fame), who hired none other than Kenneth Arnold to investigate the Maury Island affair. Arnold, whose own, historic encounter came three days after Dahl's encounter at Maury Island, delved deeply into the story, and was later joined by two Air Force investigators, Captain William Lee Davidson and First Lieutenant Frank Mercer Brown, who were working under General Nathan Twining to collect information on the then-current wave of UFO encounters that was being widely reported across the United

States.

Crisman would turn over samples of the mysterious debris collected at Puget Sound to the Air Force investigators, who intended to fly it to their final destination at Wright Field, Ohio. Fate would have another outcome, however. Shortly after Brown and Davidson departed from Washington State, their plane crashed, killing both men. A team was dispatched to clean up the site. Reportedly, however, the strange debris could not be located.

Many commentators (including Captain Edward Ruppelt of Project Blue Book fame) have stated that the entire Maury Island event was nothing more than an unfortunate hoax that had a tragic outcome for Brown and Davidson. Kenn Thomas's intense and dedicated research, however, has shown that the affair might not be so black-and-white as has previously been assumed. Most significant, are Crisman's links with the Intelligence community: In 1968, Fred Crisman was subpoenaed by New Orleans District Attorney Jim Garrison, as part of Garrison's investigation into the assassination of President Kennedy.

In a well-known report titled *The Torbitt Document*, Crisman is named as one of the three "hoboes" picked up in the rail yard behind the infamous Grassy Knoll at Dealey Plaza, Dallas where, some maintain, a "second gunman" was located during the killing of Kennedy. The fog of time has effectively resulted in certain aspects of the Maury Island case remaining unresolved – and perhaps, unfortunately, permanently. For some, the case is still nothing but a tragic hoax. For others, however, it is seen as one of the most important cases of all, involving the actual recovery of debris from a malfunctioning UFO. The involvement of shadowy players on the periphery of the Intelligence community; the possibility of the deliberate murder of Air Force personnel in possession of the strange materials recovered at Maury Island; and even both direct and indirect links to the JFK assassination, all serve to ensure that the controversy surrounding the Maury Island affair continues.[9]

Clay Shaw

According to the *Majestic 12 1ˢᵗ Annual Report*, some of the debris from Maury Island was turned over by Crisman (described in the document as a Counter Intelligence Corps operative) to a CIA agent named "Shaw." Kenn Thomas suggests that this was Clay Shaw –

one of three people that Jim Garrison attempted to indict during his quest for the truth surrounding the JFK assassination. And although Shaw was eventually acquitted, his role as a CIA asset has since then been well documented, and finally admitted officially by the Agency. For his part, Garrison claimed that his prosecution of Shaw was a "toe-hold" to a larger conspiracy in which Fred Crisman may have been an assassin working on behalf of the aerospace industry, which had its own reasons for wanting JFK dead. Shaw himself died on August 14, 1974.[10]

Jim Garrison

Jim Garrison, the New Orleans District Attorney, the author of the book, *On the Trail of the Assassins*, and the man portrayed by actor Kevin Costner in Oliver Stone's film *JFK*, is one of the most-talked about figures within the assassination controversy. Although UFOs do not appear in Garrison's book, he had identified key players with links to UFOs and bio-warfare as being implicated in the assassination. Plus, Garrison had pre-assassination links with FBI agent Guy Banister, and may have been aware of the Maury Island case.

Consider the following in Garrison's own words from his book *On the Trail of the Assassins*: "Upon my return to civilian life after World War II, I followed my family tradition and went to law school at Tulane, obtaining both Bachelor of Laws and Master of Civil degrees. Shortly thereafter I joined the FBI. As a special agent in Seattle and Tacoma, I was very impressed with the competence and efficiency of the Bureau."

On his pre-assassination days with Guy Banister, Garrison stated: "I knew Banister fairly well. When he was in the police department, we had lunch together now and then, swapping colorful stories about our earlier careers in the FBI. A ruddy-faced man with blue eyes which stared right at you, he dressed immaculately and always wore a small rosebud in his lapel."

As this shows, Garrison was acquainted with Banister, he was based in Tacoma where the Maury Island incident occurred, and he had identified several key players in the JFK assassination who were also involved in the recovery for official of UFO debris and materials. The possibility that Garrison and Banister discussed some of the UFO investigations that Banister was implicated in during his time with the FBI is something that cannot be dismissed lightly, given Garrison's admission that they "swapped colorful stories" from their FBI days.[11]

Michael Riconosciuto

Arrested in 1991 on drug charges, Michael Riconosciuto was a key player in a saga that investigative journalist Danny Casolaro was pursuing for his proposed book *The Octopus*, the subject matter of which was a shadowy, powerful group of people within the military, government and intelligence community – the Octopus of the book's title – that was deeply involved in a host of issues, including UFOs and biological warfare. Casolaro was found dead under very dubious circumstances in a hotel room on August 10, 1991.

Riconosciuto worked with people tied to the shadowy Octopus - a group that also had ties to Iran-Contra; the Lockerbie, Scotland, Boeing 747 crash in 1988; gunrunning; and the so-called *October Surprise* controversy. Interestingly, Michael's father, Marshall, was a close business associate of Fred Crisman. Riconosciuto claims to know the true story behind Maury Island and Fred Crisman. He also claims knowledge of MJ-12 and to have witnessed an alien autopsy. Kenn Thomas and the late Jim Keith's book *The Octopus* tells the whole murky saga, and reveals that Riconosciuto made cryptic comments about Crisman and the JFK assassination to Thomas that he, Riconosciuto, declines to elaborate upon. However, Riconosciuto does offer the possibility that the Maury Island UFOs were some sort of "advanced radar platform" flown by the military, and that they were either nuclear-powered or had nuclear materials on board.[12]

Colonel Philip Corso

The author of the book *The Day After Roswell* that detailed his alleged secret knowledge of the Roswell UFO crash of July 1947, Colonel Philip Corso was an investigator for Senator Richard Russell, who was on the Warren Commission that investigated the assassination of President Kennedy. At the time of his death, Corso was planning a follow-up book with the working title of *The Day After Dallas* that would, he said reveal the truth about the JFK assassination. How curious that someone who claimed to know the truth about Roswell also maintained intimate knowledge of Kennedy's death.[13]

Senator Richard Russell

Russell had a major UFO sighting while visiting Russia in 1955 that was subsequently investigated, extensively, by both the CIA and the Air Force. It is known, from cryptic comments that he made, that Russell received a classified briefing on the UFO subject from the CIA. Interestingly, Russell was the one member of the Warren Commission who believed that a conspiracy lay behind Kennedy's death.[14]

William Holden

Formerly with the United States Air Force, William Holden served aboard the presidential aircraft *Air Force One* during Kennedy's tenure as President. Nick Redfern interviewed Holden in 1997 when he, Holden, was visiting England. Holden told Redfern that he was aboard the plane at the time that Kennedy was due to give his famous "Ich bin ein Berliner" speech, and saw Kennedy reading a newspaper that contained an article on UFOs. Kennedy, Holden told Redfern, saw him looking at the feature and asked him what he thought about UFOs. Holden replied to the President that he believed they existed. Holden further advised Redfern that Kennedy told him he was correct: UFOs *did* exist. Holden stated additionally to Redfern that Kennedy, "wanted to tell the public the truth about UFOs," but that, ominously, his "hands were tied."[15]

Dorothy Kilgallen

In 1955, gossip-columnist Dorothy Kilgallen was clandestinely fed a crashed UFO story by a still-unknown person attached to the British Government. She also leaked parts of the Warren Commission report on JFK's assassination in 1964, and was the last person to interview Jack Ruby – the man who shot and killed Lee Harvey Oswald. Kilgallen was, she said, going to blow the JFK assassination out of the water with some startling new information. She died in 1965, under circumstances that many view with suspicion, and before she had a chance to reveal her story.[16]

Marilyn Monroe

The UFO author and researcher Linda Moulton Howe has

uncovered information from two scientists that relates to a visit to Area 51 by President Kennedy shortly after becoming president, allegedly to view the remains of recovered alien spacecraft. This may be connected to a story related within an unauthenticated CIA document on Marilyn Monroe, that asserts that JFK (who had an affair with the actress) had secretly told her the details of his visit to a, "secret air force base for the purpose of inspecting things from outer space." Monroe died under controversial circumstances in August 1962, at the exact time when she was threatening to reveal classified government data that she had recorded in her "diary of secrets."[17]

The Biological Warfare Angle

According to MJ-12 documents secured by Timothy Cooper, in the period leading up his assassination, Kennedy had been making inquiries with NASA, with James Angleton, with Allen Dulles, and with others in the intelligence community, about opening up the classified UFO files of the United States Government to the public, and possibly, even, to the Soviets too, and that this prompted those implicated in the secrecy to insist on the President's termination with extreme prejudice.

There is another interesting piece to this jigsaw. On November 21 (two days before the assassination) a planned event was organized at Brooks Air Force Base, Texas. JFK was to dedicate six new aerospace medical research buildings there that were said to be vital to the American space program. Interestingly, there have been rumors that JFK may have seen "other" things during his visit to Brooks – chiefly the biological remains of alien cadavers recovered from a UFO crash in New Mexico in 1947.[18]

This story is made all the more intriguing by the fact that among those that JFK was scheduled to meet at Brooks, one was Major General Theodore C. Bedwell, Jr. Born in Texas in 1909 he attended Southern Methodist University in Dallas and received his Doctor of Medicine degree in 1933. His first assignment was Fitsimons General Hospital, Denver, Colorado, where he served until 1939. He served at various locations and in various positions during the Second World War.

Notably, however, from 1946 to 1947 he served as Deputy Surgeon and Chief, Industrial Medicine, Air Materiel Command at Wright

Field, Ohio. He also spent time at the School of Aviation-Medicine at Randolph Field, Texas; a military base that appears on the distribution list for a 1947 *Air Accident Report* dealing with a collision between an aircraft and an unidentified object. In other words, only forty-eight hours before he was shot, JFK was about to meet someone who was arguably in a prime position to see the bodies brought into Wright Field in 1947.[19]

Also during the visit to Brooks, an arrangement was made for Kennedy to meet with Colonel Harold V. Ellingson, USAF, who had received a Bachelor of Science degree in Bacteriology in 1935. Ellingson held a number of posts, the most interesting being that of Post Surgeon and Hospital Commander at Fort Detrick - where, according to a number of MJ-12-related papers, research into alien viruses was being undertaken.[20]

The 6570th Aerospace Medical Research Laboratories

Another part of the itinerary planned for JFK on his visit to Brooks AFB involved the president receiving a briefing from the staff of the 6570th Aerospace Medical Research Labs, which happened to be based at Wright-Patterson AFB. Their work centered upon the feasibility of putting a man into space from a medical and biological perspective.[21]

Is it only coincidence that two days before he died (and at a time that he was at loggerheads with James Angleton, Allen Dulles, and the CIA, about releasing MJ-12 data to the public and to the Russians) JFK met with one man who held a high-ranking medical posting at Wright Field in the summer of 1947, met with another man who had held a senior post at Ft. Detrick, and received a briefing on aero-medical research undertaken at Wright-Patterson? It is not an impossible that Kennedy was due to receive data at Brooks that would assist his efforts to break the secrecy barrier concerning UFOs. That Kennedy's life was ended only days later in Dallas may not be without significance.

Interestingly, FBI agent and alleged assassination player Guy Banister also had ties to biological warfare issues of a type that were of concern to Fort Detrick personnel such as Ellingson. At the Hearings of the Louisiana Joint Legislative Committee on March 7, 1957 at the Louisiana State Capitol Building, Baton Rouge, Banister discussed his knowledge of an outbreak of foot-and-mouth disease in cattle herds in Canada that was suspected of being a deliberate release of the virus. Similarly, he also investigated cases of "wheat stem rust" that attacked wheat in Montana and Dakota in the early 1950s, as it was suspected that this was another example of early biological warfare assaults on the United States by unidentified sources. Notably, on the issue of bio-warfare as it relates to the two above examples, Banister stated to the Committee that he had personally consulted with "the nation's leading pathologists."[22]

Here, then, is an example of a man linked with all of the key ingredients of the MJ-12 papers – (a) the Kennedy assassination; (b) crashed saucers; and (c) biological warfare operations.

An intriguing character known to Banister was David Ferrie. A homosexual who typically wore a bizarre wig and had painted-on eye-brows to hide the fact that he was utterly hairless over his entire head and body, Ferrie was an investigator for Banister, he was associated with Clay Shaw, and a tie-in can be found that links Ferrie with Lee Harvey Oswald as far back as the 1950s. Ferrie is known to have been involved in flying missions in and out of Cuba, and he has been identified by a number of sources as being involved in a plan to fly the real assassins of JFK out of Dallas. Ferrie also had a fascination with both cancer cures and plans to induce cancer in people as a form of covert assassination. Ferrie died, under suspicious circumstances, before Jim Garrison could call him as a witness in his trial against Clay Shaw. Edward T. Haslam's book *Mary, Ferrie and the Monkey Virus* provides a wealth of data on Ferrie's cancer research, as does the unpublished manuscript of Judyth Vary, a woman who alleges she had an affair with Lee Harvey Oswald in the period leading up to the assassination of Kennedy in November 1963.[23]

And it should not be forgotten that there is a curious, central theme to many of these JFK-UFO links. For the most part, they all deal with not UFO sightings or general alien encounters, but specifically *UFO crashes*. Guy Banister investigated a possible crashed UFO; Fred Crisman handled unidentified debris; CIA asset Clay Shaw (according to the MJ-12 papers) was provided with some of the Maury Island debris; Michael Riconosciuto claims to know the true story of Maury Island and claimed to have seen an alien autopsy; Dorothy Kilgallen was fed a crashed UFO story in 1955; Colonel Philip Corso allegedly worked with UFO materials recovered at Roswell and saw an alien body; Marilyn Monroe had knowledge of crashed spacecraft and bodies; and the staff at Brooks AFB that had arranged to meet JFK two days before his death worked at key locations reportedly involved in the analysis of alien biology and viruses, namely Ft. Detrick and Wright Field (later Wright-Patterson Air Force Base).

Shaw, Banister, Crisman and Ferrie may have had knowledge of the ultimate secret that MJ-12 was hiding and that Kennedy was trying to disclose. They may also have had a collective, and vested, interest in having Kennedy eliminated from the picture on that fateful and fatal day in 1963 to protect their involvement in the MJ-12 saga.

There is one more piece of data worth recording, too: on June 30, 1999, Timothy Cooper received a typed, one-page letter from a source who described himself as a "retired CIA counterintelligence officer who worked for Jim Angelton from 1960 to 1974." It should be noted that the source misspelled Angleton's name. This may of course have simply been an error during the typing of the letter. However, the November 12, 1963 memorandum that refers to Kennedy's plans to share with the Soviets MJ-12-originated data on the "knowns and the unknowns," also misspells Angleton's name as Angelton.

It seems odd that two people who allegedly worked closely with Angleton should spell his name both identically and incorrectly. We should not, therefore, dismiss the possibility that the same person was responsible for producing both documents, and that they may have been fabricated for purposes unknown. With that in mind, related below is the content of the June 30, 1999 letter to Timothy Cooper:

"Mr. Cooper: I am a retired CIA counterintelligence officer who worked for Jim Angelton [sic] from 1960 to 1974. When Jim died it was my responsibility to go through his secret files and take inventory of sensitive files that would connect MJ-12 to JFK's murder."

The author forwarded to Cooper under cover of this letter a series of MJ-12-related "directives," explaining to Cooper that: "I literally snatched the 'Directives' from the fire and have kept them safe from review. To allow a review would compromise future directors and put the agency in a difficult position."

He continued: "I feel the time is fast approaching when the files of the Majestic...project will be pried loose and the public's right to know should begin. We in CI [Note from the authors: Counterintelligence] have monitored civilian UFO research for a long time and have played a major role in keeping the UFO community busy. Salina [Note from the authors: allegedly the first name of Thomas Cantwheel's daughter] requested that the MJ-12 Directives be sent to you and hopefully, be disseminated in a responsible manner."

In conclusion, he wrote: "I think your decision to work with Dr. [Robert] Wood was a good one. He has credibility and good science skills...I don't think you realize it but you and Dr. Wood have started a shit storm. Nixon's SCEO ordered all MJ-12 documentation purged and destroyed. This one was not. [Note from the authors: this same claim concerning Nixon is made by another source, whose account is related in a later chapter, titled *The Area 51 Revelations 2006.*] This carbon copy is the only link to MJ-12 and don't expect any more in the future. Everything is now on computers and there is no existing paper trail to my knowledge. If you play your cards right, you should make progress with what you have. I caution you to be careful about who you talk to and trust with this information."

Interestingly, a hand-written note at the foot of the letter states: "Not everyone has good intentions. Watch your ass."[24]

If only President Kennedy had done likewise...

* * *

Chapter 12 Notes:

1. National Security Memorandum from President John F. Kennedy to Director, Central Intelligence Agency, June 28, 1961. Available at www.majesticdocuments.com by downloading: http://209.132.68.98/pdf/kennedy_ciadirector.pdf.

2. *The MJ-12 Project, Operations Review*, Allen W. Dulles, November 5, 1961. Available at www.majesticdocuments.com by downloading: http://209.132.68.98/pdf/MJ-12opsreview-dulles-61.pdf.

3. Ibid.

4. *Classification review of all UFO intelligence files affecting National Security*, Memorandum from President John F. Kennedy to Director, Central Intelligence Agency, November 12, 1963. Available at www.majesticdocuments.com by downloading: http://209.132.68.98/pdf/kennedy_cia.pdf.

5. Ibid.

6. *UFO Working Groups*, November 12, 1963, National Security Agency Intercept of the "Hot Line." Available at www.majesticdocuments.com by downloading: http:// 209.132.68.98/pdf/umbra.pdf.

7. *On the Trail of the Assassins: My Involvement and Prosecution of the Murder of President Kennedy*, Jim Garrison, Sheridan Square Press, 1988. *Guy Banister*, www.spartacus.schoolnet.co.uk/JFKbannister.htm.

8. *Tacoma News Tribune*, July 12, 1947.

9. *Maury Island UFO*, Kenn Thomas, IllumInet Press, 1999. *The Secret Life of Fred Crisman*, Anthony L. Kimery, *UFO Magazine*, Vol. 8, No. 5, 1993. *Notorious Fred Crisman*, Part II, Kalani & Katiuska Hanohano, *UFO Magazine*, Vol. 9, No. 1, 1994. *Maury Island UFO: The Crisman Conspiracy*, Kenn Thomas, *UFO Crash Retrieval Conference Proceedings*, November 14-16, 2003, Las Vegas, NV. *Majestic 12 1ˢᵗ Annual Report.*

10. *Maury Island UFO: The Crisman Conspiracy*, Kenn Thomas, *UFO Crash Retrieval Conference Proceedings*, November 14-16, 2003, Las Vegas, NV. *Majestic 12 1ˢᵗ Annual Report.*

11. *On the Trail of the Assassins: My Involvement and Prosecution of the Murder of President Kennedy*, Jim Garrison, Sheridan Square Press, 1988.

12. *The Octopus: The Secret Government and Death of Danny Casolaro*, Kenn Thomas & Jim Keith, Feral House, 1996.

13. *The Day After Roswell*, Colonel Philip J. Corso (Ret.) with William J. Birnes, Simon & Schuster, 1997.

14. *Observations of Traveler in USSR*, Air Intelligence Information Report, October 14, 1955.

15. Interview with William Holden, October 1997.

16. *Kilgallen*, Lee Israel, Dell Publishing, 1980. *The Death of Dorothy Kilgallen*, Robert D. Morningstar. See: www.jfkresearch.com/morningstar/kilgallen.htm.

17. *Cosmic Crashes: The Incredible Story of the UFOs That Fell to Earth*, Nick Redfern, Simon & Schuster, 1997.

18. *News Release*, Office of Information, HQ USAF Aerospace Medical Division, November 8, 1963.

19. Ibid.

20. *News Release*, Office of Information, HQ USAF Aerospace Medical Division, November 9, 1963.

21. *News Release*, Office of Information, HQ USAF Aerospace Medical Division, November 11, 1963.

22. Statement from Guy Banister to the Committee on Segregation, Louisiana State Senate, March 1957. See: www.ajweberman.com/nodules/nodule11.htm.

23. *Mary, Ferrie & the Monkey Virus: The True Story of an Underground Medical Laboratory*, Edward T. Haslam, Wordsworth Communication Service. *Should We Believe Judyth Baker?* See: http://mcadams.posc.mu.edu/judyth.htm.

24. Letter from unknown source to Timothy Cooper, June 23, 1999. Available at www.majesticdocuments.com by downloading: http://209.132.68.98/pdf/burnedmemo coverletter-pdf.

Chapter 13
The Big Thicket UFO Retrieval, 1964

One of the most intriguing, but little known, UFO crash-retrieval cases that has a direct bearing upon the "alien virus" data contained within the pages of this book occurred in February 1964 in a heavily forested area of southeast Texas known as the Big Thicket, and involved the recovery of a small UFO by a combination of military personnel stationed at Fort Polk, Louisiana and at Fort Hood, Texas. Particularly notable is the fact that this was not the first time that Fort Polk was allegedly involved in the retrieval of a crashed UFO. Moreover, the area in which the 1964 crash occurred has been the site of strange and unexplained aerial activity for decades.

Fort Polk is located in west-central Louisiana, about 250 from New Orleans, and 180 miles from Houston, Texas. Construction of what was then called Camp Polk began on January 28, 1941 on the broad, rolling plains that, at the time, contained little but pine forests, a few dilapidated shacks and some range-wire fencing. The camp's first commander, Colonel Otto Wagner, arrived at the post with a few soldiers in March 1941; in the wake of which thousands of wooden barracks were constructed to support an Army preparing to battle Axis forces on the North African, European and Pacific fronts. Camp Polk - named for Confederate Lieutenant General and Episcopal Bishop Leonides Polk - was officially completed on August 1, 1941.

After the War, the post, which had been scaled down in size, was opened on a fuller basis for the Korean War and then closed. It wasn't until the 1961 Berlin Crisis that Fort Polk was reactivated on a more permanent basis, and it became an infantry-training center in 1962. Subsequently, it was selected to conduct Vietnam-oriented advanced training. As soldiers prepared for combat in Southeast Asia, commanders made the most of Fort Polk's 198,000 acres - especially a small portion filled with dense, jungle-like vegetation. For the next 12 years, more soldiers were shipped out to Vietnam from Fort Polk than from any other American training base.

The 5th Infantry Division became Fort Polk's major tenant in

1974, and the post became one of the most modern installations in the Army. In 1993, Fort Polk's 5th Division, designated as the 2nd Armored Division, moved to Fort Hood, Texas. On March 12, 1993, Fort Polk officially became the home of the Joint Readiness Training Center, which relocated from Arkansas. Fort Polk is also home to Warrior Brigade that contains several combat support units.

Soldiers of Fort Polk have been called to serve around the world in recent history. They fought in Panama during Operation Just Cause, and in the Persian Gulf in Operation Desert Storm. Currently Fort Polk is supporting the war on terrorism by providing contingency training for the Army's light infantry and special operations forces, and by deploying home station and reserve component forces in support of Operations Enduring Freedom, Noble Eagle, and Iraqi Freedom.[1]

In his 1982 status report titled *UFO Crash/Retrievals: Amassing the Evidence*, the late author and researcher Leonard Stringfield revealed the testimony of a source identified as Sergeant HJ, who saw duty in Korea with the Army's Infantry, and who claimed direct and personal knowledge of a crashed UFO event in Louisiana in the summer of 1953. According to HJ, he was stationed at Fort Polk at the time, and was on maneuvers in the area on one particular day when, at around dusk, "an egg-shaped object" crash-landed close to them in "soft sandy soil."

HJ added that the object was "ovoid," "large," and was surrounded by a fin-like protrusion at its equator. "Top brass and medics" quickly arrived on the scene, Stringfield was told, and a small body was removed from the craft along with three living creatures, each approximately four feet in height and displaying large heads. After having been placed in isolation, all reportedly died soon afterwards. The fact that medics were present and that the recovered creatures were placed in isolation, suggests the possibility that they, like the entities recovered in the 1947 crashes in New Mexico, represented a potential biological hazard. With that in mind, it is decidedly intriguing that, a decade later, personnel from Fort Polk were involved in a similar recovery.[2]

The source of this account, Will, served at Fort Polk for a number of years in the 1960s and was involved in training troops in the jungle-style, forested environment around Fort Polk for future deployment to Vietnam. One night, in February 1964, Will was ordered by his immediate superior to prepare both himself and a small team of personnel for immediate deployment to an area of southeast Texas known as the Big Thicket.[3]

The Big Thicket truly lives up to its name: an 83,000-acre area of East Texas's Piney Woods, it is a sprawling mass of rivers, swampland, and incredibly dense forestland comprised of cypress trees, short-leaf pines, and huge trees of oak and beech, where, according to local legend: "You'll find every critter in there from crickets to elephants." Not quite true, but the Thicket *is* home to a whole host of beasts, including armadillos, alligators, panthers, bobcats, and an array of snakes. And had you been there 10,000 years ago, you would have come across bison, camels, tapirs, giant sloth, beavers, saber-toothed tigers, and ferocious packs of wolves. And the area of the Big Thicket where the 1964 crash-retrieval occurred is home to something else too: the Bragg Road Ghost Light.[4]

Bragg Road, or Ghost Road, as it is known locally, is situated in the heart of the Big Thicket. It begins at a bend on Farm-to-Market Road 787 that is 1.7 miles north of the intersection of FM 787-770, near Saratoga. In 1902, the Santa Fe Railroad hacked a survey line from Bragg to Saratoga, bought right-of-way, and opened the Big Thicket forest with a railroad, and the Saratoga train began its daily trips to Beaumont, carrying people, cattle, oil and logs. When the area's oil booms and virgin pine gave out, road crews pulled up the rails in 1934, and the right-of-way was purchased by the county, and the tram road became a county road. And tales of a ghostly light started to gather steam in the 1940's, '50s and '60s as more people traveled to the road.

Explanations for the Ghost Light are varied and descriptive. Some people believe the light is the merely the reflection of car lights, while scientists believe it may be a gaseous substance. Other theorists suggest that the lights are similar to the so-called Marfa Lights (also of Texas), while there are those who consider the Bragg Road lights to be indicative of a longstanding UFO presence in the area.[5]

And it is against this backdrop of collective weirdness, that the Big Thicket UFO crash of 1964 occurred. According to Will, at around 9.00 p.m. on the night in question in February 1964, he and approximately eight or nine colleagues were driven in the back of a military truck from Fort Polk to an area of the Big Thicket which was literally only around a quarter of a mile from Bragg Road. They were met there by two men in suits "who looked like classic CIA," and two high-ranking military officers. Will and his team were ordered to remain vigilant in the area, and patrolled the road and the outskirts of the woods, in the event that anyone not cleared to be in the vicinity happened to stumble upon the military operation. Shortly afterwards, said Will, a team of four - all dressed from head-to-toe in what looked like a "biological protection suit or nuclear protection suits," as Will described the scene - headed into the woods, apparently "looking for something."

A little less than two hours later, they exited the woods, carrying between them a sealed, metal container that was about five feet square. The container was loaded aboard the back of a truck that was parked next to the one that Will had arrived in, and the truck exited the area with not a word spoken by any of the Fort Hood personnel. Will and his team were warned in *severe* terms not to talk about what had occurred, and were duly ordered back to Fort Polk.

Inevitably, there were people at Fort Polk who had heard about the strange events in the Big Thicket, and gossip began spreading like wildfire. According to Will, he was told by a friend at Fort Polk that he had served with on a reconnaissance mission in Vietnam in 1963, that the team from Fort Hood had responded to a report from a military pilot in the area who had seen a small bright light descend slowly into the woods on the previous evening at around 11.15 p.m.

Will speculates that the reason why the operation in the forest occurred on the following night, however, was because the original crash-landing itself occurred on a Sunday night. And, it was felt that there would be groups of teenagers driving around with it being a weekend night. So, by delaying the recovery until Monday when the area would probably be quieter, there was a better chance of successfully completing the mission without compromise or discovery. Again, Will stresses that this is merely conjecture on his part and is not based upon anything concrete.

Will states that he got the "full story" from the same Vietnam comrade, who advised him (having, himself, received the story from his brother-in-law, who was based at Fort Hood) that the object found within the Big Thicket was a circular, white-colored object that was basketball-sized object, that looked solid, but that had a "fluid" outer coating which seemed to "shimmer and move" when touched. Will's contact said that his brother-in-law had said that this was the third such identical device that had been recovered within the previous five years. The other two having been found, respectively, somewhere in Arizona in 1958, and in northern New Mexico, near Taos, in 1961.

Most disturbing of all was the fact that, as the military had learned to its cost in the 1958 and 1961 recoveries, when the retrieval teams got within around four or five feet of the objects, they were overcome with nausea and dizziness, and at least two died of a "flesh-eating virus – kind of like Ebola," as Will described the situation. In the Big Thicket case, the military took no chances, hence the presences of the team from Fort Hood garbed in biohazard protection suits.

Significantly, Will was advised that the object was later shipped to Fort Detrick, Maryland where it was placed in a sealed room. In the late 1970s, Will was told directly by his contact's brother-in-law that no investigation of the object was undertaken for approximately four years by personnel at Fort Detrick, who were highly fearful of unleashing a virus of unknown origins and power on an unsuspecting world. Most disturbing of all, was the fact that personnel at Fort Detrick had come to the unsettling conclusion that these devices were being "deliberated crash-landed" by alien intelligences as part of an on-going plot to "poison the human race" with unstoppable viruses of extraterrestrial origin. To this day, says Will, he wonders how many more of the spheres may have landed, unbeknownst to the military, and may have possibly unleashed such viruses upon the local population.

Will remains intrigued by the fact that the strange device was recovered in an area of the Big Thicket that has for decades been plagued by so-called "Ghost Lights," and wonders if this is evidence of the possibility that the UFO intelligences use certain areas as "worm-hole windows" to enter our reality from other dimensional planes. He also remains highly concerned and troubled by the disturbing nature of the secrets that he learned as a result of the Big Thicket recovery of 1964.[6]

* * *

Chapter 13 Notes:

1. *Joint Readiness Training Center and Fort Polk*: www.jrtc-polk.army.mil/aboutpolk.htm. *Fort Polk - Joint Readiness Training Center (JRTC)*: www.globalsecurity.org/military/facility/fort-polk.htm.

2. *UFO Crash/Retrievals: Amassing the Evidence*, Leonard Stringfield, published privately, 1982.

3. *Bragg Road: The Ghost Road of Hardin County, Texas*: www.bigthicketdirectory.com/ghostroad.html. *The Bragg Road Ghost Lights*: www.qsl.net/w5www/bragg/html. *In the Big Thicket*, Rob Riggs, Paraview Press, 2001.

4. Ibid.

5. Ibid.

6. Interview with Will, January 14, 2

Chapter 14
Fort Detrick and
The Andromeda Strain, 1972

In the latter part of April 2003, Nick Redfern posted a message to various members of an online *Yahoo* discussion group that he was subscribed to that focused its attention upon biological and chemical warfare. In an effort to try an determine the truth behind the *1st Annual Report*, Redfern asked if any of the group's subscribers had specific knowledge of the term "retro-virus" and its potential usage prior to the 1960s. Redfern included his telephone in the posting. No one was aware of the usage of the term in the pre-1960s time frame. However, Redfern received one telephone call from a man who asked if his question was in relation to the usage of the term as it appeared within the *1st Annual Report*. Redfern confirmed to the caller that it was. As a result, the man said that he would be interested in speaking with Redfern and an arrangement was made for him to call on the morning of May 5, 2003. For the purposes of this book, a follow-up interview was conducted on December 14, 2005.

Redfern agreed to protect the man's identity and concluded that, from the sound of his voice, he was in his sixties or perhaps older. While Redfern is keen to stress that he is unable to validate the data imparted to him by the source, he does not believe that the man is himself being deceitful. However, in the hall-of-mirrors that is the subject of UFOs, the question of whether or not the source himself was deceived is open to debate.

According to the man, from 1965 to 1975 he worked at Fort Detrick, Maryland, in an administrative position in its archives. He states that he was responsible in part for the security procedures concerning the dissemination of classified documentation.[1]

The source stated that the 1969 book *The Andromeda Strain* (written by Michael Crichton of *Jurassic Park* fame), and the subsequent 1971 movie spin-off of the same name were of deep interest and concern to staff at Fort Detrick because of the central theme of the book – namely a terrestrial space vehicle that returns to Earth containing alien microbes that subsequently unleash a lethal virus upon the population - and then-current research being undertaken at Fort Detrick into biological warfare and both manufactured and modified viruses.[2]

Redfern's informant claimed that approximately nine months after the movie version of *The Andromeda Strain* was released, a document came across his desk titled *Andromeda: Fact or Fiction?* Redfern's source was keen to stress that the document was not an officially sanctioned document. Instead it had been researched and prepared by an employee of Fort Detrick in his free time. The man had reportedly submitted the document to his superiors in the event that it was deemed to be of interest to Fort Detrick employees, as well as for future research and consideration.

Redfern's source further elaborated that the report addressed *The Andromeda Strain* scenario and looked deeply into whether or not such a nightmare could become a reality. The report ran to 194-pages; and while it did not discuss UFOs in any way, shape or firm, it did concentrated on two controversial issues:

(A)   An alien virus finding its way to Earth (possibly on a meteorite) and;

(B)   Contamination of the Earth by an alien virus as a direct result of astronauts bringing back samples from the Moon or, perhaps later, Mars.

The report allegedly dug deep into the way in which an out-of-control, extraterrestrial virus could spread wildly, and how world authorities might be forced to deal with it, what precautions would need to be taken if matters escalated, and how a viable vaccine might be created; if indeed such a vaccine even *could* be created. The report also discussed how, in a truly nightmarish scenario, a possible vaccine might remain completely elusive; the resultant effect being that the virus would mutate into a "doomsday virus" for the Human Race. The report, he says, was placed into the Fort Detrick document archive and was occasionally pulled out and read by interested parties that were employed there.

The interviewee stated that although the original copy of the document never left Fort Detrick, on one occasion something distinctly strange occurred: one of the three copies of the document that had been made was subsequently forwarded to the CIA's Office of Science and Technology, and remained with the "S&T people" for several months. Interestingly, when the document was returned to Fort Detrick, it quickly became clear that its contents had been closely scrutinized, to the extent that various "red-pencil changes" had been made to the document and certain sections had been underlined. Most notable of all, there was a red stamp on the front of the report that was about four-inches wide and one-inch high and that read: *Majestic 12-12-12 Approved, Spike-Back.*

The man advised Redfern that he asked his immediate superior what this meant or what Majestic 12 (or, as the document stated Majestic 12-12-12). His boss claimed not to know and advised him "in strong terms" not to talk about the annotated version of the document with anyone else. Redfern's contact added that this particular copy of the report was still held at Fort Detrick when he retired and stated, curiously, that there were no security restrictions surrounding its usage to "us."

The man admitted that he knew (but declined to elaborate precisely upon *how* he knew) that, "all the copies are gone [from Fort Detrick] now – today, I mean." The source stressed carefully to Redfern that he saw nothing else in his career that referenced Majestic 12, nor does he profess to know why the copy of the report should have been sent back to Fort Detrick, when it only succeeded in making people – who presumably did not have "need-to-know" – curious about what Majestic 12 was.

In what he claimed to be an effort to be helpful, the man stated that one person who "knew it all about the document at Detrick," was one Dr. Charles Rush Phillips, who, the man stated "definitely read the original document, but outside of Fort Detrick," and saw and handled the specific copy that had the Majestic 12 stamp on it.[3]

Dr. Charles Rush Phillips arrived at Camp Detrick in 1943 as a junior enlisted man and his work with gaseous sterilization and decontamination techniques ultimately revolutionized applied science. According to Fort Detrick authority Norman Covert: "His work between 1943 and 1969 made it possible for scientists to have and maintain the tools they needed to develop medical knowledge about microorganisms. The result has been the development of vaccines for a variety of diseases and an understanding of how disease spreads." Interestingly, Phillips died in May 1987 – the same month that the so-called *Majestic 12 Eisenhower Briefing Docu-*

ment surfaced publicly.[4]

Redfern's source openly speculated upon the possibility that perhaps the copy of the document in question had been returned in error to Fort Detrick by the CIA, as unlikely as such a scenario might sound. He said that as far as the document is concerned, there is nothing else that he can say or stress beyond one fact: in the early 1970s he read a document that addressed the potential threat posed by alien viruses (specifically outside of a UFO context); and that the same document had a Majestic 12 stamp on it.

He explained further that he had largely forgotten the term, Majestic 12, until the late 1980s, and specifically until the Majestic 12 controversy surfaced. The source expanded on this and stressed that his interest in the Moore-Shandera documents was not prompted by the UFO angle but specifically as a direct result of the fact that the documents asserted Detlev Bronk was a member of MJ-12.

Redfern was told that Bronk was "kind of a hero of mine;" and when Bronk's association with the Majestic 12 documents was brought to the man's attention, he began to dig deeper into the story.

The source stated that he has shown the *1ˢᵗ Annual Report* to about twenty former colleagues at Fort Detrick. None, he said, claimed any knowledge of the possibility that alien viruses or extraterrestrial DNA were held at Fort Detrick in the 1950s. And most, when questioned, said that the term "retro-virus" was not in use in any form prior to the 1960s. He also stated that, unanimously, all those that read the report said it was absolutely false that the name "Fort Detrick" was in use prior to 1956 – in any form whatsoever. Indeed, as detailed earlier, there are no officially declassified documents in the public domain that refer to "Fort Detrick" by that name before 1956.

Redfern was further informed by the source that, in his personal opinion, Tim Cooper may well have acquired "some information about lethal viruses held at Fort Detrick" from one of his sources, and perhaps, even, received data to the effect that those same viruses were "extraterrestrial originated." The man stressed, though, that he had seen no firm evidence in support of that hypothesis, and that it was merely his own opinion. But of one thing he is completely certain: in 1971 he had the opportunity to view a document that linked a group called Majestic 12 with the issue of lethal viruses held at Fort Detrick.[5]

* * *

Chapter 14 Notes:

1. Interview, December 14, 2005.

2. *The Andromeda Strain*, Michael Crichton, Ballantine Books, 1992. *The Andromeda Strain*, Review by Mark Wilson: www.scifi.com/sfw/issue80/classic.html.

3. Interview, December 14, 2005.

4. *Cutting Edge: A History of Fort Detrick Maryland*, Norman Covert, United States Army, May 1993. See also: http://www.detrick.army.mil/cutting_edge/index.cfm?chapter=chapter6.

5. Interview, December 14, 2005.

Chapter 15
Bodies on the Berwyns
January 1974

On the night of January 23, 1974, an event occurred on the Berwyn Mountain range in North Wales that for some within the UFO researcher community has come to be known as the definitive *British Roswell*. As researcher Andy Roberts stated: "Prehistoric man lived and worshipped on the mountains leaving behind him a dramatic, ritual landscape dotted with stone circles...Folklore tells us that these mountains are haunted by many types of aerial phenomena, including the spectral Hounds of Hell: those who saw them recalled how they flew through the night sky baying as though pursued by Satan himself. To the south of the Berwyn's at, Llanrhaedr-ym-Mochnant, the locals were plagued by a 'flying dragon' – intriguingly, a common name for UFOs in times gone by."

And as Roberts also carefully noted: "It is against this backdrop of history and myth that on the evening of January 23, 1974 an event took place on the Berwyn Mountains that was to perplex locals and spawned a veritable cascade of rumours, culminating in an incredible claim that, if true, would irrevocably change our view of history and make us revise our plans for the future of both our planet and our species. The claim was that a UFO piloted by extraterrestrials crashed, or was shot down, on the mountain known as Cader Berwyn and that the alien crew, some still alive, were whisked off to a secret military installation in the south of England for study."[1]

Since then, the issue of what *did* or did *not* occur on the Berwyn Mountains on the fateful night in question has been the subject of several books, intense controversy, heated debate, and, at times, unbridled fury. That *something* happened at around 8.30 p.m. on the night in question is not in doubt, however.

"I saw this bright light hanging in the sky," said Mrs. Anne Williams of Bro Diham, Llandrillo. "It had a long fiery tale which seemed to be motionless for several minutes, going dim and then very brilliant, like a dormant fire which keeps coming to life. It would have been like an electric bulb in shape, except that it seemed to have rough edges. [It] then fell somewhere behind the hills at the back of my bungalow and the earth shook."[2]

That the events caused considerable excitement and concern was something also noted by Police Constable Gwilym Owen, who was off-duty at the time and having a pint of beer in the nearby *Dudley Arms* public house. He stated shortly afterwards: "There was a great roar and a bang and the glasses shook. The sky was lit up over the mountains. The color was yellowish but other people in the valley described seeing blue lights." Five miles away, Police Sergeant Gwyn Williams was at home in Corwen: "The walls shook and the mirror swung away from the wall," he recalled. "My first thought was that a big lorry had hit the cinema – it was that kind of a roar and bang. Everyone ran into the street."[3]

At 8:38 p.m., the Global Seismology Unit of the Institute of Geological Sciences at Edinburgh, Scotland, recorded an earth tremor between 3.5 and 4 on the Richter scale. In response to questions posed by eager journalists, Dr. Roy Lilwall, the Senior Scientific Officer at the Institute, said that he had been told that a meteorite had possibly come down on the mountain and, had it been responsible for the "earthquake" that had been recorded at Edinburgh, it would have to have weighed several hundred tons.[4]

Approximately ninety minutes after the events on the Berwyns, Ken Haughton of Betws-y-coed viewed a "luminous sphere," some 400 feet across and traveling at an approximated height of 15,000 feet. It was Haughton's opinion that as he watched the sphere, it proceeded to descend into the sea in the area of the town of Rhyl, or possibly in the Dee Estuary.[5]

On the following day, January 24, a Royal Air Force mountain rescue team from Anglesey was dispatched to the Berwyn Mountains and, along with personnel from Gwynedd Police, searched the location for any sign of the object or its impact point. In turn, they received assistance in the search from the RAF station at Valley, Anglesey, who flew two aircraft to conduct a detailed photographic survey of the area. Nothing was reportedly found.[6]

And only hours later, an unusual aerial object was seen by David Upton at nearby Gobowen. As he went out of the backdoor of his home at about 7.15 p.m., he was immediately struck by the brightness of an object in the western sky and quickly ran back into the house for a pair of field glasses. To his complete amazement, these revealed a disc-shaped object that seemed to be divided up into four distinct sections, each of which was of a different color – red, green, yellow, and purple. David Upton's sister, Elizabeth, a twenty-year-old bank clerk, then took over the glasses, followed shortly thereafter by their mother, Mary Upton. Both verified David's description.

"I had been watching it for about ten minutes and thought perhaps I should tell someone about it," said Elizabeth Upton. She telephoned the local police, and they said that they would dispatch someone to the area. A minute or so after the call, the UFO disappeared behind a cloud. "We waited for the cloud to pass and when it did the disc had gone too," she explained, adding: "When I first came out of the house the light from the object was dazzling, like a street lamp. When we looked through the field glasses we could define its overall disc-shape and the four sections."[7]

Two people known to have been involved in the affair were Doctors Ron Maddison and Aneurin Evans of Keele University. Both expressed the theory that a meteorite was possibly the culprit. However, if the object *was* a meteorite they said, then it had to have (a) completely disintegrated upon impact; and (b) not left a crater, as Dr. Maddison noted carefully that: "the only changes we could see were recent disturbances of surface soil in some areas, but we were hampered to some extent by light snowfall."[8]

Two days later, it was stated in the local press that "police and RAF rescue experts" had come to the conclusion that the strange lights seen throughout the area were due to meteorite activity seen – coincidentally - at the same time that a group of men were out on the mountain range hunting hares with powerful lamps. Any link with the "earthquake" was entirely coincidental. RAF search team leader, Sergeant H. Oldham, said that another search of the area was "unlikely" to occur unless further information surfaced that attributed the lights to another source.[9]

Perhaps not surprisingly, the "hare" explanation received short shrift with the local witnesses, as can be seen fin the following extract taken from a letter sent to the *Wrexham Leader* newspaper: "Regarding your front page article '*Mystery Tremor*' in the issue of January 25, I find the explanation given absolutely ludicrous. The tremors shook houses over a 60-mile radius, and the lights were seen clearly miles away – this was reported by the national press and radio. I know nothing about 'Hare hunting' but unless the hunters use aircraft searchlights and kill their prey by lobbing a small atom bomb at them, then I fail to see how anyone can accept such an explanation."[10]

So what, exactly, *did* happen on that fateful night of January 23, 1974? Did the strange lights provide firm evidence that a malfunctioning UFO was hurtling towards its doom on the Berwyn Mountains? And was the so-called "earthquake" evidence that this same UFO had almost immediately thereafter slammed at high speed into the bleak and harsh mountain known as Cader Berwyn? Or was the entire event the result of a large-scale misperception of a curiously synchronistic combination of a meteorite shower, an earth tremor, and a group of men hunting for hares on the mountain and armed with powerful lamps – all in the same location and at practically the same time?

Andy Roberts firmly believes the latter theory to be the correct one. He also cites the fact that some of the tales about a crashed UFO having been found on the mountain range may have had their origins in the 1982 crash in the same area of a Royal Air Force Harrier jet-plane that was carrying top-secret equipment. Other British investigators of the case, such as Jenny Randles, Margaret Fry, Tony Dodd and Matthew Williams, are less certain that Roberts has resolved all of the many and varied aspects of the Berwyn affair.

Of the many controversies that continue to surround the Berwyn enigma, there can be no doubt whatsoever that the most sensational allegation is that, three nights *before* the incident on January 23, 1974, a number of alien bodies and several still-living extraterrestrial creatures were recovered from the mountainside by an elite team of military personnel, and were transferred under cover of tight security to an official installation in the South of England for study. Moreover, that official installation was allegedly Porton Down – the British equivalent of Fort Detrick.

Of course, this sounds like a conspiracy theorists' wildest dream come true; and despite vociferous attacks from the more skeptical researchers in the UFO research community, it has steadfastly remained an integral part of the story ever since it first surfaced – publicly, at least – in 1996.

The original source of the story was the UFO investigator Tony Dodd, a retired North Yorkshire police sergeant with a quarter of a century of service in the Force to his credit. At the time that the account was first revealed in the pages of the popular newsstand publication, *UFO Magazine*, Dodd refused to reveal the real name of his source for the story, as he continues to do to this very day, and instead gave him the pseudonym of "James Prescott." Dodd also claims to have seen Prescott's military records.[11]

According to Prescott, in January 1974 he was stationed at an Army barracks in the south of England. "I cannot name my unit or barracks as they are still operational," Prescott stressed to Dodd as he detailed how on 18 January 1974 he and his colleagues were put on "stand-by at short notice." Twenty-four hours later, the unit was directed to make its way towards the city of Birmingham.

"We then received orders to proceed with speed towards North Wales," Prescott elaborated. "We were halted in Chester in readiness for a military exercise we believed was about to take place. On 20 January, the communication to us was 'hot.' At approximately 20.13 hours we received orders to proceed to Llangollen in North Wales and to wait at that point." On arrival at Llangollen, recalled Prescott, the unit noticed a great deal of "ground and aircraft activity" in the area. Extraordinary events were unfolding. But it was shortly after 11.30 p.m. when things really began to take shape.

"We, that is myself and four others, were ordered to go to Llanderfel and were under strict orders not to stop for any civilians," said Prescott. The team soon reached Llanderfel, whereupon they were ordered to load two large oblong boxes into their vehicle: "We were at this time warned not to open the boxes, but to proceed to [the Chemical and Biological Defense Establishment at] Porton Down, [Wiltshire], and deliver the boxes." A number of hours later, they reached Porton Down and the mysterious cargo was quickly taken inside the facility. "Once inside," explained Prescott, "the boxes were opened by staff at the facility in our presence. We were shocked to see two creatures which had been placed inside decontamination suits."

The staff at Porton began the careful task of opening the suits. "When the suits were fully opened it was obvious the creatures were clearly not of this world and, when examined, were found to be dead. What I saw in the boxes that day," Prescott told Dodd, "made me change my whole concept of life.

"The bodies were about five to six feet tall, humanoid in shape, but so thin they looked almost skeletal with a covering skin. Although I did not see a craft at the scene of the recovery, I was informed that a large craft had crashed and was recovered by other military units."

Most remarkable was what Prescott had to say next: "Sometime later we joined up with the other elements of our unit, who informed us that they had also transported bodies of 'alien beings' to Porton Down, but said that their cargo was still alive."

In conclusion, Prescott added that this was "the only time I was ever involved in anything of this nature. This event took place many years ago and I am now retired from the Armed Forces."[12]

Although work at Porton Down had originally begun in March 1916; it was not until 1940 that the installation became the central hub of British interest in biological warfare. Following the start of the Second World War, a highly secret and independent group – the Biology Department, Porton - was established by the War Cabinet, with a mandate to investigate the reality of biological warfare and to develop a means of retaliation in the event that biological warfare was utilized against the United Kingdom. By 1946, the name of the wartime group had become the Microbiological Research Department. A decade later, the biological warfare research of Porton Down's staff had become solely defensive in nature; and in 1957 it was re-named the Microbiological Research Establishment.

By the 1970s it was decided that the MRE should be placed under the aegis of a civil authority, and on 1 April 1979, it became known as the Center for Applied Microbiology and Research. In 1995, the Establishment became part of the Defense Evaluation and Research Agency, and six years later DERA split into two organizations: QinetiQ, a private company, and the Defense Science and Technology Laboratory, which remains an agency of the Ministry of Defense. Today, Porton Down is known as DSTL, Porton Down.[13]

Were live aliens really loose on the Berwyn Mountains? Did an incident that pre-dated the key events of January 23, 1974 by three days occur? Can such claims be substantiated and corroborated or should we relegate them to the worlds of myth and fantasy? Or can there be yet another, even more intriguing, explanation?

A whole variety of UFO researchers, authors, and investigators have looked into the claims surrounding James Prescott, including Matthew Williams: "I spoke to Tony Dodd at the Cardiff UFO Conference just after this story came out, and I also spoke with him on the phone. Tony won't reveal the real name of James Prescott because he thinks that the guy will be traced back to the Army camp or the operational unit he worked for. So if Tony does reveal his name, he'll end up being given a very hard time by the government.

"But as I said to Tony: 'There aren't going to be many people who (a) were at a UFO crash-retrieval in North Wales with a specific set of circumstances; and (b) who are now talking about it. I'm pretty sure that the government are going to find out who he is, anyway, aren't they?'

"The obvious problem was that if the Army or the government got to Prescott before he had the chance to speak with anyone else, he would be in a lot more trouble than if his name was out in the open. That way, if the Army did anything against him, they'd be seen doing it.

"If Prescott does exist – and I think he probably does exist – he'd be far better off talking to people. But Tony said that the guy was on an Army pension and was concerned that he'd end up losing it.

"Tony says that he has checked the credentials of James Prescott. How far that goes and what it means, I don't know. But he's happy with them. Tony was happy that after all the research he'd done, Prescott was who he said he was."

From his conversations with Dodd, Williams was able to fill in some of the blanks with respect to what allegedly occurred between the time that Prescott and his unit departed from the crash site with the bodies and their arrival at Porton Down:

"The crates were loaded on to the back of an Army vehicle. They eventually got on to the main road and headed on to the motorway. At one point, they decided to pull off the motorway and stop at one of the services – just for a cup of tea. They weren't particularly worried, because at that point they hadn't been told what was contained in the crates.

"They stopped at the services; however, as they went to get out of the cab, they realized that they'd been followed by another vehicle. The people in the vehicle came up to the cab and said, 'No. Get back in your cab and get straight back on the road. Don't stop. Just get straight down to Porton Down.' And apparently they were shadowed all the way to Porton."[14]

Researcher Margaret Fry also has strong opinions with regard to the Prescott controversy: "I think Tony Dodd definitely interviewed James Prescott. The military were definitely there that night between nine and eleven. That's definite. But the bodies? I don't know. Who would ever know? James Prescott isn't going to say anything [on the record]; he'd be killed if he did.

"Tony told me that James Prescott said that his unit was parked on the B4391 road, and they were given the bodies. I don't know how. Either Tony has been told, or he hasn't told me. But there were, apparently, some soldiers already on the mountain and it was they who brought the bodies down to the little road. James Prescott was handed the bodies on the road; he didn't go on to the mountain-side at all.

"Some people...some lorries took away pieces, debris. Others took away bodies. And, according to this man, at least one was still alive. This is just evidence of one man, but all I can say is that everything I've collected since all points to the fact that this was correct."

According to Fry, Dodd told her that after the story was publicized, Prescott was indeed contacted by officialdom: "Tony says that he think that Prescott is perfectly genuine. But he's very afraid. He's had all sorts of individuals from the Ministry of Defense coming to him. The MoD don't know [sic] for certain that it's [Prescott] who is talking, but they're hinting darkly of the things that can happen if he says anything. And now, Prescott has said that he wants to let it lie. He's sorry; he doesn't want to say anything further for the moment, because he's too afraid. As I say, they don't know for certain that it's him. But his house, it's a military house; he got it by 'grace and favor' when he retired. Now they're telling him that if it is him who told Tony, he could end up losing his home. He wasn't just your common-or-garden private; he was very high up in the military. He's got a hell of a lot to lose."[15]

But how had the military been able to access the alleged crash sit with such apparent ease? According to Matthew Williams:

"Margaret [Fry] invited me up to North Wales and I went through some of the witness statements. Where the event was supposed to have taken place, we actually went there. We drove up there, stopped the car and had a look across the range to where the crash supposedly happened. It's quite a long walk, so I first looked at it from a distance through binoculars for ten to fifteen minutes. We looked at the topography to see whether or not it was possible to get somebody up there in such a short time, and Margaret's impression was that it would have to have been done on foot. It would have taken a long time to walk up there: possibly up to an hour or more.

"The fact that the military were already there to recover the bodies and maybe the UFO suggests they must have had advance notice that the crash was going to happen. We know that James Prescott said that they had a couple of days notice. So the things we found at the crash site did tend to support his account."[16]

While Williams and Fry appear convinced that the Prescott story (and all of its attendant controversies) is essentially genuine, not everyone who has addressed this aspect of the Berwyn affair is convinced that this is necessarily the case. Neither, however, are they of the opinion that this is evidence of a simple hoax, as the UFO authority and author Jenny Randles explains:

"[I]n 1995, I was lecturing in London at the *Fortean Times* [magazine] *Unconvention Conference*; I gave a talk on crashed UFO incidents and mentioned the [Berwyn] case. It was at the end of my lecture that a man came up to me. He was attached to the science editorial team of the *Sunday Express*. He said that he was fascinated by what I had to say because of something which had happened around 1993.

"The *Sunday Express* had been approached by a doctor living in the area around Bala. This doctor had told the Express that he had been building up a dossier over the previous twenty years, to indicate that there was definitely some cause of higher levels of childhood cancers in the area; and his thesis was that this was connected with a nuclear power station in the area. He'd reported it to the *Sunday Express* in that context.

"The science journalist who was at the *Unconvention* had gone to North Wales to investigate it, and spent a couple of days trying to find whether there could have been a scenario that might have caused this. He said that he couldn't find any substance to these allegations, and so the *Express* just simply wrote off the story. But as he said: 'Of course, if you are now introducing another potential source of radiation in the area twenty years ago that might have provoked things which the doctor had never even known about, it might make the story more interesting.'"[17]

Indeed it might. And what of the account given to retired police sergeant Tony Dodd? Randles's views on this matter are illuminating:

"The whole scenario of this is curious. About six weeks prior to the "alien bodies" story breaking, I had written a big article on the case for *Sightings* magazine. In that article I mentioned the possibility that the UFO story could be a cover for a nuclear accident – as I'd always done when referring to the incident.

"Then, shortly afterwards, the story appeared in which this soldier came forward to Tony Dodd, and who told Tony how he had ferried the bodies from the area. But the very day on which that story appeared in the newspapers, there was a *World in Action* program on TV which dealt with a nuclear accident at Greenham Common in the late 1950s in which radiation leaked from a nuclear weapon. Local doctors had since noted that this was apparently related to a rise in childhood leukemia in the area, and they had been trying very hard to establish a link through government documentation.

"*World in Action* stated that they had been pressuring the Ministry of Defense for the last few weeks to admit things, and they were getting the runaround. So it did occur to me that in the period between July and September 1996, you had the [Berwyn] case brought into the open in a big way through *Sightings* magazine – which [sold] about thirty to forty thousand copies per issue – and linking it with a nuclear accident at the same time.

"By coincidence, Granada Television – the makers of *World in Action* – were pressuring the Ministry of Defense on another incident which might have been very similar in nature. It's conceivable that someone in the Ministry of Defense might well have got tetchy about this, and was fearful that if Granada Television made a case for the incident at Greenham Common in the 1950's, someone might start to dig into other possibilities.

"It might have been the ideal opportunity that the Ministry of Defense needed to try to emphasize the alien-contact aspect of the [Berwyn] case by bringing out a story which reaffirmed that. Now, that is pure supposition on my part because I have no idea who this anonymous soldier is. I don't know if he believes what he's saying. But the timing was certainly interesting."[18]

If the only source for the James Prescott story about strange, humanoid creatures being found on the mountainside was Prescott himself, then one might be tempted to dismiss it out of hand as nothing more than a fanciful hoax generated by some unfortunate *Walter Mitty*-style character. However, other sources – some with official backgrounds - claim to have heard of distinctly similar stories and rumors that link the Berwyn saga of 1974 with Porton Down, the British equivalent of Fort Detrick.

* * *

Chapter 15 Notes:

1. *Fire on the Mountain*, Andy Roberts, published privately. *Out of the Shadows: UFOs, the Establishment and the Official Cover-Up*, David Clarke & Andy Roberts, Piatkus, 2002. See also: www.flyingsaucery.com.

2. *Guardian*, January 25, 1974.

3. Ibid.

4. *Times*, January 25, 1974.

5. *North Wales Weekly News*, January 31, 1974.

6. *Times*, January 25, 1974.

7. *Border Counties Advertiser*, January 30, 1974.

8. *Phantoms of the Sky*, David Clarke & Andy Roberts, Robert Hale Books, 1990.

9. *Wrexham Leader*, January 25, 1974.

10. *Wrexham Leader*, February 1, 1974.

11. *UFO Magazine*, September/October 1996.

12. Ibid.

13. *History of Porton Down*: www.mod.uk/issues/portondownvolunteers/history.htm.

14. Interview with Matthew Williams, January 17, 1997.

15. Interview with Margaret Fry, December 3, 1996.

16. Interview with Matthew Williams, January 17, 1997.

17. Interview with Jenny Randles, March 28, 1997.

18. Ibid.

Chapter 16
The Porton Down Story Continues
1974-1980

I spent thirty years in the Royal Air Force as an aircraft engineer," explains Bob Bolton. "I had various postings, including at Akrotiri in Cyprus, RAF Honnington and at RAF Valley in North Wales from 1971 to 1974. My wife [and] her family came from Corwen. At the time that the thing on the Berwyns happened, they lived up on the side of the mountain and her mom still lives there to this day. Corwen is part of the Berwyn range. From where their house is, if you walk up the path that goes behind the houses up and onto the top of the mountains, you're talking perhaps a mile and a quarter away from where it all occurred; so it's not very far away at all.

"[She] still remembers what happened on the night of 23 January [1974]. She said to me when I spoke to her about it just recently: 'I saw aircraft and heard aircraft shot down during the Blitz and it was like an aircraft coming down, but the sound was louder, bigger, heavier that anything you could imagine to do with an aircraft.'

"They didn't know what it was. They heard the noise first of all and ran out into the road. They weren't the only ones: all their neighbors ran out as well. It got louder and louder and louder and they couldn't see anything in the sky but then they felt the impact where the houses shook and she had things fall off the mantle-piece in the house.

"It was [my wife's] dad, who told me the story about bodies being found on the mountain. His real name was Harold Smith. But everyone called him Mick. He had a full-time job with Vauxhall at Elsmere Port; he was a local councilor and was also a part-time Sub-Fire Officer at Corwen. One day we got talking and got on to the subject of UFOs and he said to me: 'Oh, well, you obviously don't know about the incident up on the Berwyn Mountains.'

"I first heard the story from him around 1976. At that time he only told me that bodies had been brought down from the mountain and didn't say anything more. Nothing about who brought them down or where they were taken. But from 1979 to 1982 I was posted to

189

Germany and Mick and [my wife's mother] came out to stay with [us] for a month and it was here that he told us a lot more.

"I remember that the information that he told us had apparently come from another person in the North Wales Fire Service whose son was in the Army. But it's not surprising that he would have been told: Mick was a well-respected man and knew people throughout the North Wales Fire Service including at Bala and Wrexham. Mick told me that while the police weren't involved, the Army was – heavily. I can't give you an exact date when they visited and he told us this, but it was definitely between 1979 and 1982. He said that there were definitely lorries from Porton Down at the scene; that there was a lozenge-shaped object on the mountainside; and that bodies were taken off the mountain and driven to Porton. And to this day, [his wife] can also confirm that Mick told her the story about Porton Down and bodies too – either in the late 1970's or the early 1980's.

"I do remember Mick saying that when he had first told me this story in 1976, he didn't know that it was the Army who had taken the bodies off the mountain and he didn't know at the time that they'd been taken to Porton Down. So he must have learned that between 1976 and when he came to see us in Germany."[1]

One of the strangest – and somewhat unsavory – aspects of this affair surfaced in 1998 when rumors began circulating that the pseudonymous James Prescott was somehow connected with a very real James Prescott who lost his life in the Falklands War in 1982. It was May 17, 1982 when Staff Sergeant James Prescott of the Royal Engineers was killed while attempting to defuse a bomb on board HMS Antelope. He was later awarded a posthumous Conspicuous Gallantry Medal for his bravery.

According to Max Hastings and Simon Jenkins in *The Battle for the Falklands*: "A broadcast from the bridge announced that the bomb-disposal team would try a new method of defusing the bomb. Prescott and Phillips detonated a small charge, then walked forward to inspect the results. As they approached, the bomb exploded. Prescott seemed to be hit by a door blown free by blast, which killed him immediately."[2]

Needless to say, the fact that Tony Dodd had not related the tale until the mid-1990's effectively means that the James Prescott killed in the war of the Falklands fourteen years previously could not have been his source of the story. Moreover, a former colleague of Dodd's, and editor of the newsstand publication on espionage *Eye-Spy Magazine*, Mark Birdsall, has stated that while his brother, the late Graham Birdsall, believed that Dodd's use of the name James Prescott for his source *did* have some particular significance to it, Mark recalled that Dodd had told him that it had *no* significance and that he, Dodd, had merely conjured it up as a suitable pseudonym. In other words, the fact that there existed a *real* James Prescott in the British Army, and that Dodd decided to use that same name for his Army source, was something that amounted to nothing more than an unfortunate coincidence.[3]

Curiously, however, there *is* a Falkland's link to this story. Regrettably, it comes from another anonymous soldier who claims to have been told of the Berwyn UFO recovery by military personnel while traveling in the convoy of ships that headed for the Falkland's when war was declared. Is it possible – as *has* been postulated – that Dodd's source for the "Berwyn alien body recovery" was involved in the Falkland's campaign and that the pseudonym of James Prescott was adopted as a tribute to his fallen colleague (and perhaps as a "signal" to other colleagues) who may also been told the story on the journey to the islands? To date, this is a question that remains unanswered.[4]

The James Prescott saga aside, another account links anomalous aerial phenomena and strange, humanoid creatures in the North Wales area on the night of January 23, 1974. From Anne Owen (who now resides in France), comes the following:

"We had bought two, derelict, four-hundred-year-old cottages which we were converting. This was on a mountain above Trefriw and Llanrwst near the River Conwy. We'd taken a caravan up and a horse, as well, and our two children. We had a friend of ours visiting us at the time – a lecturer and mathematician from Toronto University – and we converted a small barn into a bit of a house with a window for him. We were in the caravan with the children, as we couldn't move into the cottages yet. That night – January twenty-three – the horse was very restless, so we put him near our caravan. But later in the night he started rocking the caravan and was in a terrible state.

"Then we suddenly saw this thing outside the window. It was like a white ball, very slow-moving. It was difficult to know how far away from us it was as it was pitch black outside, but it looked about two or three feet wide. Then suddenly there was an enormous bang, absolutely colossal. At first, we thought it had hit the place where our friend was. Luckily it didn't hit him, so we weren't actually sure where it *had* hit. But in the morning, our friend was outside looking at a rowan tree that had been forced out of the ground. What was strangest of all was that the tree had been stripped of all its bark and had been up-rooted and thrown four hundred feet.

"The only other person who was local to us was an old lady who was staring at it too. Well, she came up to me and said that she'd been woken by the bang. She also lived on the mountain and had gone to her bedroom window and had seen these 'little men' that were very small and all dressed in black – about three to four foot tall. She thought, because she'd seen the military on the mountain before that this was something to do with them. But she found it rather odd that they were so small! She described a 'little gathering' of them, about four or five, very, very early in the morning and near where the tree was. But she said that they didn't look too different, only smaller.

"When she went down to the village to tell the story, everyone thought that she was mad and then when we asked her again she wouldn't talk about it anymore. Although we did know of people in Trefriw who had had their windows broken by this thing.

"But we had a group of people come from Cardiff University and they started to photograph the tree and all around it. They said they had had some instances of UFOs in the area and had been 'sent to investigate' what had taken place. This happened within one day of this taking place. They sent us a photograph that showed a white cylinder where the tree had stood and that wasn't there when the picture was taken – you couldn't see it with the naked eye. They asked us if we knew what it was, but we had no idea.

"The oddest thing of all, though, was how the people from the university knew what had happened. They were in their forties and fifties then; so they weren't students. But the day before, and the day after, this happened a weird mist came down out of nowhere. This was nothing like a normal mist and I still remember it now. I wish I had the answers to it all, but all I can do is tell you what I remember."[5]

Having digested the witness testimony and the available evidence, can we come to any firm conclusions with respect to this particular aspect of the broader mystery of what may have occurred on the Berwyn Mountains thirty years ago?

Certainly, there is now demonstrable proof (albeit in the form of second-hand testimony) that the alien body angle of the controversy, as well as the Porton Down allegations, had been quietly disseminated amongst the closed-knit North Wales community at least as far back as 1976; and were later elaborated upon by a respected figure in the North Wales Council and Fire Service, no less, in the early 1980s to a then serving member of the Royal Air Force. In other words, Tony Dodd's informant – James Prescott – appears not to have been the original source of this account: it does have a precedent that the families of Bob Bolton and the late Harold Smith can attest to. Also, the account of Anne Owen demonstrates that the stories of live aliens being seen on the mountainside (as James Prescott asserted that he had heard was the case) also have some form of limited corroboration.

Of course, questions remain: why, for example, was James Prescott so adamant that the incident in which he was involved occurred on the evening of January 20 when – unanimously – all the other available evidence points to January 23 as being the correct date? Was this an error in recollection on his part, or were the events of January 23 only a part of a larger and even more bizarre mystery? And what of Anne Owen's mysterious visitors – allegedly from Cardiff University – who turned up conveniently out of the blue to discuss her experiences?

To this day, as is the case with so many crashed UFO incidents, we are left with a mountain of questions and very few definitive answers. But the controversy surrounding crashed UFOs, alien bodies and Porton Down does not end there.

Only months after the *Unorthodox Aircraft* file that is referenced in a previous chapter surfaced into the public domain, Nick Pope, who investigated UFO reports for the British Ministry of Defense from 1991 to 1994, wrote a novel titled *Operation Thunderchild* that centered around a hostile attack on the United Kingdom by alien forces. At the time, stories and rumors were in circulation to the effect that Pope was telling in a fictionalized format, "the truth" that he was unable to reveal in a non-fiction book. Regardless of whether or not this is the case, in *Operation Thunderchild*, alien bodies recovered from a UFO crash are taken to the Chemical and Biological Defense Establishment at Porton Down – precisely the same location where, it was alleged, that alien bodies found on the Berwyn Mountains, North Wales were taken in January 1974.[6]

When *Operation Thunderchild* was published, Nick Redfern questioned Nick Pope vigorously regarding the claims that the book was base more on fact than fiction. His comments were illuminating, to say the least.

"Even to you, Nick, I can't comment on that," said Pope. "But let's put it this way: *Operation Thunderchild* is going to be more controversial than *Open Skies, Closed Minds* or *The Uninvited* [Pope's previous non-fiction titles]. And, indeed, the Ministry of Defense may have more of a problem with it. Mainly because it's going to feature real locations, real weapon systems, real tactics, real doctrine and real crisis management techniques. It's going to blend my knowledge and experience of UFOs with my knowledge of crisis management – such as my involvement in the Gulf War where I worked in the Joint Operations Center."

"Given that you won't comment on the hypothesis that *Operation Thunderchild* relates in a fictional format the sorts of things that you were legally unable to relate in a non-fiction book, are you saying that there is more going on behind the scenes than meets the eye?' Redfern asked Pope.

Positively oozing uneasiness, Pope replied: "Well, it's very difficult to go into the details, but I'm a bit more inclined to think that there's perhaps more to this than meets the eye."

"More to what?" pressed Redfern.

Pope elaborated: "There are one or two things about the Ministry's stance over the last few years that have caused me to question things perhaps a little bit more than I did previously. I do think that there's a little bit more going on than perhaps I previously thought. I have to be very careful with every single word I say, because I know that every word, every sentence, every nuance, will be picked over by ufologists, the Ministry of Defense and a number of other agencies."

"Excuse me, Nick," said Redfern. "A number of other agencies? What do you mean by that?"

"I mean, a number of other agencies," was Pope's tight-lipped – and only - reply.[7]

Moreover, by Pope's own admission, he had a great deal of inside help when it came to researching the subject matter - as he stated in the *Acknowledgements* section of the book:

"Finally, but perhaps most crucially, there are those who, for a number of reasons, I am not able to name. I was helped with this book by a wide range of experts from various different agencies, who supplemented my own knowledge with their insights into the world of politics, science, military doctrine and much else besides."[8]

Given this statement, it is of course interesting that Pope's novel included a section on alien bodies being taken for analysis to none other than Porton Down. Of course, Pope, a regular contributor to *UFO Magazine*, would have been keenly aware of the James Prescott controversy and may simply have included the Porton Down angle in his book to help perpetuate the air of mystery and intrigue about himself that he has been careful to cultivate since publicly announcing his belief in the existence of aliens.

However, at the same time that (a) the National Archive, London, was declassifying files on UFOs and biological warfare, (b) leaked documents on those same topics were surfacing in the United States; and (c) Nick Pope's *Operation Thunderchild* was released, the British Ministry of Defense, in an unprecedented move, gave a huge amount of technical assistance and support to a BBC television production titled *Invasion Earth* that dealt with an attack on the planet by hostile aliens.

Inevitably, this led to rumors that this was all part of a less-than-subtle attempt on the part of the British Government to get the general public thinking about the possibility of humankind waging war with an alien species. Does the MoD know something that we don't? A Defense source specifically referred to Nick Redfern by Nick Pope had a number of perceptive comments to make.

"It's extremely strange," he began, "that on the one hand the MoD is publicly so dismissive about UFOs; and yet on the other it bent over backwards to provide assistance to a TV company producing a science-fiction drama which starts with the RAF shooting down a UFO.

"Normally," he continued, "the Ministry of Defense only helps film and TV companies where it believes that significant benefits will fall to the MoD in terms of recruiting, training or public relations. This was the case, for example, with our participation in the *James Bond* film, *Tomorrow Never Dies*. What, one wonders, did the MoD think it had to gain from helping to perpetuate a view that the Royal Air Force were virtually at war with extraterrestrials? Questions about our participation in this project were raised at the highest level within the Ministry of Defense."[9] And, most notable of all, in *Invasion Earth*, aliens from a captured, crashed UFO were taken to Porton Down.

And there is another, final intriguing footnote to the Porton Down controversy: Although the famous UFO incident at Rendlesham Forest, Suffolk, England of December 1980 has been the subject of half a dozen books and is considered by many to be an example of a UFO landing event rather than a crash, there are several indicators that "something" may have been retrieved from the forest.

The basics of the account are that between December 26 and 29, 1980 multiple UFO encounters occurred within Rendlesham Forest that involved United States' military personnel based at the nearby Royal Air Force stations Bentwaters and Woodbridge. According to numerous U.S. Air Force personnel, a small, triangular shaped object was seen maneuvering in the forest – as well as strange, almost spectral, alien-style entities.

In a July 31, 1994 lecture at Leeds, England, Charles Halt (formerly Colonel Charles Halt and one of those that witnessed the strange object) divulged his recollections of what had occurred fourteen years previously. During the course of his lecture, Halt astounded the audience by revealing something that had been hitherto unknown: an unscheduled C141 transporter aircraft arrived at Woodbridge just hours after the initial encounter and a group of "special individuals" departed from the aircraft, headed straight out of Woodbridge's East Gate, and disappeared into the forest.[10]

It should be noted, too, that the C141 is a huge aircraft, fully equipped to carry freight, vehicle payloads or, alternatively, up to 200 troops – ample space to also secrete a relatively small object (as the Rendlesham vehicle was described) of unknown origin.[11]

It may be relevant that during its life as an active military station, RAF Woodbridge was home to a squadron with an intriguing history, as Captain John E. Boyle of the U.S. Air Force reveals: "In the late 1960s and early 1970s, the 67th Aerospace Rescue and Recovery Squadron stationed at RAF Woodbridge [provided] standby rescue coverage for the American space flights. Of course, they were never needed to provide emergency rescue actions, but at the time, the unit was trained and available to rescue astronauts with their HH-53 and HC-130 aircraft. In early 1988, the 67th ARRS was re-designated as part of the 39th Special Operations Wing, their primary mission changing from that of rescue to supporting US Special Operations forces. Their secondary mission remains that of search and rescue and they would provide any assistance necessary in future space missions."[12]

Although the 67th's rescue and recovery skills were not needed during NASA's space missions, the question has to be asked: were they implicated in the recovery of something that originated with *somebody else's* space program in December 1980?

On this path: in her book on the Rendlesham affair, titled *You Can't Tell the People*, British writer Georgina Bruni reported on a rumor that shortly after the events at Rendlesham Forest a number of personnel from Porton Down were reportedly dispatched to the area and, dressed in some sort of full-body protection suit, entered the woods – for reasons that remain unknown.

Notably, however, the late British Admiral of the Fleet, Lord Hill-Norton, who had a personal interest in UFOs, tabled questions at an official level with British authorities on January 11, 2001 in an attempt to resolve the issue of the Porton Down allegations as they related to Rendlesham. Predictably, the response to Hill-Norton's questions, that surfaced on January 25, 2001, was to the effect that staff at the Chemical and Biological Defense (CBD) laboratories at Porton Down had made a check of their archives, but had found "no record of any such visits." Of course, it should be noted that this carefully worded statement does not state that such records did not exist; only that the specific personnel who made the search were unable to locate anything relevant. The controversy surrounding crashed UFOs and Porton Down seems destined to continue.[13]

* * *

Chapter 16 Notes:

1. Interview with Bob Bolton, November 14, 2000.
2. *The Battle for the Falklands*, Max Hastings & Simon Jenkins, Pan Books, 1997.
3. Conversation with Mark Birdsall, July 14, 2000.

4. Interview, April 10, 2000.

5. Interview with Anne Owen, August 11, 2000.

6. *Operation Thunderchild*, Nick Pope, Simon & Schuster, 1999.

7. Interview with Nick Pope, November 14, 1999.

8. *Operation Thunderchild*, Nick Pope, Simon & Schuster, 1999.

9. Interview, November 14, 1999.

10. Lecture given by Charles Halt (U.S. Air Force, Retired), Leeds, England, July 31, 1994.

11. *The Illustrated History of the United States Air Force*, Michael Roberts, Guild Publishing, 1989.

12. Letter to Nick Redfern from Captain John E. Boyle, United States Air Force, Chief, Public Affairs Office, Royal Air Force Bentwaters, Suffolk, England, September 30, 1988.

13. *You Can't Tell the People*: Georgina Bruni, Pan Books, 2001.

Chapter 17
The Chihuahua, Mexico Crash
August 1974

The following document, titled *Research Findings on the Chihuahua Disk Crash* is dated March 23, 1992, and was mailed to the researcher Elaine Douglas in July 1993. It was also sent to a number of British UFO investigators in early 1996, including Nick Redfern and Matthew Williams, bearing a Maryland postmark. If true, the document seems to have been written at an unofficial level by a source with deep knowledge of the incident at issue and who desired the release of the official evidence to interested parties. Which, in part, relates to the deaths of various individuals as a result of what may have been a lethal virus of the type described within the pages of the *1st Annual Report*.[1] The document reads thus:

"On 25 Aug. 74, at 2207 hrs., U.S. Air Defense radar detected an unknown approaching U.S. airspace from the Gulf of Mexico. Originally the object was tracked at 2,200 (2530 mph) knots on a bearing of 325 degrees and at an altitude of 75,000 feet, a course that would intercept U.S. territory about forty miles southwest of Corpus Christi, Texas. After approximately sixty seconds of observation, at a position 155 miles southeast of Corpus Christi, the object simultaneously decelerated to approximately 1700 (1955 mph) knots, turned to a heading of 290 degrees, and began a slow descent. It entered Mexican airspace approximately forty miles south of Brownsville, Texas. Radar tracked it approximately 500 miles to a point near the town of Coyame, in the state of Chihuahua, not far from the U.S. border. There the object suddenly disappeared from the radar screens.

"During the flight over Mexican airspace, the object leveled off at 45,000 feet, then descended to 20,000 feet. The descent was in level steps, not a smooth curve or straight line, and each level was maintained for approximately five minutes.

"The object was tracked by two different military radar installations, It would have been within range of Brownsville civilian radar, but it is assumed that no civilian radar detected the object due to a lack of any such reports.

"The point of disappearance from the radar screens was over a barren and sparsely populated area of Northern Mexico. At first it was assumed that the object had descended below the radar's horizon and a watch was kept for any re-emergence of the object. None occurred.

"At first it was assumed that the object might be a meteor because of the high speed and descending flight path. But meteors normally travel at higher speeds, and descend in a smooth arc, not in "steps." And meteors do not normally make a thirty-five degree change in course. Shortly after detection an air defense alert was called. However, before any form of interception could be scrambled, the object turned to a course that would not immediately take it over U.S. territory. The alert was called off within twenty minutes after the object's disappearance from the radar screen.

"Fifty-two minutes after the disappearance, civilian radio traffic indicated that a civilian aircraft had gone down in that area. But it was clear that the missing aircraft had departed El Paso International with a destination of Mexico City, and could not, therefore, have been the object tracked over the Gulf of Mexico. It was noted, however, that they both disappeared in the same area and at the same time.

"With daylight the next day, Mexican authorities began a search for the missing plane. Approximately 1035 hrs there came a radio report that wreckage from the missing plane had been spotted from the air. Almost immediately came a report of a second plane on the ground a few miles from the first. A few minutes later an additional report stated that the second 'plane' was circular shaped and apparently in one piece although damaged. A few minutes after that the Mexican military clamped a radio silence on all search efforts.

"The radio interceptions were reported through channels to the CIA. Possibly as many as two additional government agencies also received reports, but such has not been confirmed as of this date. The CIA immediately began forming a recovery team. The speed with which this team and its equipment was assembled suggests that this was either a well-rehearsed exercise or one that had been performed prior to the event.

"In the meantime requests were initiated at the highest levels between the United States and Mexican governments that the U.S. recovery team be allowed onto Mexican territory to 'assist'. These requests were met with professed ignorance and a flat refusal of any cooperation.

"By 2100 hrs, 26 Aug. 74, the recovery team had assembled and been staged at Fort Bliss. Several helicopters were flown in from some unknown source and assembled in a secured area. These helicopters were painted a neutral sand color and bore no markings. Eyewitness indicates that there were three smaller craft, very possibly UH1 Hueys from the description. There was also a larger helicopter, possibly a Sea Stallion. Personnel from this team remained with their craft and had no contact with other Fort Bliss personnel.

"Satellite and reconnaissance aircraft overflight [sic] that day indicated that both the crashed disk and the civilian aircraft had been removed from the crash sites and loaded on flat bed trucks. Later flights confirmed that the convoy had departed the area heading south.

"At that point the CIA had to make a choice, either to allow this unknown aircraft to stay in the hands of the Mexican government, or to launch the recovery team, supplemented by any required military support, to take the craft. There occurred, however, an event that took the choice out of their hands. High altitude over-flights [sic] indicated that the convoy had stopped before reaching any inhabited areas or major roads. Recon showed no activity, and radio contact between the Mexican recovery team and its headquar-ters ceased. A low altitude, high speed overflight [sic] was ordered.

"The photos returned by that aircraft showed all trucks and jeeps stopped, some with open doors, and two human bodies lying on the ground beside two vehicles. The decision was immediately made to launch the recovery team but the actual launching was held up for the arrival of additional equipment and two additional personnel. It was not until 1438 hrs. that the helicopters departed Fort Bliss.

"The four helicopters followed the border down towards Presidio then turned and entered Mexican airspace north of Candelaria. They were over the convoy site at 1653 hrs. All convoy personnel were dead, most within the trucks. Some recovery team members, dressed in bioprotection [sic] suits, reconfigured the straps holding the object on the flatbed truck, then attached them to a cargo cable from the Sea Stallion. By 1714 hrs the recovered object was on its way to U.S. territory. Before leaving the convoy site, members of the recovery team gathered together the Mexican vehicles and bodies, then destroyed all with high explosives. This included the pieces of the civilian light plane which had been involved in the mid-air collision. At 1746 hrs the Hueys departed.

"The Hueys caught up with the Sea Stallion as it re-entered U.S. airspace. The recovery team then proceeded to a point in the Davis Mountains, approximately twenty-five miles north east of Valentine. There they landed and waited until 0225 hrs. the next morning. At that time they resumed the flight and rendezvoused with a small convoy on a road between Van Horn and Kent. The recovered disk was transferred to a truck large enough to handle it and capable of being sealed totally. Some of the personnel from the Hueys transferred to the convoy.

"All helicopters then returned to their original bases for decontamination procedures. The convoy continued non-stop, using back roads and smaller highways, and staying away from cities. The destination of the convoy reportedly was Atlanta, Georgia.

"Here the hard evidence thins out. One unconfirmed report says the disk was eventually transferred to Wright-Patterson A.F. Base. Another says that the disk was either transferred after that to another unnamed base, or was taken directly to this unknown base directly from Atlanta.

"The best description of the disk was that it was sixteen feet, five inches in diameter, convex on both upper and lower surfaces to the same degree, possessing no visible doors or windows. The thickness was slightly less than five feet. The color was silver, much like polished steel. There were no visible lights nor any propulsion means. There were no markings. There were two areas of the rim that showed damage, one showing an irregular hole approximately twelve inches in diameter with indented material around it. The other damage was described as a 'dent' about two feet wide. The weight of the object was estimated as approximately one thousand, five hundred pounds, based on the effect of the weight on the carrying helicopter and those who transferred it to the truck. There was no indication in the documentation available as to whether anything was visible in the 'hole'.

"It seems likely that the damage with the hole was caused by the collision with the civilian aircraft. That collision occurred while the object was traveling approximately 1700 knots (1955 mph). Even ignoring the speed of the civilian aircraft, the impact would have been considerable at that speed. This is in agreement with the description of the civilian aircraft as being 'almost totally destroyed'. What was [sic] being taken from the crash site were pieces of the civilian aircraft. The second damage may have resulted when the object impacted with the ground. The speed in that case should have been considerably less than that of the first impact.

"No mention is made of the occupants of the civilian aircraft. It is not known if any body or bodies were recovered. Considering the destruction of the civilian light aircraft in mid-air, bodies may well not have come down near the larger pieces.

"Unfortunately what caused the deaths of the Mexican recovery team is not known. Speculation ranges from a chemical released from the disk as a result of the damage, to a microbiological agent. There are no indications of death or illness by any of the recovery team. It would not have been illogical for the recovery team to have taken one of the bodies back with them for analysis. But there is no indication of that having happened. Perhaps they did not have adequate means of transporting what might have been a biologically contaminated body.

"Inquiries to the FAA reveal no documents concerning the civilian aircraft crash, probably because it did not involve a U.S. aircraft nor did it occur over U.S. airspace.

"It should be noted that the above facts do not tell the complete story. Nothing is known of the analysis of the craft or its contents. Nothing is known about the deaths associated with the foreign recovery team. Nor is it known if this craft was manned or not.

"Other questions also remain, such as why would a recovered disk be taken to Atlanta? And where did the disk come from? It was first detected approximately 200 miles from U.S territory, yet U.S. air defenses extend to a much greater distance than that. If the object descended into the atmosphere, perhaps NORAD space tracking has some record of the object. Alternate possibility is that it entered the Gulf of Mexico under radar limits then 'jumped' up to 75,000 feet. Considering prior behavior exhibited by disks of this size, it is probable that the entry was from orbital altitude.

"The facts that are known have been gathered from two eye witness accounts, documentation illegally [sic] copies, and a partially destroyed document. This was done in 1978 by a person who is now dead. Only in February of this year did the notes and documents come into the hands of our group."[2]

While the description of the crash and recovery of the unknown object broadly conforms to the data presented in other reports, the reference to an apparently lethal biological agent present at the scene is *very* worrying. However, as we have seen time and again – and via numerous examples - it is most definitely not at all without precedent.

*   *   *

Chapter 17 Notes

1. *Research Findings on the Chihuahua Disk Crash*, March 23, 1992. See also: *UFO Crash/Retrievals: Search for Proof in a Hall of Mirrors, Status Report VII*, Leonard Stringfield, 1994. For further details, see: *Majic Eyes Only: Earth's Encounters with Extraterrestrial Technology*, Ryan S. Wood, Wood Enterprises, 2005.

2. Ibid.

Chapter 18
The FBI and Cattle Mutilations
1974-1980

As has been noted in the chapter titled *Animals and Biological Warfare 1947-1948*, the cattle mutilation issue is one that has been linked with the key controversy contained within this book: lethal viruses of extraterrestrial origin that may be designed to wipe out the human species. But first, in this chapter, some vital background data on this strange and grisly mystery.

For the majority of investigators of animal mutilation incidents, the premier event was that of September 1967, when Lady, a three-year-old horse belonging to Nellie Lewis, was found killed and mutilated under shocking circumstances on the ranch of her brother, Harry King, in southern Colorado. While the body of Lady was left essentially intact, the flesh from her neck and head had been completely removed in what seemed to be a surgical-like procedure.

From his Alamosa home, Nellie Lewis's husband, Berle, commenting on the sudden increase in UFO sightings which accompanied Lady's death, said: "We see something – I won't say what it is – every night." A further account came one month after the events at the King ranch from two witnesses who caught sight of a pair of high-flying, cigar-shaped objects – each about half the size of a football field – on a course that would have taken them over the southern Colorado area.[1]

In mid-1974, at least five cattle were found slain and mutilated in Madison County, Nebraska. In all cases the genitalia of the animals were removed, and in one instance the cow was reported to be minus one ear and eye, as well as its nose, mouth and tongue. Again, unusual aerial activity was reported. One witness, Harold Kester, described seeing an object that "looked as if it had a bluish-green light on each side with a glow surrounding it. It was behind a tree and moved from one side of the tree to the other. We couldn't tell how close it was or how fast it was moving."[2]

In July 1975 six cows were found mutilated forty miles north of Council, Idaho. Again, tongues, genitalia and the udders of the animals were removed. In a series of similar findings in Colorado, the cattle had been entirely drained of blood.

"We didn't find any [blood] at all," commented Sheriff Jim Hileman of Adams County. "It could have been washed away by rain, but I'd have to say that not finding any blood in this sort of a case is highly unusual."[3]

"I'm not scared, just uneasy," reported a citizen of Elsberry, Missouri, following a series of mutilations that hit the town in June 1978. As in Madison County, Nebraska, in 1974, and Council, Idaho, in 1975, the animals were missing vital organs and body parts including teeth, eyes, tongues and ears. And, more baffling, the animals were again drained of blood in some vampire-like fashion.[4]

Greeley, Colorado, was the target of the mutilators in September 1980. A Briggsdale rancher, Roland Ball, commenting on two cattle found slaughtered, said: "That's the first one I've ever seen this way. We found another west of the one that had been dead for two days, but it had been dead for quite a while. But it had one ear gone and I could tell it wasn't a predator." In addition to the removed organs, one of the cattle had a four-inch diameter circle of hide removed from the area of its navel. "They had just taken the navel out and everything around it. It was just as neat a cut as could be," said Ball.[5]

At 9.45 p.m. on December 13, 1993, Christopher O'Brien, a journalist of southern Colorado, received a telephone call from a Crestone resident house-sitting in the Baca Grants, who reported that a "glowing white object" had fallen to the ground south of the Baca, north of Hooper.

The next day, a 1,700-pound bull was found dead on the Dale and Clarence Vigil ranch in the nearby Costilla County. In addition to the usual signs of mutilation, broken tree branches were found where the animal lay, and, six feet up, red hair and blood were found on the tips of other branches, giving the impression that the bull had been physically lifted off the ground.[6]

What was certainly one of the most controversial statements made with respect to animal and cattle mutilations came in 1997 from the late Lieutenant-Colonel Philip J. Corso (who served on President Eisenhower's National Security Council staff, the Operations Coordination Board, and the US Army Staff's Foreign Technology Division):

"In the Pentagon from 1961 to 1963, I reviewed field reports from local and state police agencies about the discoveries of dead cattle whose carcasses looked as though they had been systematically mutilated. Local police reported that when veterinarians were called to the scene to examine the dead cattle left in fields, they often found evidence not just that the animal's blood had been drained but that the entire organs were removed with such surgical skill that it couldn't have been the work of predators or vandals removing the organs for some depraved ritual."

Corso continued that the first thought on the part of the U.S. military was that this was the work of the Soviets. However, he added, this was not the case, according to the colonel:

"[I]t wasn't the Soviets who were going after our cattle. It was the *EBE's* [Note from the authors: *EBE* is an abbreviation of *Extraterrestrial Biological Entity* – a term allegedly used within US Intelligence circles to describe alien beings] who were experimenting with organ harvesting, possibly for transplant into other species or for processing into some sort of nutrient package or even to create some sort of hybrid biological entity.'[7]

Of course, the UFO-mutilation link has been made on other occasions, too: notably, in the pages of the *Interplanetary Phenomenon Unit Summary* of July 22, 1947. It states with respect to the issue of "animal parts" found in the vicinity of a UFO crash in New Mexico in the summer of 1947: "The most disturbing aspect of this investigation was there were other bodies found not far from LZ-1 [a designation for the Foster Ranch where William Brazel found unusual debris that has become a part of the Roswell story] that looked as if it had been dissected as you would a frog. It is not known if army field surgeons had performed exploratory surgery on these bodies. Animal parts were reportedly discovered inside the craft at LZ-2 [which was a site reportedly twenty miles northwest of the town of Socorro, NM] but this cannot be confirmed. The team has reserved judgement on this issue."[8]

For some of the most fascinating data on cattle mutilations, however, we have to turn our attention to the Federal Bureau of Investigation (FBI). All of the currently available evidence suggests that FBI knowledge of the phenomenon began in the early months of 1973, when a cluster of reports surfaced in Iowa. Later that year yet further incidents occurred in at least a dozen counties in Kansas, with more still extending into Nebraska. Many of the killings were associated with sightings of unidentified aerial lights, unmarked helicopters – and an absolute lack of any incriminating evidence to suggest who (or what) was perpetrating these disturbing crimes.

With public anxiety rising, rumors began to circulate to the effect that the mutilations were the work of a powerful and extraordinarily well-equipped band of devil-worshippers who were killing the unfortunate cattle and excising various body parts for use in their satanic ceremonies. To illustrate this, on September 4, 1974, US Senator Carl T. Curtis wrote the following to FBI Director, Clarence M. Kelley:

"This will refer to my previous letter of August 21 to you regarding the series of incidents stretching from Oklahoma to Nebraska in which cattle have been dismembered in some kind of strange witchcraft cult. Enclosed is a newspaper article which appeared in the Hastings, Nebraska, Daily Tribune concerning these weird events. Articles similar to this one have appeared in many of the Nebraska newspapers. I thought you would want to see this article in order to substantiate the claims which have been made. I am wondering if your good offices have instigated an investigation into this situation either in Nebraska or any of the other states experiencing similar acts of mutilation to livestock. I will appreciate hearing from you."

The *Daily Tribune* article to which Senator Curtis referred made an intriguing revelation: "Cattle killings aren't the only strange happenings in northeast Nebraska. There have been numerous reports of unidentified flying objects in both Antelope and Knox counties." This was something expanded upon by Sheriff Herbert Thompson. Quoted by the newspaper, he stated: "We don't know if they are helicopters or strange lights for the most part. There were several reported over the weekend. The people who reported them called them strange lights. Previously we had two positive identifications of helicopters."[9]

Despite the phenomenal number of mutilations and the repeated sightings of anomalous aerial lights, all of which suggested that some form of coordinated operation was under way, at the time all the FBI was willing to state to Senator Curtis was: "It appears that no Federal Law within the investigative jurisdiction of the FBI has been violated, inasmuch as there is no indication of interstate transportation of the maimed animals."

Four months later, an Airtel was sent from the FBI office at Minneapolis to the FBI laboratory, which played down the theory that the mutilations were the work of some unidentified entity, and asserted that, in all probability, they were caused by "other varmints, believed to be foxes." A report citing the testimony of Richard Hilde, Chief Agent with the North Dakota Crime Bureau, stated: "[Hilde] said the dead animals in North Dakota had been found in scattered locations, and the Bureau believed they died of natural causes and then small animals such as foxes had eaten the soft part of the animals."

This does not account for the mystery helicopters, nor the strange lights reported time and again in the areas of mutilation sites. Nor does it explain whey there was a total lack of similar reports prior to the late 1960s. And when there was an alarming outbreak of mutilations in Colorado in 1974 and 1975, it became more than apparent that this was the work of something far stranger than the local animal population.

On August 29, 1975, Floyd K. Haskell, Senator for the State of Colorado, wrote an impassioned letter to Theodore P. Rosack, Special Agent in Charge of the FBI at Denver, Colorado, imploring the FBI to make a full investigation into the cattle mutilations, in an attempt to resolve the matter once and for all. His letter stated:

"For several months my office has been receiving reports of cattle mutilations throughout Colorado and other western states. At least 130 cases in Colorado alone have been reported to local officials and the Colorado Bureau of Investigation (CBI); the CBI has verified that the incidents have occurred for the last two years in nine states. The ranchers and rural residents of Colorado are concerned and frightened by these incidents. The bizarre mutilations are frightening in themselves: in virtually all the cases, the left ear, rectum and sex organ of each animal has been cut away and the blood drained from the carcass, but with no traces of blood left on the ground and no footprints."[10]

Our old friend, the unmarked helicopter, was also out in force in Colorado, as Senator Haskell was only too well aware. He continued:

"In Colorado's Morgan County area there has [sic] also been reports that a helicopter was used by those who mutilated the carcasses of the cattle, and several persons have reported being chased by a similar helicopter. Because I am gravely concerned by this situation, I am asking that the Federal Bureau of Investigation enter the case. Although the CBI has been investigating the incidents, and local officials also have been involved, the lack of a central unified direction has frustrated the investigation. It seems to have progressed little, except for the recognition at long last that the incidents must be taken seriously. Now it appears that ranchers are arming themselves to protect their livestock, as well as their families and themselves, because they are frustrated by the unsuccessful investigation. Clearly something must be done before someone gets hurt."[11]

Stressing that the loss of livestock in at least twenty-one states under similar circumstances suggested an interstate operation was being coordinated, Senator Haskell closed his letter to FBI Agent Rosack thus: "I urge you to begin your investigation as soon as possible, and to contact my office to discuss in more detail the incidents I have described. We stand ready to give you all possible assistance."[12]

In addition to contacting Agent Rosack, Senator Haskell issued a press release, informing the media that he had asked the FBI to investigate the mutilations. This caused the *Denver Post* newspaper to comment on September 3: "If the Bureau will not enter the investigation of the mysterious livestock deaths in Colorado and some adjacent states then Senator Floyd Haskell should take the matter to Congress for resolution."

Aware of previous FBI statements to the effect that there was nothing to indicate that the killings were within the FBI's jurisdiction, the *Denver Post* stated firmly: "The incidents are too widespread – and potentially too dangerous to public order – to ignore. Narrow interpretations of what the FBI's role is vis-à-vis state authority are not adequate to the need."

The issue of possible disregard for the law should the Bureau not wish to become involved was also something high on the *Post's* agenda: "There is already federal involvement. Consider this: Because of the gun-happy frame of mind developing in eastern Colorado (where most of the incidents have been occurring), the US Bureau of Land Management (BLM) has had to cancel a helicopter inventory of its lands in six counties. BLM officials are simply afraid their helicopters might be shot down by ranchers and others frightened by cattle deaths."[13]

This certainly concerned the FBI, and on the day after publication, Special Agents Rosack and Sebesta of the Colorado FBI made a visit to the offices of the *Denver Post*, where, in a meeting with three *Post* representatives, Charles R. Buxton, Lee Olson and Robert Partridge, the FBI's position with respect to the mutilations was spelled out: "...unless the FBI has investigative jurisdiction under Federal statute, we cannot enter any investigation."

One week later, on September 11, Senator Haskell telephoned Clarence M. Kelley at the FBI to discuss the entire issue of cattle and animal mutilation and the possibility of the FBI becoming involved in determining who, exactly, was responsible. Again, the FBI asserted that this was a matter outside of its jurisdiction.

"Senator Haskell [said that] he understood our statutory limitations but he wished there was something we could do," reported an FBI official, R. J. Gallagher. Haskell had additional reasons for wanting the mutilation issue resolved swiftly, as Gallagher recorded in an internal memorandum of September 12, 1975:

"Senator Haskell re-contacted me this afternoon and said that he had received a call from Dane Edwards, editor of the paper in Brush, Colorado, who furnished information that US Army helicopters had been seen in the vicinity of where some of the cattle were mutilated and that he, Edwards, had been threatened but Senator Haskell did not know what sort of threats Edwards had received or by whom. He was advised that this information would be furnished to our Denver Office and that Denver would closely follow the situation. Senator Haskell expressed his appreciation."[14]

The FBI ultimately determined that the unidentified helicopter issue was also outside of its jurisdiction, and that on this matter it was unable to proceed further. Curiously, however, during this same time frame, numerous reports of both UFOs and unidentified helicopters surfaced in the immediate vicinity of strategic military installations around the USA, and there is evidence that someone within the FBI was fully aware of this, and was taking more than a cursory interest in these sightings.

Proof of this comes via a number of Air Force reports forwarded to the FBI only weeks after its contact with Senator Haskell. Selected extract from these reports state:

"On 7 Nov 75 an off duty missile launch officer reported that unidentified aircraft resembling a helicopter had approached and hovered near a USAF missile launch control facility, near Lewistown. Source explained that at about 0020, 7 Nov 75, source and his deputy officer had just retired from crew rest in the Soft Support Building (SSB) at the LCF, when both heard the sound of a helicopter rotor above the SSB. The Deputy observed two red-and-white lights on the front of the aircraft, a white light on the bottom, and a white light on the rear.

"On 7 Nov 75, Roscoe E. III, Captain, 341 Strategic Missile Wing, advised that during the hours of 6-7 Nov 75, two adjacent LCFs, approximately 50 miles south of aforementioned LCF, reported moving lights as unidentified flying objects (UFO). During this period there were no reports of helicopter noises from personnel at these LCFs.

"This office was recently notified of a message received by security police MAFB, MT., detailing a similar nocturnal approach by a helicopter at a USAF weapons storage area located at another USAF base in the Northern Tier states. Local authorities denied the use of their helicopters during the period 6-7 Nov 75."

That these particular reports should have been of interest to the FBI is perplexing, given the statements made to Senator Haskell that the unidentified helicopter sightings reported in Colorado were outside of the FBI's jurisdiction. One might be forgiven for wondering if a directive had come from on high in the US Government, ordering the FBI to steer clear of the mutilation and unidentified helicopter issues.

It is also notable that a currently unauthenticated MJ-12 document leaked to the researcher William Moore, refers to the Northern Tier helicopter and UFO sightings of 1975, and expresses concern that, in view of the fact that the media had picked up on the stories, there was a need on the part of some authority to develop an effective disinformation plan to counter the developing interest that was surrounding the sightings. Could this be why the FBI professed no interest in the Colorado helicopter encounters?[15]

Moving on from the mutilations of 1975, the next indication of FBI involvement in the subject came in the final months of 1976. In September of that year, *Oui* magazine published a large and comprehensive article outlining the history of the cattle mutilations, the theories surrounding who or what was responsible, and the opinions of numerous persons one way or another implicated in the whole affair. Under the cover of the following memorandum, a copy of the article was sent to FBI headquarters at Washington, D. C., by the special agent in charge at the Springfield, Illinois, FBI office:

"Enclosed for the Bureau is one copy of an article entitled 'The Mutilation Mystery', which allegedly appeared in *Oui* Magazine, September 1976 issue. For the information of the Bureau, Sheriff Russell Crews, Illinois, on 9/30/76, furnished enclosed article to SA Donald R. Sorensen since it pertained to widespread incidents such as those set forth in referenced Airtel. [Note: The 'referenced airtel' has yet to be released by the FBI.] This is furnished to the Bureau in view of numerous references in this article to Federal investigative agencies and also theories that these mutilations of cattle are only a forerunner for later mutilations of human beings."[16]

That the FBI should have taken particular note of a magazine article that, in part, referred to the animal mutilations as being a forerunner for later mutilations of human beings is notable for one particular reason.

Don Ecker spent ten years as a police investigator and is now a writer living in Los Angeles. Whilst looking into claims that human beings have been mutilated in a similar fashion that reported in animals and predominantly cattle, Ecker contacted an active police detective friend, Scot, who had been involved in the investigation of a number of cattle mutilation incidents.

"I relayed my various information on human mutes to [Scot], and asked if he would be willing to send an inquiry through his Department's computer to the National Crime Information Center, operated and maintained by the FBI in Washington, D. C," states Ecker. Several days later, Scot, sounding troubled, got back in touch with Ecker: "Someone is sitting on something, big as Hell." Contact was made with a further source, this time in the Department of Justice, who would only state that: "if all were smart, they would simply leave this issue alone."[17]

As tempting as it would be to dismiss this particularly controversial aspect of the mutilation mystery as nothing more than a hoax or a friend-of-a-friend tale, the verifiable fact that, as far back as 1976, the FBI had on file records pertaining to "later mutilations of human beings" must, by definition, mean that we keep this matter open for possible future debate and consideration.

An examination of the animal mutilation files that the FBI has declassified reveals that between September 1976 and early 1978, the Bureau had no further significant involvement in the mutilation issue. By mid-1978, however, it had become clear that this was a matter that the FBI could afford to ignore no longer. With the assistance of local police authorities, medical sources and concerned ranchers, the FBI came to accept slowly that this sickening mystery was all too real, even if the perpetrators remained disturbingly anonymous and free to conduct their butchery on a country-wide scale.

When the mutilators focused their attention on Rio Arriba County, New Mexico, it marked the turning point in convincing the FBI that, whoever was responsible for the strange killings, they were here to stay.

Following a series of mutilations between 1976 and 1978, Manuel S. Gomez, a rancher who had himself lost a number of cattle, approached the Senator for New Mexico (and a former astronaut), Harrison Schmitt, and requested that enquiries be made to determine if, finally, some form of investigation could be instigated to settle the problem.

Schmitt duly complied and on July 10, 1978 wrote to Chief Martin E. Vigil of the New Mexico State Police and informed him of the concerns of Manuel Gomez and other ranchers in the area, many of who were also losing livestock to the elusive mutilators with worrying regularity.[18]

Aware that Police Officer Gabe Valdez of Espanola had investigated a number of such cases, Vigil asked Captain P. Anaya of the Espanola Police to forward him copies of all relevant paperwork, which could in turn be made available to Senator Schmitt, should he wish to take matters further. As a result, by October 1978, Schmitt was in receipt of Valdez's files and, armed with the evidence that something truly mind-blowing was taking place, mailed a letter voicing his concern to the Attorney General of the Department of Justice, Griffin B. Bell:

"During the past several years, ranchers throughout the West, including my home state of New Mexico, have been victimized by a series of cattle mutilations. As a result, these ranchers have as a group and individually suffered serious economic losses. While an individual cattle mutilation may not be a federal offense, I am very concerned at what appears to be a continued pattern of an organized interstate criminal activity. Therefore, I am requesting that the Justice Department re-examine its jurisdiction in this area with respect to the possible re-opening of this investigation."[19]

Attorney General Bell responded with speed and assured Senator Schmitt: "I have asked Philip Heymann, head of the Criminal Division to look into our jurisdiction over the cattle mutilation problem with which you are concerned," adding that: "I must say that the materials sent me indicate the existence of one of the strangest phenomenons [sic] in my memory." That Bell took all of this seriously is evident from the following note attached to a letter to Heymann: "Please have someone look into this matter at an early date. Senator Schmitt is our friend and there have been about 60 mutilations in New Mexico in recent months."

For his part, on March 2, 1979, Assistant Attorney General Heymann wrote the following, one-page memorandum for the attention of the FBI, under the cover of which were sent copies of Officer Gabe Valdez's files:

"For several years the Criminal Division has been aware of the phenomenon of animals being mutilated in a manner that could indicate that such acts are performed by persons as part of a ritual or ceremony. The report that some of the mutilations have occurred in Indian country is our first indication that Federal Law may have been violated. It is requested that the Federal Bureau of Investigation conduct an appropriate investigation of the 15 mutilations and any others that occur in Indian country as a possible crime on an Indian reservation."[20]

And so the FBI's deep involvement in the animal mystery began in earnest. For the men and women pf the FBI assigned to deal with the animal mutilations, the fist step was to review the files of Police Officer Gabe Valdez.

Between August 1975 and the summer of 1978, almost thirty cases of animal mutilation had been recorded in the Rio Arriba area, with many indicating that the attacks were the work of some well-equipped intelligence. One report that stands out, and demonstrates that the genuine mutilations are not the work of predators, was filed by Valdez in June 1976.

"At 8.00 p.m. on 13 June, Valdez was contacted by the rancher Manuel Gomez and advised that he had found a three-year-old cow on his ranch that bore all the classic signs of mutilation. As Valdez listened, Gomez stated that the cow's left-ear, tongue, udder and rectum had been removed with what appeared to be a sharp instrument. Yet there was absolutely no blood in the immediate vicinity of the cow, nor were there any footprints in evidence; however, there were marks of some sort: marks that gave every impression that some form of aerial object had landed and carried out a grisly attack on the unfortunate animal.

"At 5.00 a.m. on the following day, Valdez set off for the Gomez ranch along with Paul Riley of the New Mexico Cattle Sanitary Board, where both intended examining the evidence for themselves. On arriving, Officer Valdez and Riley were confronted by a scene of carnage. There was the cow, just as Gomez had described: three years old, laying on its right side, vital body parts having been removed with the utmost precision. But that was not all. There were also strange landing marks. In a two-page report written shortly afterwards and declassified by the FBI, Valdez recorded the details:

"Investigations continued around the area and revealed that a suspected aircraft of some type had landed twice, leaving three pod marks positioned in a triangular shape. The diameter of each pod was 14 inches. Emanating from the two landings were smaller triangular shaped tripods 28 inches and 4 inches in diameter. Investigation at the scene showed that these small tripods had followed the cow for approximately 600 feet. Tracks of the cow showed where she had struggled and fallen. The small tripod tracks were all around the cow. Other evidence showed that grass around the tripods, as they followed the cow, had been scorched. Also a yellow oily substance was located in two places under the small tripods. This substance was submitted to the State Police Lab. The Lab was unable to detect the content of the substance. A sample of the substance was submitted to a private lab and they were unable to analyze the substance due to the fact that it disappeared or disintegrated. Skin samples were analyzed by the State Police Lab and the Medical Examiner's Office. It was reported that the skin had been cut with a sharp instrument."

Three days later, Valdez contacted Dr. Howard Burgess, a retired scientist from Sandia Laboratories, and asked him to conduct a radiation test at the scene. The results were astounding. All around the tripod marks and in the immediate tracks, the radiation count was found to be twice that of normal. Valdez came up with an intriguing hypothesis as to why this should have been so: "It is the opinion of this writer that radiation findings are deliberately being left at the scene to confuse investigators."

Valdez discovered something else too. In the days between his first visit to the Gomez ranch and the second visit with Dr. Howard Burgess, the mysterious aerial object had returned. It led to a distressing discovery:

"There was also evidence that the tripod marks had returned and removed the left ear. Tripod marks were found over Mr. Gomez's tire tracks of his original visit. The left ear was intact when Mr. Gomez first found the cow. The cow had a 3-month-old calf which has not been located since the incident. This appears strange since a small calf normally stays around the mother even though the cow is dead."

Valdez also noted in his report that this particular incident was typical of those he had investigated over the course of a sixteen-month period. "They all carry the same pattern," he asserted. Perhaps most pertinent, Valdez had been able to determine that in at least one case, the animal in question was found to have had a high dose of atropine in its blood system. "This substance is a tranquilizing drug," reported Valdez.

There was also concern on the part of Valdez that "government associated laboratories are not reporting complete findings." For that reason, Valdez ensured that samples from the slain cattle were later submitted to private chemists for analysis.

Fully aware of the theories that all of the mutilations were the work of either satanic cults or natural predators, Valdez added:

"Both [theories] have been ruled out due to expertise and preciseness and the cost involved to conduct such a sophisticated and secretive operation. It should also be noted that during the spring of 1974 when a tremendous amount of cattle were lost due to heavy snowfalls, the carcasses had been eaten by predators. These carcasses did not resemble the carcasses of the mutilated cows. Investigation has narrowed down to these theories which involve (1) Experimental use of Vitamin B12 and (2) The testing of the lymph node system. During this investigation an intensive study has been made of (3) What is involved in germ warfare testing, and the possible correlation of these 3 factors (germ warfare testing, use of Vitamin B12, testing of the lymph node system)."

As Valdez's files make abundantly clear, such reports proliferated, including the following of May 1978:

"This four year old cross Hereford and Black Angus native cow was found lying on left side with rectum, sex organs, tongue, and ears removed. Pinkish blood from [illegible] was visible, and after two days the blood still had not coagulated. Left front and left rear leg were pulled out of their sockets apparently from the weight of the cow which indicates that it was lifted and dropped back to the ground. The ground around and under the cow was soft and showed indentations where the cow had been dropped. 600 yards away from the cow were the 4-inch circular indentations similar to the ones found at the Manuel Gomez ranch on 4-24-78. This cow had been dead approximately [illegible] hours and was too decomposed to extract samples. This is the first in a series of mutilations in which the cows' legs are broken. Previously the animals had been lifted from the brisket with a strap. These mutilated animals all dehydrate rapidly (in one or two days)."

A third document, also of 1978, refers to another incident where abnormal radiation traces were found:

"It is believed that this type of radiation is not harmful to humans, although approximately 7 people who visited the mutilation site complained of nausea and headaches. However, this writer has had no such symptoms after checking approximately 11 mutilations in the past 4 months. Identical mutilations have been taking place all over the Southwest. It is strange that no eyewitnesses have come forward or that no accidents [have] occurred. One has to admit that whoever is responsible for the mutilations is very well organized with boundless financing and secrecy. Writer is presently getting equipment through the efforts of Mr. Howard Burgess, Albuquerque, N.M. to detect substances on the cattle which might mark them and be picked up by infra-red rays but not visible to the naked eye."[21]

Strange landing-marks, elevated radiation readings, tranquilizing drugs, animals covertly air-lifted out of the area: what on Earth (or off it) was going on? What had Officer Valdez stumbled upon? Was this some form of highly secret U.S. Government or military operation centered on germ warfare testing, or something even more bizarre? It is evident from examining the surrounding FBI documentation generated as a direct result of Valdez's police reports, that the Bureau took very seriously the evidence and official testimony that the officer had collected. A four-page Airtel from Forrest S. Putman, FBI Special-Agent-in-Charge at Albuquerque, to the Director of the FBI and summarizing the events in question, makes this abundantly clear:

"For the past seven or eight years mysterious cattle mutilations have been occurring throughout the United States and for the past four years have been occurring within the State of New Mexico. Officer Gabe Valdez, New Mexico State Police, has been handling investigations of these mutilations within New Mexico."

Putman went on to describe the way in which Valdez theorized that the mutilations were taking place:

"Information furnished to this office by Officer Valdez indicates that the animals are being shot with some type of paralyzing drug and the blood is being drawn from the animal after an injection of an anti-coagulant. It appears that in some instances the cattle's legs have been broken and helicopters without any identifying numbers have reportedly been seen in the vicinity of these mutilations. Officer Valdez theorizes that clamps are being placed on the cow's legs and they are being lifted by helicopter to some remote area where the mutilations are taking place and then the animal is returned to its original pasture. The mutilations primarily consist of removal of the tongue, the lymph gland, lower lip and the sexual organs of the animal. Much mystery has surrounded these mutilations, but according to witnesses they give the appearance of being very professionally done with a surgical instrument, and according to Valdez, as the years progress, each surgical procedure appears to be more professional. Officer Valdez has advised that in no instance, to his knowledge, are these carcasses ever attacked by predator or scavenger animals, although there are tracks which would indicate that coyotes have been circling the carcass from a distance."

Special Agent Putman then informed the Director of the results of Valdez's dealings with officialdom:

"He also advised that he has requested Los Alamos Scientific Laboratory to conduct investigation for him but until just recently has always been advised that the mutilations were done by predatory animals. Officer Valdez stated that just recently he has been told by two assistants at Los Alamos Scientific Laboratory that they were able to determine the type of tranquilizer and blood anti-coagulant that have been utilized."

The sheer scale of the events that Valdez had an awareness of, was then spelled out by Putman:

"Officer Valdez stated that Colorado probably has the most mutilations occurring within their State and that over the past four years approximately 330 have occurred in New Mexico. He stated that of these 330, 15 have occurred on Indian Reservations but he did know that many mutilations have gone unreported which have occurred on the Indian reservations because the Indians, particularly in the Pueblos, are extremely superstitious and will not even allow officers in to investigate in some instances. Officer Valdez stated since the outset of these mutilations there have been an estimated 8,000 animals mutilated which would place the loss at approximately $1,000,000."

Putman further informed the Director that on the previous day, February 15, 1979, he had met with Officer Gabe Valdez, Senator Harrison Schmitt, R. E. Thompson, United States Attorney (USA) and Bureau Special Agent Samuel Jones, and it had been decided that the best course of action was for a conference to be convened in Albuquerque, no later than April, where "those who have suffered cattle mutilation [can] discuss this matter to determine what has been developed to date and to recommend further steps to be taken to solve this ongoing problem." He continued:

"It is obvious if mutilations are to be solved there is a need for a coordinated effort so that all material available can be gathered and analyzed and further efforts synchronized. Whether the FBI should assume this role is a matter to be decided. If we are merely to investigate and direct our efforts toward the 15 mutilated cattle on the Indian reservation we, I believe, will be in the same position as the other law enforcement agencies at this time and would be seeking to achieve an almost impossible task. It is my belief that if we are to participate in any manner that we should do so fully, although this office and the USA's office are at a loss to determine what statute our investigative jurisdiction would be in this matter. If we are to act solely as a coordinator or in any other official capacity the sooner we can place this information in the computer bank, the better off we would be and in this regard it would be my recommendation that an expert in the computer field at the Bureau travel to Albuquerque in the very near future so that we can determine what type of information will be needed so that when the invitation for the April conference is submitted from Senator Schmitt's Office that the surrounding States will be aware of the information that is needed to place in the computer. It should be noted that Senator Schmitt's Office is coordinating the April conference and will submit the appropriate invitations and with the cooperation of the USA, Mr. Thompson will chair this conference. The FBI will act only as a participant."

Up until this point, Putman had not discussed with the Director the theories of who, precisely, was responsible for the mutilations. That situation was about to change:

"Since this has not been investigated by the FBI in any manner we have no theories whatsoever as to why or what is responsible for these cattle mutilations. Officer Gabe Valdez is very adamant in his opinion that these mutilations are the work of the U. S. Government and that it is some clandestine operation either by the CIA or the Department of Energy and in all probability is connected with some type of research into biological warfare. His main reason for these beliefs is that he feels that he was given the "run around" by Los Alamos Scientific Laboratory and they are attempting to cover up this situation. There are also theories that these are cults (religious) of some type of Indian rituals resulting in these mutilations and the wildest theory advanced is that they have some connection with unidentified flying objects."

Putman concluded his four-page Airtel as follows:

"If we are to assume an investigative posture into this area, the matter of manpower, of course, becomes a consideration and I am unable to determine at this time the amount of manpower that would be needed to give this our full attention so that a rapid conclusion could be reached. The Bureau is requested to furnish its comments and guidance on this whole situation including, if desired, the Legal Counsel's assessment of jurisdictional question. An early response would be needed, however, so that we might properly, if requested to do so, obtain the data bank information. If it appears that we are going to become involved in this matter, it is obvious that there would be a large amount of correspondence necessary and Albuquerque would suggest a code name be established of BOVMUT."[22]

On April 20, 1979, the proposed conference came to pass, and was detailed in FBI memoranda one week later. Such was the concern surrounding the cattle mutilations that nearly two hundred people attended the meeting, which was held at the Albuquerque Public Library.

A report to FBI headquarters from Albuquerque, dated April 25, outlines the flavor of the conference, and addresses the various opinions of those in attendance:

"Forrest S. Putman, Special Agent in Charge (SAC), Albuquerque Office of the FBI, explained to the conference that the Justice Department had given the FBI authority to investigate those cattle mutilations which have occurred or might occur on Indian lands. He further explained that the Albuquerque FBI would look at such mutilations in connection with mutilations occurring off Indian lands for the purpose of comparison and control, especially where the same methods of operation are noted. SAC Putman said that in order for this matter to be resolved, the facts surrounding such mutilations should be gathered and computerized.

"District Attorney Eloy Martinez, Santa Fe, New Mexico, told the conference that his judicial district had made application for a $50,000 Law Enforcement Assistance Administration (LEAA) Grant for the purpose of investigating the cattle mutilations. He explained that there is hope that with the funds from this grant, an investigative unit can be established for the sole purpose of resolving the mutilation problem. He said it is his view that such an investigative unit could serve as a headquarters for all law enforcement officials investigating the mutilations and, in particular, would serve as a repository for information developed in order that this information could be coordinated properly. He said such a unit would not only coordinate this information, but also handle submissions to a qualified lab for both evidence and photographs. Mr. Martinez said a hearing will be held on April 24, 1979, for the purpose of determining whether this grant will be approved.

"Gabe Valdez, New Mexico State Police, Dulce, New Mexico, reported he has investigated the death of 90 cattle during the past three years, as well as six horses. Officer Valdez said he is convinced that the mutilations of the animals have not been the work of predators because of the precise manner of the cuts. Officer Valdez said he had investigated mutilations of several animals which had occurred on the ranch of Manuel Gomez of Dulce, New Mexico.

"Manuel Gomez addressed the conference and explained he had lost six animals to unexplained deaths which were found in a mutilated condition within the last two years. Further, Gomez said that he and his family are experiencing fear and mental anguish because of the mutilations."

The FBI then reported on the nature of the lectures delivered by a variety of speakers that had been invited to attend and speak at the conference. Their opinions – as diverse as they certainly were – make for notable reading:

"David Perkins, Director of the Department of Research at Libre School in Farasita, Colorado, exhibited a map of the United States which contained hundreds of colored pins identifying mutilation sites. He commented that he had been making a systematic collection of data since 1975, and has never met a greater challenge. He said, "The only thing that makes sense about the mutilations is that they make no sense at all."

Tom Adams of Paris, Texas, who has been independently examining mutilations for six years, said his investigation has shown that helicopters are almost always observed in the area of the mutilations. He said that the helicopters do not have identifying markings and they fly at abnormal, unsafe, or illegal altitudes.

"Dr. Peter Van Arsdale, Ph. D., Assistant Professor, Department of Anthropology, University of Denver, suggested that those investigating the cattle mutilations take a systematic approach and look at all types of evidence is [without] discounting any of the theories such as responsibility by extraterrestrial visitors or satanic cults.

"Richard Sigismund, Social Scientist, Boulder, Colorado, presented an argument which advanced the theory that the cattle mutilations are possibly related to activity of UFOs. Numerous other persons made similar type presentations expounding on their theories regarding the possibility that the mutilations are the responsibility of extraterrestrial visitors, members of Satanic cults, or some unknown government agency.

"Dr. Richard Prine, Forensic Veterinarian, Los Alamos Scientific Laboratory (LASL), Los Alamos, New Mexico, discounted the possibility that the mutilations had been done by anything but predators. He said he had examined six carcasses and in his opinion predators were responsible for the mutilation of all six.

"Dr. Claire Hibbs, a representative of the State Veterinary Diagnostic Laboratory, New Mexico State University, Las Cruces, New Mexico, said he recently came to New Mexico, but that prior to that he examined some mutilation findings in Kansas and Nebraska. Dr. Hibbs said the mutilations fell into three categories: animals killed and mutilated by predators and scavengers, animals mutilated after death by "sharp instruments" and animals mutilated by pranksters.

"Tommy Blann, Lewisville, Texas, told the conference he has been studying UFO activities for twenty-two years and mutilations for twelve years. He explained that animal mutilations date back to the early 1800's in England and Scotland. He also pointed out that animal mutilations are not confined to cattle, but cited incidents of mutilation of horses, dogs, sheep, and rabbits. He also said the mutilations are not only nationwide, but international in scope.

"Chief Raleigh Tafoya, Jicarilla Apache Tribe, and Walter Dasheno, Governor, Santa Clara Pueblo, each spoke briefly to the conference. Both spoke of the cattle which had been found mutilated on their respective Indian lands. Chief Tafoya said some of his people who have lost livestock have been threatened.

"Carl W. Whiteside, Investigator, Colorado Bureau of Investigation, told the conference that between April and December 1975, his Bureau investigated 203 reports of cattle mutilations."

At the conclusion of the conference, a meeting was convened in Albuquerque and which was attended heavily by the FBI, law enforcement officers from New Mexico, and numerous official investigators from Nebraska, Colorado, Montana, and Arkansas. One of the highlights of the meeting, which had not been divulged during the public conference, was the revelation that in Arkansas, the authorities had investigated twenty-eight cases of cattle mutilation, all of which "were the work of intentional mutilators and not of predators" – something with which the investigator from Montana concurred.[23]

As a result, during May 1979, the District Attorney's Office for Santa Fe, New Mexico, received a $50,000 Law Enforcement Assistance Administration (LEAA) grant, to enable a comprehensive review of the evidence to begin in earnest. It was decided, however, that the investigation would be limited to a study of those livestock found solely on Indian land in New Mexico. Oddly, an FBI memorandum of June 1, 1979 stated that, following the announcement that an official investigation was to begin, "there have been no new cattle mutilations in Indian country."

Four days later, however, the low-profile approach to which the FBI was hoping to adhere was shattered when the *National Enquirer* newspaper devoted one page of its June 5 edition to a discussion of the FBI's involvement in the mutilation issue.

Among those cited by the *Enquirer* was one Henry Monteith, an engineering physicist at Sandia Laboratories. Monteith, having spoken with a number of Indians, had no doubt that the mutilations were the work of extraterrestrials, and went on to disclose that amongst those Indians to whom he had spoken, there were some who claimed to have seen "spaceships land and unload star people who chase down animals and take them back to the spaceship." And in a moment of light relief, District Attorney Eloy Martinez of Espanola, New Mexico, admitting that "UFOs are a possibility," stated: "I might be the first district attorney in the country to prosecute an alien from outer space." Had it come to pass, that would indeed have been a court case worth seeing.[24]

Armed with the $50,000 LEAA grant, investigations began in earnest, under the three-person team of Director Kenneth M. Rommel, Jr. (who had served with the FBI for twenty-eight years); Diana S. Moyle, Coordinating Secretary; and an investigator: Cipriano Padilla. Many, however, were critical of the investigation.

In July 1979, the *Rio Grande Sun* reported that the finding of "the county's freshest mutilation so far," which curiously went un-investigated. "I was really disgusted," said Dennis Martinez, a rancher, who had discovered the mutilated carcass within three hundred yards of his Truchas farm. "The news media said investiga-tors would come as soon as they were called." For seven hours Martinez waited, but no investigator arrived.

"I don't blame them for being upset," commented Senator Harrison Schmitt, expressing his concern that the finding on the Martinez ranch remained practically unacknowledged. And when advised that Kenneth Rommel had still to contact Officer Gabe Valdez, whose files acted as the catalyst that prompted Schmitt to initiate high-level enquiries with the FBI, he responded: "That doesn't sound like complete investigating."

There were other stories in circulation, too, concerning the LEAA-funded investigation, as the *Rio Grande Sun* was only too well aware. Citing a number of confidential sources who had expressed dissatisfaction with Kenneth Rommel's study, the *Sun* stated: "Persons who have spoken to the investigator complain he is brusque or too flippant, or he doesn't take their ideas or their reports seriously, and they'd rather not discuss with him further mutilation phenomena."

This may of course represent nothing more than a marked difference of opinion over the source of the mutilations. However, darker rumors were also in circulation. "Other persons express fears that not only Rommel, but the District Attorney and the State Police, are working together to cover up whatever is behind the mutilations and rumors are spreading fast," added the newspaper.[25]

On July 17, 1979, Senator Schmitt announced that the State Appropriations Committee had directed the FBI to continue its investigations. Such action, said Schmitt, is "necessary due to the continuing widespread problem of cattle mutilations and the need for federal coordination of the investigation. I hope that the Committee's endorsement of this proposal will increase the FBI's investigative activity so that the answer to this bizarre and grisly mystery will be found." Within two weeks, however, the FBI office at Albuquerque noted:

"Since being instructed to investigate this matter, there have been no reports of mutilations on Indian lands in New Mexico. In view of this, no investigation is currently being conducted regarding mutilations, and the Albuquerque Office is placing this matter in a closed status."

Come January 1980, the situation had changed little, as an FBI report to Washington discloses:

"On January 15, 1980, Kenneth M. Rommel advised [that] his office has pursued numerous investigative leads regarding the possible mutilation of animals in New Mexico. He said that to date, his investigative unit has determined that none of the reported cases has involved what appear to be mutilations by other than common predators. Rommel said he has travelled to other states and conferred with investigators in those areas regarding mutilations, and to date has received no information which would justify the belief that any animals have been intentionally mutilated by human beings. Rommel added that regarding all the dead animals he had examined, the damage to the carcasses has always been consistent with predator action.

"On January 15, 1980, this matter was discussed with Assistant US Attorney Richard J. Smith, US Attorney's Office, Albuquerque. Assistant US Attorney Smith said that in his opinion there is no Federal interest in continuing an investigation in this matter in the absence of further reports of acts of suspected mutilation of animals on Indian land in New Mexico."[26]

Two months later Rommel's feelings were set forth in a letter to the FBI laboratory at Washington:

"For your information, since approximately 1975, New Mexico and other states, primarily those located in close proximity to New Mexico, have had incidents referred to by many as 'the cattle mutilation phenomena'.

"Stock animals, primarily cattle, have been found dead with various parts of the carcass missing such as one eye, one ear, the udder, and normally a cored anus. Most credible sources have attributed this damage to normal predator and scavenger activity. However, certain segments of the population have attributed the damage to many other causes ranging from UFOs to a giant governmental conspiracy, the exact nature of which is never fully explained. No factual data has been supplied supporting these theories."

In writing to the FBI laboratory, Rommel requested that an analysis be carried out on some material that was believed to be identical to flakes found on the hides of cattle in the Dulce, New Mexico, area. He stated: "I would appreciate it if through the use of a GS mass-spectroscopy test or any other logical test, that these flakes can be identified. This in itself would go a long way to assisting me to discredit the UFO-Cow Mutilation association theory." Rommel was informed that the flakes were nothing more than enamel paint.[27]

By the summer of 1980, Rommel had prepared a bound report, entitled *Operation Animal Mutilation*, copies of which were circulated throughout the FBI. The final entry in the FBI's cattle mutilation file reads: "A perusal of this report reflects it adds nothing new in regard to potential investigation by the Albuquerque FBI of alleged mutilations on Indian lands in New Mexico."[28]

And there matters stand to this day. For all the efforts of Senators

Harrison Schmitt and Floyd Haskell, Police Officer Gabe Valdez, numerous ranchers, media sources, private and official investigators, the final report generated by the LEAA's $50,000 grant concluded that the mutilations were the work of nothing more than scavengers. A detailed study of the data set forth in FBI files, however, clashes acutely with the conclusions of *Operation Animal Mutilation*.

Firstly, the decision to limit investigations to those cattle found mutilated on Indian land in New Mexico is curious, particularly in view of the fact that, when it was announced that Rommel's study was beginning in earnest, such killings ceased! Whilst individual mutilations outside of Indian land might not technically have been within the FBI's jurisdiction, surely a detailed comparison with such cases would have been warranted? Indeed it would, and this was something, it will be recalled that, Forrest S. Putman, Special Agent in Charge of the FBI at Albuquerque noted in early February 1979:

"If we are merely to investigate and direct our efforts toward the 15 mutilated cattle on the Indian reservation we, I believe, will be in the same position as the other law enforcement agencies at this time and would be seeking to achieve an almost impossible task. It is my belief that if we are to participate in any manner that we should do so fully."

Putman's proposal was certainly laudable and it is baffling why the investigation did not fully address the mutilation issue on a nationwide scale. There are other anomalies too.

In his letter of March 5, 1980 to the FBI, Kenneth Rommel wrote that with respect to the claims that the mutilations were the work of UFOs or a "giant government conspiracy," no factual data to support either theory existed. But what of the files of Police Officer Gabe Valdez? They may not confirm that aliens from some far off world are systematically butchering our cattle, but they do confirm the presence of unidentified aerial vehicles in the immediate vicinity of mutilation sites.

The disturbing report written up by Valdez after his visit of June 14, 1976 to the ranch of Manuel Gomez is a perfect example. "Investigations continued around the area and revealed that a suspected aircraft of some type had landed twice," stated Valdez. And what of the pod marks, scorched ground, elevated radiation readings and the unidentified, yellowy, oily substance found at the site? Is this not the factual data that Rommel asserted was so noticeably absent?

Moreover, the reports collected by Valdez in 1978, implying that animals had actually been lifted into the air by some unknown object, are also convincing evidence of a phenomenon beyond mere predators: "Both cows were laying on their left side with left front leg and left rear leg broken which indicates that animals were lifted by their extremities," reported Valdez.

We also note that investigations in Arkansas had concluded that no fewer than twenty-eight cases of cattle mutilation had been recorded, and that in Colorado, a phenomenal 203 accounts had surfaced. Yet, the project sponsored by the Law Enforcement Assistance Administration insisted on focusing solely on the aforementioned fifteen New Mexico-based incidents. And it should not be forgotten too that Dane Edwards, editor of a Brush, Colorado-based newspaper, had informed Senator Floyd Haskell that not only had US Army helicopters been seen in the vicinity of local cattle mutilations, but that he too had been "threatened" by unknown parties.

Is it possible that the *Rio Grande Sun* was close to the truth when it stated that: "Other persons express fears that not only Rommel, but the District Attorney and the State Police, are working to cover up whatever is behind the mutilations, and rumors are spreading fast"?

Did the FBI uncover something about the mutilations that was deemed so shocking that the public and the media had to be kept in the dark at all costs? Emil P. Moschella of the FBI has informed us that the Bureau has not conducted any investigation of cattle mutilation since 1980 and that all material on the FBI's involvement in the New Mexican mutilations has been released into the public domain without any excisions. A similar assurance comes from the Justice Department. And yet the perplexing points noted above (that suggest the existence of a real phenomenon of unknown origin and intent) remain. But can they be resolved? Possibly.

We have seen that there has been a veritable abundance of such reports since the late 1960's and that those same reports seem to be allied in many cases with sightings of unmarked helicopters, Army helicopters and unusual and unidentified aerial lights. Is it really the case, as suggested by the late Colonel Philip J. Corso that alien creatures are carrying out these macabre acts? Or is there a more down-to-earth possibility? There is. And it is one that is even more terrifying in view of its implications.

As a police officer in Fyffe, Alabama, Ted Oliphant investigated over thirty cases of cattle mutilation in a six-month period from October 1992 to May 1993. Oliphant has reported that in a number of such cases, pharmaceuticals had been found in bovine blood, including barbiturates, anti-coagulants and synthetic amphetamines. The drugs found are *not* veterinary drugs, stresses Oliphant: they are pharmaceuticals associated with human beings. Among those law enforcement agents who have thoroughly investigated these bovine excision sites, says Oliphant, there is a consensus that some kind of medical testing is taking place.

Oliphant makes a noteworthy observation with respect to the body-parts excised from the animals: "The jaw is an important part because enzymes are produced there. Enzymes that can kill viruses and bacteria; it's an antibody factory. The digestive track also acts as a filter that absorbs, collects and stores traces of any chemical or toxin introduced. The rectum is a similar filter as are [the] ears. They store traces of toxins and chemicals like a library. Because many diseases (like [Creutzfeldt Jakob Disease] and [Bovine Spongiform Encephalopathy]) can be inherited, the reproductive system may be a good place to find look for clues on how it passed to the next generation. With BSE & CJD being such devastating new diseases, is it possible that many alleged cases of cattle mutilations are actually evidence of our tax dollars at work?"[29]

A practically identical theory is advanced in Colm Kelleher's 2005 book *Brain Trust* that paints a highly disturbing picture of the United States' beef industry, and that delves deep into the issue of emerging viruses and the way in which they are advancing into the food chain, and from there into the human species.[30]

But the most controversial theory concerning cattle mutilations, that has a major bearing upon the data contained within this book, is still to come and will be expanded upon in a later chapter.

* * *

Chapter 18 Notes:

1. *Pueblo Chieftain*, October 7, 1967. *An Alien Harvest*, Linda Moulton Howe, Linda Moulton Howe Productions, 1989.

2. *Argus Leader*, August 30, 1974.

3. *Idaho Statesman*, July 6, 1975.

4. *Elsberry Democrat*, June 22, 1978.

5. *Greeley Tribune*, September 18, 1980.

6. *The Leading Edge*, No. 66, 1994.

7. *The Day After Roswell*, Lt. Col.. Philip J. Corso & William J. Birnes, Simon & Schuster, 1997.

8. *Interplanetary Phenomenon Unit Summary*, July 22, 1947. Available at: www.majesticdocuments.com by downloading: http://209.132.68.98/pdf/ipu_report.pdf.

9. Letter from United States Senator Carl T. Curtis to FBI Director Clarence M. Kelley, September 4, 1974.

10. Letter from United States Senator Floyd K. Haskell to Special-Agent-in-Charge Floyd K. Haskell, FBI, Denver Office, August 29, 1975.

11. Ibid.

12. Ibid.

13. *Denver Post*, September 3, 1975.

14. FBI memorandum prepared by R. J. Gallagher, September 12, 1975.

15. *The MJ-12 Documents: An Analytical Report*, William L. Moore & Jaime H. Shandera, Fair Witness Project, 1990.

16. *The Mutilation Mystery, Oui Magazine*, September 1976.

17. *UFO*, Vol. 4, No. 3 and Vol. 5, No. 2.

18. Letter from Senator Harrison Schmitt to Chief Martin E. Vigil, Chief, New Mexico State Police, July 10, 1978.

19. Letter from Senator Harrison Schmitt to Attorney General of the Department of Justice, Griffin B. Bell.

20. Letter from Assistant Attorney General Heymann to the FBI, March 2, 1979.

21. New Mexico State Police Files, 1975-1978.

22. FBI memorandum, *Cattle Mutilations Occurring in Western States*, from FBI Special Agent Forrest S. Putman to Director, FBI, February 16, 1979.

23. FBI report, *Cattle Mutilations*, April 25, 1979.

24. *National Enquirer*, June 5, 1979.

25. *Rio Grande Sun*, various editions (undated photocopies in FBI records), July 1979.

26. FBI memoranda, January 28, 1980.

27. Letter from Kenneth M. Rommel to FBI Laboratory, March 5, 1980.

28. *Operation Animal Mutilation*, Kenneth M. Rommel, 1980.

29. *The Anomalist*, No. 6, 1998.

30. *Brain Trust*, Colm Kelleher, Paraview-Pocket Books, 2005.

Chapter 19
Somaliland and Varginha, 1996

It is intriguing that in 1996, the same year that Tony Dodd's source in the British Army, James Prescott, surfaced with a story about alien bodies taken to the Government's chemical and biological research establishment at Porton Down in 1974, two accounts surfaced that linked alleged UFO crashes with what appear to be lethal viruses of unknown origin - one in Somaliland and the other in South America.

The facts concerning the Somaliland event, brief as they are, can be found in a three-page document titled *Somaliland President Egal Speaks On Mysterious Bomb Blast* that was declassified by the Central Intelligence Agency in 1999 and concerns a series of "mysterious explosions" that had occurred in the vicinity. The report (that was forwarded to the State Department, Defense Intelligence Agency, and Wright-Patterson Air Force Base, Dayton, Ohio, among other agencies and departments) stated:

"From the *Focus on Africa* Program:

"FBIS' [Foreign Broadcast Information Service] transcribed text there [sic] have been reports this week of mysterious explosions in the remote eastern region of the self-declared republic of Somaliland. They apparently occupied in December, but because of the remote nature of the area have been slow coming to light. The blasts have been attributed to various causes from unidentified flying objects, UFOs, to rocket tests. Well, Somaliland Leader, Mohamed Egal, has been looking into the matter. On the line to Hargesa, Timothy Ecott asked him what he thought had been going on.

"Begin recording Egal [sic]: We have these mysterious reports from our nomadic population there, and then, I sent a four-man commission, two doctors, a veteran doctor, and one minister, and they have submitted to us a report, which is very, very alarming. They said that they went there almost a fortnight after this thing has taken place and the found most of the animals in the area are still in a sort of a demented stage. They were not grazing, they were just stampeding all over the place.

"Ecott: You said the animals were demented. What about the people living there?

"Egal: Some of them, who were very close to the area, have got skin rashes, and some of them are almost shredding their outer skin. There are boils all over the place, and some of them are having stomach aches, you know, and very unusual motions – stomach motion – and a lot of symptoms have been reported. We are sending back some doctors to actually evaluate the human damage and the animal damage that has been done.

"Ecott: Did anyone get an eyewitness account of what this explosion might have been caused by?

"Egal: The people who were there, you know, the stories they tell is [sic] that they heard no noise. Apparently whatever exploded was moving at a supersonic speed, because there was no prior noise or anything like that. You know, they just heard a very, very, very loud explosion which has taken place and the light, you know, the light of the explosion in the air. The area is so big that they didn't have the capability or the time to investigate the whole ground and try and pick up any debris that might have fallen. They haven't been able to do that.

"Ecott: Whatever your authority is claiming that this might have been, some of the news agencies are talking about UFOs.

"Egal: No, no, no, no. We are not making any claims of that or any fantastic claims like that, you know. What we think happened is that there must have been a missile fired from somewhere, which has exploded either deliberately over our country or whether it has exploded inadvertently, we can't tell. So, what we are asking now, people like the English, and French, and especially the Americans who monitor the world, they must know what happened, you know. They definitely know what happened. If it was Saddam Hussein who fired the missile, it would have been in the headlines all over the world. But apparently whoever fired the missile is still in the good books of those who know, and they don't want to publicize it. But we want to know what happened to us so that at least we will know how to deal with it.

"Ecutt: Is anybody offering you help to investigate and to look after the people you say have been injured?

"Egal: Well, we have sent it...yes...to the American Embassy. You know. We have sent it to the British Embassy, we have sent it to the French Embassy, and we have sent to the BBC, and to the Reuters and people like that, you know. Nobody has yet responded, but we have made the appeal and we are still making it."[1]

Notably, the reference to people having suffered adverse physical reactions to the presence of the unidentified object, is not unlike the references contained within the *Majestic 12 1st Annual Report* that describes individuals having fatal reactions to what was reported as a particularly lethal form of alien virus present at a UFO crash site in New Mexico in 1947.

From the research team of A.J. Gevaerd and Dr. Roger Leir comes the following, based upon their in-depth research into a spectacular series of alleged alien body recoveries in the Varginha area of Brazil – also, notably, in January 1996 - that appears to have connections to the "alien virus" controversy.

As the pair states: "On 20 January 1996, around 8:30 a.m., the Varginha military police headquarters began to receive telephone calls from the district of Jardim Andere of Brazil, with reports that something strange was being seen in the neighborhood. Apparently some children had reported seeing a strange creature that looked half man and half animal and that was making a sound like "a sharp anguished cry." The entity moved only when someone threw a pebble at it. The local police command then informed the ESA (Escola de Sargentos das Forças Armadas - School of Sergeants of the Armed Forces) in the neighboring town of Três Corações that something suspicious was being sighted and reported from Jardim Andere. The ESA sent off a military truck with two soldiers and a sergeant to the scene in Varginha. About 9 p.m., the 13th Company of Special Fire Brigade was ordered to send a garrison to the place under command of Major Maciel, Sergeant Palhares, Corporal Rubens, and privates Nivaldo and Santos.

"Curious civilians were gathering around but were strictly told to evacuate the area. An hour later, a creature was spotted. It was captured with a net to catch animals, offering little resistance, and it was placed within a wooden box loaded on the ESA truck. As it was put onto the truck, according to the Fire Brigade militaries, the alien let off a faint humming sound. The military truck headed at full speed for the city of Três Corações. Just prior to the capture, shots were heard by witnesses who later saw troops carrying bags with something moving inside.

"Later that day, around 3 p.m., the young women who would turn out to be the main witnesses of the case, Liliane de Fátima Silva, 16, her sister, Valquíria Aparecida Silva, 14, and their friend, Kátia Xavier, 21, were cutting across a pathway on their way home, in the district of Jardim Andere when they were startled by what appeared to be an odd-looking creature that seemed to be in great pain. The creature was crouched and leaning against the wall of a car-repair shop. It had large, bulky lidless red eyes with no irises, and they seemed to be fixed on the witnesses. Its head was disproportionably large with bumps on top and large veins on its base extending from the shoulders up the neck. Its skin seemed to be covered with a thick, shiny and wet oily substance. Scared as they were, the three witnesses ran off. Later, as they were interviewed by the researches, the girls would say the strange bumps on the creature's head resembled horns.

"Still on 20 January, between 6:15 and 7:30 p.m., two officers from the Intelligence Service, Marco Eli Chereze and Eric Lopes, probably had the most unusual experience in their military lives, and that would end up being fatal to one of them. By then, the three girls' story was spreading quickly. Ordered to patrol the Jardim Andere area after a most unusual rain that had fallen over the city, Chereze and Lopes saw something move out of the shadows in a nearby construction work and cross the path in front of their car. The officer driving the vehicle braked immediately. Both men left.

"Chereze saw it first. The apparent 'animal' looked either hurt or too feeble as it went into the pasture nearby. As both policemen approached the creature, they realized it was certainly not an animal. It was a person: a very different, weird, and apparently deformed person. It was naked, and probably dying. In spite of the somewhat repugnant looks of the creature, they put it in their car and drove at once to a first-aid station. There, the attendant was appalled at the sight of thing, realizing that it was something odd and refused to let it in. The man was scared and recommended that it be taken to a hospital or a zoo, concluding with: 'I don't wanna be in trouble here!' The two officers took the creature to the Hospital Regional de Minas, in downtown Varginha, where vain attempts were made to keep it from dying. The hospital suddenly got crowded with police and military personnel. In an attempt to help the dying alien breathe easier, someone set it up with oxygen breathing apparatus, which was probably the cause of its accelerated death.

The body was then transferred to Hospital Humanitas.

"Dr. Fernando Eugênio Prado, responsible for the E.R. patients in the Hospital Regional that day, was barred from getting in by a stranger wearing medical gloves and apron; but he saw the inert body afterwards – as a matter of fact, he would declare during a medical congress towards the end of 1996 that he could not be sure whether it was a dead extraterrestrial, but it was certainly the strangest thing he'd ever seen. Unfortunately, though, when he was interviewed by two UFO researchers investigating the case, Dr. Prado denied the truth of his statement, explaining that he'd said that only to put a stop to the mockery by some of his colleagues that were teasing him about the Varginha's ET because he lived in the town of Varginha, and that was why he said he'd actually seen something odd, so everyone would stop mocking about his town.

"On 22 January, a military convoy headed for the School of Sergeants of the Armed Forces, in the city of Três Corações carrying an awkward cargo, all sealed in heavy boxes. The next day, military vehicles would rush to Campinas, in the State of São Paulo, going straight to Unicamp, the State University in the city of Campinas, carrying two boxes. In one box was the body taken away from Hospital Humanitas, Varginha. The other box contained something living. It could be the creature captured earlier by the Fire Corps on the 20th.

"One of the creatures was taken to an underground laboratory in [on] the premises of the state university. The box, with two holes on each side, was carried by two Army men. In the days that followed, a whole staff of scientists and physicians began to virtually live in those quarters of Unicamp, among whom Dr. Fortunato Badan Palhares. Foodstuff was brought in at most irregular hours, including vegetables, fruit, milk, mixed soup and yogurt. There was no contact between the employees who carried the food around and the working doctors. The food would be passed quickly through a door, which was just as quickly closed. Eventually, serum was requested.

"On the 26th, American militaries, including some NASA officials, arrived at Unicamp. The official purpose of the visit was to discuss the possible participation of Brazilian scientists in future space missions. One of the most serious and regrettable facts involving the sequence of events in the whole incident was the death of Corporal

Marco Eli Chereze. He was one of the officers from the Intelligence Service of the Military Police who took part in the capture of the second creature on the night of 20 January 1996. Witnesses say that the officer might have died of general infection after having touched the alien, which was specified in the necropsy report. However, his death certificate presents no defined cause for his death. A witness said that at the moment of its capture, the being made a slight movement that led the man to touch its left arm without his gloves.

"On the 23rd, Chereze's father asked his son what was 'all the nonsense' people had been talking about, with rumors of the military having captured a little monster or a strange being. With a serious countenance, Marco Eli Chereze replied that 'it was no nonsense,' adding that a lot was yet to be said about the affair; and on the 26th, as his family were watching the evening news talking about the Varginha's ET, he said, sternly, 'Do not watch that sort of thing. It's no good.'

"On February 6th, a little tumor similar to a furuncle appeared in Chereze's armpit. The officer complained about severe pains in his back and was taken to the hospital. He underwent a small surgery to have the tumor removed and then sent back home. On the 10th of the same month, Chereze complained of pains in his back and high fever and was sent to Hospital Bom Pastor where he was seen by a cardiologist named Dr. René. The doctor and his staff were unable to produce a precise diagnosis of his illness. He was transferred to Hospital Regional do Sul de Minas, where he died on the 16th, of acute respiratory deficiency, septicemia and bacterial pneumonia.

"Examinations included urine tests, X-rays from his back, spine, and sacrum, and an orthopedic evaluation performed by Dr. Rogério Lemos. A disc hernia was possible. Blood tests showed a blood count with leucocytosis, left deviation, and toxic granulations of the neutrophils.

"'These are signals of a significant infection, with high capacity to cause toxemia — not to my surprise, there were toxic granulations.' Two antibiotics were prescribed: penicillin and gentamicin, since doctors thought that it might be a case of pneumonia due to the location of the pain or to the urinary infection. HIV tests were also undertaken, 'since it was realized that he had an immunodeficiency and a simple urinary infection or pneumonia — or both. This would not lead a person to a septicemia condition, taking two antibiotics.

This is almost impossible and it only occurs in cases of immunodeficiency.' Despite the antibiotics, the infection was getting worse. Six hours later, he died.

"His body was taken for autopsy, which revealed a urinary tract infection caused by enterobacteria that was confirmed by examinations at Hospital Bom Pastor. There was also a lung infection: a small pneumonia. The doctor explained it could not have been a case of congenital immunodeficiency, otherwise he could not have lived to 23 in good health, and: 'he didn't have that for sure or at least didn't have immunodeficiency the day he died. For this reason, it [the immunodeficiency] was surely acquired. How he acquired that, no one knows. I say the cause of death was not found because it wasn't pneumonia, or the urinary infection and the abscess that killed him. We still don't know the cause.'

"The blood count issued by the laboratory of clinical analysis of Hospital Bom Pastor revealed the following information: 'Presence of cytoplasm vacuoles. Presence of fine toxic granulations in 8% of neutrophils. Little poikilocytosis.' Interpreting these data, cardiologist Cesário Furtado stated that 'the fine toxic granulations appear in the neutrophils of a person when he is being attacked by highly virulent bacteria. That forms a mass of combat; let's call it like that that could reach 50% to 60%. The report shows 8% because it was the first blood test. It already shows an infection, which made us prescribe the two antibiotics.'

"Their presence indicates a significant and serious infection. 'It's not very common. But in serious cases it is very frequent. In all serious infections you often have the possibility of finding them in numbers ranging from 5% to 50%, or even more.' The immediate cause of death was precise. 'But what led to death is yet unclear. An immunodeficiency, for sure. Well, the attack of three bacteria in three different parts of the body in that space of time is a hard thing to deal with.'

"'I assure you that no abscess can cause an immunodeficiency. An abscess may even cause septicemia, but it can't kill a person. Besides, any antibiotics can cure it. That was not the case. It was not the bacteria penetrating the arm that caused the infection. It was a strange death without any clear explanation. During my professional life, I've seen two people around 25 dying of an infection like that, but both were reportedly immunodeficient [sic]. And both had the spleen removed [splenectomy] due to past accidents.'

"According to Dr. Furtado, Marco Eli Chereze had a 'strange death, without a rational explanation. In the course of my professional life, I have already seen two individuals, aged about 25, die of an infection, but we knew that both had immune deficiency. Both of them, if I recall, had had removal of the spleen (splenectomy) following a past accident. After a certain delay, that causes immunodeficiency. In that situation, the person may decease rapidly if he finds himself in the condition of a septicemia. But, once again, it was not the case.'

"In the same year – 1996 - and not long after the creature's appearance as reported by Liliane, Valquíria and Kátia, as well as by other civilian and military witnesses, other mysterious incidents were reported in Varginha that may or may not be related to the 'ET' from Varginha, as the creature – or better yet, the creatures – came to be known, but which certainly bring to mind the affairs involving the capture of both beings on January 20

'On April 21st, around 9 p.m., Ms Terezinha Galo Clepf, 65, was at a birthday party at a Hall used for celebrations in a wooded area nearby Varginha's zoo. She went out to smoke and suddenly glimpsed among the bushes something that nearly scared her out of her wits. It was a creature standing on a guardrail, leaning against it. She described it as 'very ugly,' apparently wearing an elm on its large head, and it had bright red eyes. Terezinha was frightened, went back inside and told her husband she wanted to go home. Prior to that, during the first week of April, several animals in the zoo had appeared dead for no apparent reason. Their entrails were sent to Belo Horizonte, the State's capital, for a thorough analysis, but the cause of death was not determined. Dr. Elaine Maria Santos Gomes, veterinarian in Belo Horizonte, stated that the finds suggested the presence of a caustic toxin. Some of the animals had had a diffuse hemorrhage.

"Nearly a month later, on May 19th, at 7 p.m., Hildo Gardingo, 20, was driving to Varginha and suddenly saw illumined by the headlights of his car, a creature in the middle of the road that was approximately 5.25 feet tall and was trying to run across the road from a farm. Gardingo described an almost identical creature to the one described by Liliane, Valquíria and Kátia, sighted on January 20th, except he thought he saw hairs covering its body. As the beam from the car lights focused on the 'animal' it covered its eyes with its hand and ran back into the bushes by the side of the road. The young man was scared and drove away from the scene as fast as he could.

"Before Gardingo's frightening experience, however, on April 28th a disturbing episode involving two of the three girls occurred bringing to mind the idea of an inevitable cover-up around the Varginha's sightings. On that same date, Luzia Helena Silva, and her daughters, Liliane and Valquíria were visited by four men who refused to identify themselves and who were not wearing military uniforms. The men were ready to pay a huge amount of money to make the women go public and deny their story. If the girls had accepted, they would have had interviews on a TV channel and said what the strange visitors had coached them to say. They refused to comply, though.

"Whether or not the military was involved in the attempted bribes may be a matter of speculation. Fact is, though, that aiming to cover up the evidence presented by the UFO investigators, the head department of the School of Sergeants of the Armed Forces, under orientation of General Sérgio Pedro Coelho Lima, started on 10 May 1996 an internal investigation to find who among its members were in any way linked to the events revealed about the case.

"General Lima also summoned a press conference, promising everything would be explained. It was a tense and eagerly expected moment, for it could be the second time the Brazilian authorities would go public about the UFO phenomenon. The first time was in 1986 when the minister for the Aeronautics had confirmed in a press conference that fighter planes had actually chased several unidentified flying objects over Brazilian territory. But when General Coelho Lima spoke up, he vehemently denied that his men and instruments had had any involvement whatsoever with the so-called UFO sighting or retrieval and with the capture of possible alien beings. He concluded by saying that '... we'll be at your disposal here in the School to discuss anything that involves our end-activity. We will always be open to your inquiries.'

"As a TV reporter approached him later, the general, refusing to give an interview, and said: 'Whatever I had to declare, I have just done it in my official note.' The reporter pressed on asking, 'Where are those militaries that were cited by the UFO researchers on the day of the incident?' And the commander replied, 'Working for the Army and for the Nation.' 'Can this be proven?' asked the reporter, to which the general replied, 'Proven to whom, and why?' 'Well,' said the reporter, unsatisfied, 'the goal is to prove facts, isn't it?' The general then said, firmly, 'I don't have to prove anything. Whatever I had to say, I've already said.' And he left the room.

"Some time after, a serious contradiction came to the surface. Major Calza, who together with General Lima took part in the release of the official version, appeared on a BBC video saying that 'that day there was a malformed and mentally disabled dwarf who was injured by a hailstorm and, therefore, wandered by Varginha scaring residents together with his wife, another dwarf, who, besides that, was pregnant and just about going into labor.' However, during the sequence of the interview, Major Calza slipped by saying, 'That was when we [The Army] caught that creature.'

"A further attempt at forcing the main witnesses to withdraw their story was made in early 1997. On January 18th, when Luzia Helena was leaving her job around 2:00 a.m. (she worked as a housekeeper) she was approached by two of the same men who had showed up in her house before, offering her money. The men wanted to convince her at any cost to say that everything was nothing but a joke. They did not threaten her, but were very insistent. 'They tried to silence me,' says Luzia. But she still wouldn't give in to them. Later on, seeing that it was useless to waste time on her, the same men approached Luzia Helenas's employee and tried to persuade her to convince Luzia to agree with them and deny the whole alien story. The woman, who was an employee at Varginha's Forum and has a Bachelor's degree in Law, wished to remain unknown and does not want her name made public amongst the UFO research community.

"As if those bribe attempts were not enough, many UFO investigators and others in charge of the case were threatened with mysterious phone calls. The calls were made by unidentified people who had the clear intention of scaring or discouraging the researchers. Early in 2003, American UFO researcher and orthopedic surgeon Roger Leir was in Varginha to gather information about the case. At that time, he talked to another physician who refused to reveal his name but he had assisted in the capture of the creature at Hospital Regional. According to the Brazilian doctor, the body had different kinds of injuries, but he was sure that the creature was alive at the moment it entered the hospital.

"He stated that when trying to examine the injuries of the creatures, he suddenly felt 'as if my hands were automatically driven,' and also believed that 'it was as if the lights in the room had suddenly changed, becoming yellowish,' it also appeared that 'the perception increased somehow.' However, he could not understand well the physiological constitution of the body he was examining, although it was anthropomorphic — with a head, trunk, and limbs.

"The doctor did not hear any sound that might possibly have been made by the creature, nor did he mention the existence of the much commented 'thin and bifurcate tongue,' reported by other medical and military witnesses. But he confirmed seeing the being's slow movements when showing life signals, and refused to say that the creature seemed to breathe.

"On January 12th, Brazilian UFO researcher Fernando Tejo was scanning the skies over the city of Cruzeiro (State of São Paulo) after hearing rumors of strange moving lights. He did notice what appeared to be stars moving about, and soon afterwards two of those luminous points stopped just under the Alfa star in the Centaur constellation. Next, the objects began to move again and this time in a straight line towards each other, giving the impression they would mingle; but they suddenly broke apart. One of the light points moved towards Serra do Mar (a mountain range along the coast) and the other shot towards the frontier with the State of Minas Gerais.

"Also prior to the sighting and capture of the alien creatures, researchers have dug out the somewhat polemical report of a possible UFO crash not too far away from Varginha. The first references to the crash date to January 13th. The NORAD (North American Aerospace Defense Command) alerted Brazilian authorities about an unidentified artifact flying over the southern region of the State of Minas Gerais. It appeared to be about to crash.

"Glider pilot Carlos de Souza was driving on route BR-381 (connecting São Paulo to the city of Belo Horizonte (Minas Gerais) when he saw an elongated, cigar-shaped flying object move about the sky at an unsteady altitude, leaving behind an apparent trail of smoke or fog. The object disappeared suddenly and Souza assumed it had crashed. He pulled over next to a farm where the UFO had probably crashed, and he found pieces of metallic-like debris which was light at the touch and that returned to its original shape after being crumpled in the witness's hand, similar to what was reported in the 1947 Roswell incident, in the USA. The place reeked of ammonia. Subsequently, a police corporal approached Souza, accompanied by other militaries and severely admonished him, demanding that he leave the place immediately and refrain from talking about the incident. Though apparently bombastic, Souza's testimony would help explain the promptness with which ESA's officers appeared on the spot to capture the alien creature in the district of Jardim Andere, a few days later (January 20th), probably having been informed about and in pursuit of something unidentified since the 13th, or even before that.

"Still on January 13th, Walter Xavier da Silva, mayor of Monsenhor Paulo, a town 23,7 miles from Varginha, and his wife were driving to their farm in the neighborhood when they saw in the sky a large elongated object ("shaped like a train car," he would say later) with four lights around it. Static at first, the UFO suddenly began to move, making a strong roaring noise like an activated vibrating engine, until it disappeared behind some hills. The sighting was immediately followed by a glare that illumined the ground. Mayor Silva felt sick and had conjunctivitis for several days."[2]

Essentially, that is where the case stands to this day. Gevaerd and Leir, however, continue their investigations.

* * *

Chapter 19 Notes:

1. Central Intelligence Agency Intelligence Report: *Somaliland President Egal Speaks On Mysterious Bomb Blast*, January 1996.

2. *The Essential Varginha Incident*, A.J. Gevaerd & Dr. Roger Leir, 2005. *Varginha: Brazil Crash Retrieval Case*, Dr. Roger Leir, *3rd Annual Crash Retrieval Conference Proceedings*, November 4-6, 2005, Wood & Wood Enterprises.

Chapter 20
The AIDS-Cattle Mutilation
Controversy, 1999

There can be absolutely no doubt at all that the most controversial, and some would say outrageous, development in this particular story is one that surfaced in 1999, when researcher Philip Duke, PhD, suggested that both cattle mutilations and alien abductions were connected with a nefarious extraterrestrial plot to conquer the Earth by infecting the human population with HIV.

According to Duke: "Cattle mutilations are logically explainable only as Extraterrestrial activities. The mutilation body materials taken all correspond with sites of HIV transmission or replication (blood) in humans, except for the ear, which may contain a locator device. Circumstantial evidence suggests cattle are mutilated primarily to harvest HIV antibodies and virus from blood in quantity, and to obtain information relating to possible HIV transmission in humans, by study of the materials taken from corresponding cattle mutilation sites. The left ear is always taken, presumably to facilitate locator retrieval. Healthy, live fetuses are also taken from animals to be mutilated. The primary reason for cattle mutilations may be to harvest HIV antibodies. Cattle mutilation phenomena support the AIDS-ET Connection."

Duke asks: "Why do the aliens want the relatively large amounts of HIV and antibodies (so far entirely in theory) to be found in the mutilated cattle blood they harvest? Why are they going to such trouble to obtain these materials in quantity? What uses might they be put to?"

Duke answers the question himself: "According to the work of Dr. David Jacobs, some abductees will be usefully employed prior to and during the colonization process. Then it would be only logical to protect these valued abductees against HIV. And, it may be necessary to protect the aliens themselves against HIV infection, especially if HIV should become much more readily transmissible.

"According to the AIDS-ET Connection concept, the gray aliens may require ongoing sizable production and research sources of the virus and its antibodies for new strains. Although at least three different pandemics are well underway, BW [Biological Warfare] theory dictates the development and deployment of different strains, as well as continual monitoring of present strain performances (by examination and testing of human abductees)."[1]

Duke elaborates on this highly contentious scenario:

"Why have they come here? To answer that, ask yourselves, what would we be doing in their place? Obviously exploration comes first; and then taking for our advantage. Explorers have always done this. What do they want? We have a whole new wonderful world, teeming with life, just waiting for them. There is only one thing standing in their way; that is us. Attack us openly, we would retaliate, and they would inherit a radioactive biosphere wasteland. No, the smart thing is to secretly destroy our civilization, and with it our means of organized (atomic) retaliation. By employing a Biological Warfare (BW) agent. That agent is HIV. When enough people are sick, dying and dead from AIDS, then alien colonization will proceed openly. Other people know about the alien agenda and have published concerning it."[2]

Certainly, Duke's theories have provoked a huge amount of debate. It should be noted that a variation on this theory exists, suggesting that the United States Government engineered AIDS as a form of biological warfare. History has shown, however, that the original allegations to this effect surfaced from disinformation experts and psychological warfare operatives within the former-Soviet Union's KGB. While there is certainly a wealth of data at our disposal suggesting that utterly lethal alien viruses may very well be a reality, such is the sensitivity surrounding the AIDS crisis that a wealth of additional research definitely needs to be undertaken if such controversial claims are to be firmly embraced or discarded.

Background data on the KGB's involvement in spreading rumors to the effect that the United States Government deliberately engineered HIV as a weapon of biological warfare, were addressed in a 2005 paper that originated with the Department of State. Titled *AIDS as a Biological Weapon*, it states:

"When the AIDS disease was first recognized in the early 1980s, its origins were a mystery. A deadly new disease had suddenly appeared, with no obvious explanation of what had caused it. In such a situation, false rumors and misinformation naturally arose, and Soviet disinformation specialists exploited this situation as well as the musings of conspiracy theorists to help shape their brief but highly effective disinformation campaign on this issue.

"In March 1992, then-Russian intelligence chief and later Russian Prime Minister Yevgeni Primakov admitted that the disinformation service of the Soviet KGB had concocted the false story that the AIDS virus had been created in a US military laboratory as a biological weapon. The Russian newspaper *Izvestiya* reported on March 19, 1992:

"'[Primakov] mentioned the well known articles printed a few years ago in our central newspapers about AIDS supposedly originating from secret Pentagon laboratories. According to Yevgeni Primakov, the articles exposing US scientists' 'crafty' plots were fabricated in KGB offices.' The Soviets eventually abandoned the AIDS disinformation campaign under pressure from the U.S. Government in August 1987."

In a section of the document titled *The Real Origins of AIDS*, the Department of State notes:

"In the mid-1980s, there was still considerable confusion about how AIDS had developed, although scientists universally agreed that it was a naturally occurring disease, not one that was man-made. In the intervening years, science has done much to solve this mystery. There is now strong scientific evidence that the AIDS virus originated as a subspecies of a virus that commonly infects the western equatorial African chimpanzee, Pan troglodytes troglodytes. An article in the February 4, 1999, issue of *Nature* magazine called *Origin of HIV-1 in the Chimpanzee Pan Troglodytes*, explained how scientists used mitochondrial DNA analysis to determine that 'all HIV-1 strains known to infect man' were closely related to a simian immunodeficiency virus (SIV) found in the Pan troglodytes chimpanzee. The article also notes that the natural range of Pan troglodytes chimpanzees 'coincides precisely with the areas of HIV-1 group endemicity.' The less common HIV-2, which also causes AIDS, had previously been determined to be related to a virus infecting another African primate, the Sooty Mangebey."

The Department of State elaborated:

"Dr. Beatrice Hahn of the University of Alabama and her colleagues made this discovery after analyzing frozen blood and tissue samples from four chimpanzees, including a lab chimp named

Marilyn, which had died in 1985. Modern tests for HIV reactivity were not available at that time, and Marilyn's tissue and blood samples were rediscovered only in 1998, making the new analysis possible.

"Dr. Hahn and her colleagues estimate that SIV may have existed in Pan troglodytes chimpanzees for as long as several hundred thousand years. Although it cannot be known with certainty how the virus gained a foothold in humans, hunting chimpanzees for food, which is common in west equatorial Africa, could have provided a source for transmission from chimpanzees to humans.

"Other scientific discoveries place the oldest known human case of HIV as occurring in 1959. A February 5, 1998, article in *Nature*, 'An African HIV-1 sequence from 1959 and implications for the origin of the epidemic,' reported that a plasma sample obtained in early 1959 from an adult Bantu male living in what is now Kinshasa, Democratic Republic of the Congo (DRG) had tested positive for HIV-1.

"In 2000, scientists at the Los Alamos National Laboratory used their powerful supercomputers to analyze the relationships among various strains of HIV-1. Their calculations showed that the main HIV-1 virus probably established itself in humans in about 1930, as explained in an article in the June 8, 2000, issue of *Science* magazine called, *Timing the Ancestor of the HIV-1 Pandemic Strains*.

"Thus, although a simian immunodeficiency virus appears to have existed for very long periods of time in Pan troglodytes chimpanzees, it did not lead to a pandemic in humans before the 20th century. The beginnings of modernization and urbanization in western equatorial Africa in the early 1900s may have contributed to the rise of the AIDS pandemic. Between 1900 and 1961, the population of what is now Kinshasa, DRG increased approximately 100 times, from a few thousand in 1900 to 420,000 in 1961. This exponential growth in urbanization and related dislocations of traditional rural life may have led to conditions that were conducive to the spread of AIDS. Such possibilities are explored at greater length in an article *Origin of HIV Type 1 in Colonial French Equatorial Africa?* published in the journal *AIDS Research and Human Retroviruses* (volume 16, number 1, 2000, pp. 5-8)."

The Department of State document concludes:

"HIV-1, the virus that caused the AIDS pandemic, could not be man-made because direct evidence shows that AIDS has existed in humans at least since 1959 and scientific analysis shows that it was probably present some 75 years ago, which is long before humans had the means to genetically engineer microbes.

"HIV-1 is very closely related to a similar virus found in equatorial West African chimpanzees

"The scientific evidence indicates that the HIV-1 virus resulted from cross-species transmission, which is known to occur in other human diseases, including influenza, plague, tuberculosis, and many other diseases, especially since this species of virus has a strong predilection for frequent mutation, making adoption to humans relatively easy.

"Social and economic conditions in western equatorial Africa changed dramatically in the 20th century, which could explain why the AIDS pandemic emerged at this time and not previously."[3]

The data contained within the pages of this book strongly suggests that we should not ignore the theories of researcher Philip Duke, PhD. However, we should also not forget that Russia's KGB was busy in the 1980s concocting bogus stories (and perhaps even concocting bogus documents similar to some of the MJ-12 documents that refer to lethal viruses of undetermined origins), designed to reinforce allegations that the United States Government had created HIV. As a result of these two observations, it behooves us to tread very carefully in this emotion-driven area.

*   *   *

Chapter 20 Notes:

1. *Cattle Mutilation Phenomenon and HIV*, Philip S. Duke, PhD, 1999. See: www.geocities.com/Area51/Shadowlands/6583/cattle038.html.

2. *The AIDS-ET Connection*, Philip S. Duke, PhD., Cosmos Press, 1999.

3. *The Real Origins of AIDS*, Department of State, July 27, 2005. See: http://usinfo.state.gov/media/Archive/2005/Jul/27-595713.html and usinfo.state.gov/media/Archive/2005/Jan/14-777030.html.

Chapter 21
Strange Deaths
2001-2005

From the latter part of 2001 to 2005, numerous individuals working within the elite field of microbiology (which is defined as the study of organisms that are too small to be seen with the naked eye, such as bacteria, viruses and yeasts), and in various countries around the world, died under circumstances that some within the media and the general public have come to view as highly suspicious in nature.

Many of the deaths appear, at first glance at least, to have prosaic explanations. There are those, however, who maintain that the sheer number of such deaths, the majority of which occurred within a matter of months, cannot be explained away so easily. More intriguing is the fact that many of those dead microbiologists had links to worldwide intelligence services, including the United States' CIA, Britain's MI5 and MI6; and Israel's Mossad.

Inevitably, this strange cluster of deaths, in such a tightly knit area of cutting-edge research, has led to a proliferation of theories in an attempt to resolve the matter. Some believe that a cell of deep-cover terrorists, from the Middle East, is attempting to wipe out the leading names within the field of microbiology as part of an on-going plot to prevent Western nations from developing the ultimate bio-weapon.

A darker theory suggests that this same weapon has *already* been developed, and now, with their work complete, the microbiologists are being systematically killed, one by one, by Western Intelligence, in an effort to prevent them being kidnapped by terrorists who will then force them to work for the other side.

And an infinitely more intriguing scenario - borne out of the admittedly intriguing fact that some of the microbiologists were working on theoretical ways to counteract the effects of a deadly plague that might surface on the Earth if a virus of unknown origins was brought to our planet by meteorite - has led to assertions that just such an "alien virus" has been found, studied, understood, and finally harnessed in the event that it may one day be needed as an offensive weapon.

The controversy largely began on November 12, 2001, when Dr. Benito Que, a cell biologist working on infectious diseases, including HIV, was found dead outside of his laboratory at the Miami Medical School. Police said that he was possibly the victim of a mugger. *The Miami Herald* stated that his death occurred as he headed for his car, a white Ford Explorer parked on Northwest 10th Avenue. Furthermore, according to the *Herald*, the "word" was that Que had been attacked by four men equipped with baseball-bats. This was later recanted, however, and it was stated that Dr. Que had died of cardiac arrest. Police later refused to comment on the death.[1]

Eleven days later, Dr. Vladimir Pasechnik, a former microbiologist for Biopreparat, a bio-weapons production facility that existed in Russia prior to the collapse of the Soviet Union, was found dead near his home in the county of Wiltshire, England. At the time, the *London Times* newspaper stated: "The defection to Britain in 1989 of Vladimir Pasechnik revealed to the West for the first time the colossal scale of the Soviet Union's clandestine biological warfare program. His revelations about the scale of the Soviet Union's production of such biological agents as anthrax, plague, tularemia and smallpox provided an inside account of one of the best-kept secrets of the Cold War.

"After his defection he worked for ten years at the UK Department of Health's Center for Applied Microbiology Research before forming his own company, Regma Biotechnics, to work on therapies for cancer, neurological diseases, tuberculosis and other infectious diseases. In the last few weeks of his life he had put his research on anthrax at the disposal of the Government, in the light of the threat from bio-terrorism."

According to British Intelligence, Pasechnik died of a stroke.[2]

On October 8, 2001 a report contained within the British *Guardian* newspaper said that the victims of "the Spanish Flu" had been victims of "the world's most deadly virus." Moreover, the newspaper added, British scientists, hoped to uncover the genetic makeup of the virus, making it easier to combat. Professor John Oxford of London's Queen Mary's School of Medicine, the British government's flu adviser, acknowledged that the exhumations and subsequent studies would have to be done with extreme caution so that the virus was not unleashed to cause another epidemic. The uncovering of a pathogen's genetic structure is the *exact* area that

Dr. Pasechnik was involved with at Regma. Pasechnik died six weeks after the planned exhumations were announced.[3]

Twenty-four hours later, on November 24, 2001, the FBI announced that it was monitoring an investigation into the disappearance of a Harvard biologist because of "his research into potentially lethal viruses," including ebola. Dr. Don C. Wiley, 57, had last been seen in Memphis, Tennessee, where he attended the annual meeting of the Scientific Advisory Board of the St. Jude Children's Research Hospital. His rented car was found at 4.00 a.m. on 16 November on a bridge over the Mississippi River, with a full fuel tank, and the key still in the ignition. Wiley had left the Peabody Hotel just four hours previously. He was due to meet his wife and two children that same day in Cambridge, Massachusetts. FBI agents took an interest in Wiley's disappearance because of this expertise and as a direct result of "our state of affairs post-September 11," said Memphis-based FBI agent William Woerne. Wiley was a Harvard biochemistry and biophysics professor, and was considered a national expert on Ebola, HIV, herpes and influenza. In 1999, Wiley and another Harvard professor, Dr. Jack Strominger, won the Japan Prize for their discoveries of how the immune system protects humans from infections.[4]

Wiley's sister-in-law said that it was uncharacteristic for him not to leave a message. Days earlier, for example, he *had* left a note for his 85-year- old father telling him when he would be back from a jog. Why he did not do so on this occasion is a mystery. Wiley was last seen only hours before his disappearance at the St. Jude's Children Research Advisory Dinner at the Peabody Hotel, Memphis, where he was reported to be in good spirits and not in any way depressed or showing suicidal tendencies. Wiley is known to have left the hotel around midnight; however, the bridge where his car was found is only 5 minutes drive from the hotel – which leaves 4 hours unaccounted for. According to Walter Crews of the Memphis Police Department: "We began this investigation as a missing person investigation. From there it went to a more criminal bent."[5]

Notably, on the same day that authorities were searching for Wiley, three more microbiologists were killed when a Swissair flight from Berlin to Zurich crashed during its landing approach. Twenty-two were killed and nine survived. Among those killed were Dr. Yaakov Matzner, 54, dean of the Hebrew University School of

Medicine; Amiramp Eldor, 59, head of the Hematology Department at Ichilov Hospital in Tel Aviv and a world-recognized expert in blood clotting; and Avishai Berkman, 50, director of the Tel Aviv Public Health Department.[6]

On December 12, 2001, it was revealed in the media that a leading researcher on DNA sequencing analysis had been found dead in the secluded northern Virginian farmhouse where he lived alone. Robert M. Schwartz had been found by neighbors, on 10 December, after co-workers at his place of employment reported that he had skipped work and had missed a meeting. "We're all stunned," said Anne Armstrong, president of the Virginia Center for Innovative Technology, a non-profit agency where Schwartz worked. "We don't know anything. What we're assuming is maybe he walked in on something." Loudon County Sheriff Stephen Simpson said that detectives had "some leads." Schwartz was a founding member of the Virginia Biotechnology Association, worked at the center for almost fifteen years, and had served as the executive director of research and development and university relations. He also worked on the first national online database of DNA sequence information.[7]

On the other side of the world, forty-eight-hours later, equally disturbing events were occurring. Set Van Nguyen was a microbiologist who worked at the Commonwealth Scientific and Industrial Research Organization's Animal Diseases Establishment at Geelong, Australia, and had been employed there for fifteen years. According to Police at Victoria, Australia: "Set Van Nguyen, 44, appeared to have died after entering an airlock into a storage laboratory filled with nitrogen. His body was found when his wife became worried after he failed to return from work. He was killed after entering a low temperature storage area where biological samples were kept. He did not know the room was full of deadly gas which had leaked from a liquid nitrogen cooling system. Unable to breathe, Mr. Nguyen collapsed and died."[8]

It was at this same establishment that, as *Nature* magazine reported in January 2001: "Australian scientists, Dr Ron Jackson and Dr Ian Ramshaw, accidentally created an astonishingly virulent strain of mouse-pox, a cousin of smallpox, among laboratory mice. They realized that if similar genetic manipulation was carried out on smallpox, an unstoppable killer could be unleashed."[9]

Also on the same day, much publicity was given to a story that had originally appeared on November 15, 1998 in the London *Times*, and that discussed how Israel was working on a biological weapon that would harm only Arabs.

The *Times* had reported that: "The intention is to use the ability of viruses and certain bacteria to alter the DNA inside their host's living cells. The scientists are trying to engineer deadly microorganisms that attack only those bearing the distinctive genes. The program is based at the biological institute in Nes Tziyona, the main research facility for Israel's clandestine arsenal of chemical and biological weapons. A scientist there said the task was hugely complicated because both Arabs and Jews are of Semitic origin. But he added: 'They have, however, succeeded in pinpointing a particular characteristic in the genetic profile of certain Arab communities, particularly the Iraqi people.' Dr Daan Goosen, head of a South African chemical and biological warfare plant, said that in the 1980s, his group was ordered to develop a 'pigmentation weapon' that would only target black people."[10]

It was announced on December 15, 2001 that three people had been charged with murder in the case of the scientist Robert M. Schwartz. Police revealed that he had been killed with a 2-foot sword in a "planned assassination" and that an "X" had been carved into his back. "I have no idea what this means," said the prosecutor, Robert Anderson. Police in Maryland arrested Kyle Hulbert, 18, Michael Pfohl, 21, and Katherine Inglis, 19. They were acquaintances of the victim's daughter, Clara Schwartz, a James Madison University student, said Loudon County Sheriff Stephen Simpson. "We don't know how familiar they were with the father, but we know they knew him," Simpson said.

Police revealed that Hulbert had an interest in witchcraft, was widely read on the subject, always dressed in black, and had been planning to form a "coven." A local, Fran Broomall, who let Hulbert stay in his home during the fall, stated that he had seen no evidence of any sort of occult practices on Hulbert's part. Hulbert's father told the *Washington Post* that his son had been diagnosed with schizophrenia and bipolar disorder, and had been off his medication for months. Pfohl had lived with Inglis after his parents kicked him out of the family home. An unidentified source said that the killing had "cult overtones."

It was additionally revealed that there was no sign of a forced entry into the Schwartz home. The victim's wife had died of cancer some years previously. Colleagues of Schwartz described him as a brilliant man who was skilled at translating complex scientific data to computers so it could be more easily analyzed.

The next day, a revelation surfaced to the effect that one of those arrested in the killing of scientist Robert Schwartz, namely Katie Inglis, had in January 2001 reported to the Naval Recruit Training Command Center in Great Lakes, Illinois. Navy officials stated that she had been trained to work in aviation but had suddenly left on May 28. One of the other suspects, Michael Pfohl, had expressed an interest in joining U.S. Special Forces.[11]

Four days later, Police announced that they had located the body of missing Harvard University scientist, Don C. Wiley. A body carrying identification was found on December 18 near a hydroelectric plant in the Mississippi River, and about 300 miles from where Wiley was last seen. Police Lt. Joe Scott said that a positive identification was planned when the body was returned to Memphis for an autopsy. A number of scientific organizations, including St. Jude's Children's Research Hospital where Wiley worked, put up rewards totaling $26,000 for information leading to the "arrest and charge" of anyone responsible for Wiley's disappearance. "As soon as the body gets in our morgue, the medical examiner will begin the autopsy to help answer a lot of questions," said Memphis Police Director Walter Crews.[12]

Interestingly, *Reuters* news service stated that Wiley's death had "triggered alarm bells," due to the "current bio-warfare fears" and the nature of his work, but did not elaborate as to who the alarm bells had been triggered with. The FBI stated that it was leaving the investigation of Wiley's death in the hands of the police. Friends and family of Wiley stated that he would not commit suicide.[13]

On January 14, 2002, a medical examiner, O.C. Smith, stated that Wiley's death was not murder or suicide but was "accidental." Smith added that Wiley's end was just the result of a tragic series of accidents that began when he hit a series of construction signs on the Hernando DeSoto Bridge, a mile-long span over the Mississippi that connects Tennessee and Arkansas. After the 6-foot-3-inch, 165-pound professor stopped to investigate the damage to his rental car, said investigators, he was swept off the 135-foot-high bridge by a gust of wind, possibly from one of the many 18-wheel trucks that cross the bridge at that time. Smith said Wiley had drunk several glasses of wine and suffered from a "seizure disorder that sometimes caused dizziness when he was tired or under stress." Smith ruled out suicide because he said that there were indications that Wiley's body had struck a support beam as he fell. Suicides, said Smith, would miss the beams if they leapt from the bridge. "The possibility of Dr. Wiley's death having been a suicide was carefully considered and rejected. The manner of death is therefore accidental," was the final verdict.[14]

Exactly two weeks later, on January 28, 2002, microbiologist, and member of the Russian Academy of Science, Alexi Brushlinski, died as the result of a "bandit attack" in Moscow.[15]

Then, on February 2, 2002, the following appeared in the *Washington Post*, under the heading *Daughter Charged in Slaying of Scientist*:

"A daughter of the respected Loudoun County scientist who was stabbed to death with a sword was arrested yesterday and accused of conspiring with friends to kill her father, authorities said. Loudoun County sheriff's deputies arrested Clara Jane Schwartz, 21, about 4:30 p.m. at James Madison University and charged her with first-degree murder. Schwartz planned the killing of her father, Robert M. Schwartz, 57, with at least one of the suspects already charged in his death, the Loudoun County sheriff's office said, citing unspecified documents recovered in a search. Clara Schwartz appeared before a Loudoun County magistrate last night and was denied bail. She was being held at the county jail and did not yet have an attorney."[16]

The newspaper continued that:

"Robert Schwartz, one of the nation's leading researchers on DNA sequencing analysis, worked at Virginia's Center for Innovative Technology. He was slain in his secluded Mount Gilead home Dec. 8. Investigators, who have described the killing as a 'premeditated assassination,' said Schwartz had been stabbed and cut repeatedly. An 'X' was carved in the back of his neck, they said. Three friends of Clara Schwartz -- Kyle, 18; Katherine Inglis, 19; and Michael Pfohl, 21 -- were charged with murder Dec. 12. Court papers allege that Hulbert, with a two-foot sword strapped to his side and wearing a black trench coat, strode alone into Robert Schwartz's log-and-fieldstone farmhouse, saying he had a 'job to do.'"[17]

Then, on February 9, 2002, microbiologist Victor Korshunov, 56, was hit over the head and killed at the entrance of his home in Moscow, Russia. He was the head of the microbiology sub-faculty at the Russian State Medical University and an expert in intestinal bacteria.[18]

And four days after that revelation, a similar story surfaced from England, as the *Times* newspaper of February 13 demonstrated:

"Detectives were last night trying to unravel the circumstances in which a leading university research scientist was found dead at his blood-spattered and apparently ransacked home. The body of Ian Langford, 40, a senior Fellow at the University of East Anglia's Center for Social and Economic Research on the Global Environment, was discovered on Monday night by police and ambulance men. The body was naked from the waist down and partly wedged under a chair. It is understood that doors to the terraced house were locked."

It was stated further by the newspaper that a post-mortem had failed to establish how Dr. Langford, who lived alone in the house in the English city of Norwich, had died. His work began in 1993 after he gained his PhD in childhood leukemia and infection following a first-class honors degree in environmental sciences. He had worked most recently as a senior researcher assessing risk to the environment.

Professor Kerry Turner, director of the center, said: "We are all very shocked by this appalling news. Ian was without doubt one of Europe's leading experts on environmental risk, specializing in links between human health and environmental risk. He was known for his work on the effects on health of bathing water and air pollution, for example. He was one of the most brilliant colleagues I have ever had."[19]

Forty-eight hours after the events in England, the media began reporting on the fact that on October 4, 2001, a commercial jetliner traveling from Israel to Novosibirsk, Siberia, had been shot down over the Black Sea by an "errant" Ukrainian surface-to-air missile, killing all on board. The missile was over 100 miles off-course. Despite early news stories reporting it as a charter, the flight (Air Sibir 1812) was a regularly scheduled flight.

According to several press reports of February 2002, the plane was carrying five passengers who were all leading microbiologists.

Notably, both Israel and Novosibirsk are homes for cutting-edge microbiological research. Novosibirsk is known as the scientific capital of Siberia. There are over 50 research facilities there, and 13 full universities for a population of only 2.5 million people. At about the time of the Black Sea crash, Israeli journalists had been sounding the alarm that two Israeli microbiologists had also been murdered.[20]

Also on February 15, it was revealed that the representative of British Intelligence that had informed the media that the aforementioned microbiologist, Dr. Vladimir Pasechnik, had died of a stroke in England was Dr. Christopher Davis, presently living in Virginia. Dr. Davis was also the member of British Intelligence who debriefed Dr. Pasechnik at the time of his defection. When he was asked why a former member of British intelligence would be the person announcing the death of Dr. Pasechnik to the U.S. media, Dr. Davis replied that it had come about during a conversation with a reporter he had had a long relationship with.[21]

Journalist Michael Davidson made the following, intriguing comments and observations about Pasechnik: "Vladimir Pasechnik spent the ten years after his defection working at the Center for Applied Microbiology and Research at the U.K. Department of Health, Salisbury. On February 20, 2000, it had been announced that, along with partner Caisey Harlingten, Dr. Pasechnik had formed a company called Regma Biotechnologies Ltd. Regma describes itself as 'a new drug company working to provide powerful alternatives to antibiotics.' Like three other microbiologists who died in this clearly delineated period, Pasechnik was heavily involved in DNA sequencing research."[22]

Most notable of all was the following from the British *Guardian* newspaper that also surfaced on the same day:

"Almost immediately at the outset of the anthrax scare, the Bush administration contracted with Bayer Pharmaceuticals for millions of doses of Cipro, an antibiotic to treat anthrax. This was done despite many in the medical community stating that there were several cheaper, better alternatives to Cipro, which has never been shown to be effective against inhaled anthrax. The Center for Disease Control's (CDC) own website states a preference for the antibiotic doxycycline over Cipro for inhalation anthrax. CDC expresses concerns that widespread Cipro use could cause other bacteria to become immune to antibiotics. After three months of conflicting reports it is now official that the anthrax that has killed several Americans since October 5 is from US military sources connected to CIA research. The FBI has stated that only ten people could have had access, yet at the same time they are reporting astounding security breaches at the bio-warfare facility at Ft. Detrick, MD; breaches such as unauthorized nighttime experiments and lab specimens missing.

"The militarized anthrax used by the United States was developed by William C. Patrick III, who holds five classified patents on the process. He has worked at both Ft. Detrick, and the Dugway Proving Grounds in Utah. Patrick is now a private biowarfare consultant to the military and CIA. Patrick developed the process by which anthrax spores could be concentrated at the level of one trillion spores per gram. No other country has been able to get concentrations above 500 billion per gram. The anthrax that was sent around the eastern United States last fall was concentrated at one trillion spores per gram. In recent years Patrick has worked with Kanatjan Alibekov. Now known by the Americanized 'Ken Alibek,' he defected to the U.S. in 1992. Before defecting, Alibek was the #2 man in the former Soviet Union's bio-warfare program. His boss was Dr. Vladimir Pasechnik."[23]

On February 19, 2002, the following appeared on the *Space Daily* e-newsletter:

"If microbial life is found on Mars, will it be native to the planet or something carried there from Earth? Either way, will it be safe to return samples of such organisms to Earth? Astrobiology, the search for life elsewhere, says a University of Illinois microbiologist, is making us look a lot closer at microbial life on Earth - how it adapts and its relationship to emerging infectious diseases. 'Even if we don't find life on other planets, we are learning a lot about life on the Earth, particularly microbial life,' Abigail Salyers said in an interview about her speech today at the annual meeting of the American Association for the Advancement of Science. She challenged scientists to consider far-reaching possibilities in a talk titled: *Are There Medical Implications of Geomicrobiology?*"[24]

As will become apparent shortly, the death of a microbiologist working in the fields of alien microbes and (as the media dubbed it) "space germs" would soon be added to the ever-growing list of strange deaths.

Pizza delivery may have been ambush, Suspect Later Found Dead, reported the *San Francisco Mercury News* a week later:

"Dr. Tanya Holzmayer, a pioneering scientist, was surprised Wednesday night to find a Domino's Pizza deliveryman at the front door of her Mountain View home. Moments later, a former colleague appeared out of the dark, shot her dead and ran off, police said. Guyang 'Matthew' Huang called his wife in Foster City with the news: 'I just killed my ex-boss. Now I'm going to kill myself.'

"Within an hour, a jogger found Huang's body off a path near the San Mateo Bridge. A cell phone was in Huang's pocket and a .380-caliber handgun lay near his hand. Investigators on Thursday were just beginning to put together the details of the deadly nexus between the two immigrant scientists. 'It looked like an ambush,' said Mountain View Police spokesman Jim Bennett. 'He may have used the pizza to lure her out.'

"A former colleague of both Holzmayer and Huang thinks he knows the motive: Holzmayer fired Huang from his job at PPD Discovery, a biotech company in Menlo Park, according to Dr. Igor B. Roninson. 'She told me she got orders from senior management to fire him,' said Roninson, a genomic scientist with the University of Illinois-Chicago and a consultant for PPD. 'She had to fulfill those orders, but was very upset. She had no choice, no options. But this is a year later.'

"A company spokeswoman said Huang left PPD in June, but she wouldn't confirm that he was fired. Neither Huang nor Holzmayer were still with the company. Holzmayer had quit in December to start her own biotech venture. Both Holzmayer, 46, and Huang, 38, were highly regarded in genetics.

"She was a Russian-born genomic scientist who had co-invented a tool that has helped find hundreds of molecular targets to combat cancer and HIV. He was a brilliant scholar, scoring 11th out of 230,000 students on his college entrance exams in China, and an activist who fought for reform in his homeland once he came to the United States to study in 1986."[25]

On March 24, 2002, Denver car dealer Kent Rickenbaugh, his wife, Caroline, and their son Bart were killed on this day in a plane crash near Centennial Airport. The pilot, Dr. Steven Mostow, was also killed. Kent Rickenbaugh, 64, owned two car dealerships in the

Denver area. Caroline Rickenbaugh, 62, was known for her involvement in the community. Bart Rickenbaugh, 35, lived in Bozeman, Montana.

Mostow, 63, was one of the United States' leading infectious disease experts and was associate dean at the University of Colorado Health Sciences Center. Mostow was a crusader for better health, an early advocate for widespread flu vaccinations, and more recently an expert on the threat of bio-terrorism. He was a champion for rural health care and childhood immunizations. For the past three years, he had been helping to expand the 9Health Fair, a program that benefits thousands of people in Colorado.

Investigators returned to the scene of the plane crash to try to figure out why the twin-engine Cessna 340 went down. The plane was headed to Centennial from Gunnison when Mostow reported engine trouble around 4:30 p.m., Federal Aviation Administration spokesman Jerry Snyder said.

The plane crashed near mile marker 190 in unincorporated Douglas County. Witnesses say they saw the plane go down. "As we came over the hill we saw the plane coming fairly straight toward the highway actually, and swerving from side to side, losing altitude fast," Willen Guyer said, adding: "I think the guy saw the highway and turned away from it and when he turned left he just went nose down into the ground."

The weather was cloudy with snow flurries; however, National Transportation Safety Board investigators said weather did not appear to be a factor in the crash, Douglas County Sheriff's Office spokesman Bernie Harris said. A memorial service for Dr. Mostow was held at 3 p.m. on Thursday, March 28th, at the Denison Auditorium on the University of Colorado Health Sciences campus. Funeral plans for the Rickenbaugh family have not been made public.[26]

And on the same day that Dr. Mostow was killed, another life ended (in England again) when 55-year-old microbiologist David Wynn-Williams was hit by a car while jogging near his home in Cambridge. He was an astro-biologist with the Antarctic Astrobiology Project and the NASA Ames Research Center, and was studying the capability of microbes to adapt to environmental extremes. An obituary that appeared on March 27, 2002 in the English *Times* newspaper revealed the extent of David Wynn-

Williams's work:

"A microbiologist who had for 25 years studied the survival of primitive organisms in the Antarctic environment and the implications for the wider universe, David Wynn-Williams, had been using his findings to assess the likelihood of the existence of some form of life on Mars. These studies, which had led to an exchange of ideas with NASA in the US, explored the behavior of life forms on the frontiers of existence.

"In the course of a series of ten visits to Antarctica from the mid-1970s onwards, Wynn-Williams had assessed the capability of microbes to adapt to environmental extremes, including the bombardment of ultraviolet rays and global warming conditions which might parallel those of the early Primary Era of Earth s existence, or of present day Mars. Besides his links with NASA, he had also collaborated with the Italian Antarctic program at Terra Nova Bay, with the New Zealand program at Scott Base and with American research programs in the Antarctic at McMurdo.

"In 2000 he was appointed leader of the Antarctic Astrobiology Project, which explores the effects of environmental stress at the limits of life on Earth analogous to conditions which might subsist on Mars. This drew Wynn-Williams into collaboration with the NASA Ames Research Center, the Johnson Space Center and Lunar & Planetary Institute, Houston, and Montana State University, to develop and evaluate a miniature con-focal microscope and Raman spectrometer (CMaRS) for use on a Mars landing vehicle. CMaRS has been adopted as the prime instrument for the proposed UK-led Vanguard Mars lander [sic]-rover mission, to be submitted to the European Space Agency.

"His publications were numerous and covered subjects as diverse as recent aqueous environments in Martian impact craters, the need for collaboration in astrobiology, and lichens at the limits of life. His pioneering work had been acknowledged with the award of a Polar Medal as early as 1980."[27]

Similarly, on March 28, 2002, under the heading of *Space Bug Specialist Killed in Crash*, the following was reported by Britain's BBC on its web-news site:

"A pioneering British scientist who was leading studies in Antarctica to understand the likelihood of life existing on Mars and elsewhere has been killed in a car accident. Dr David Wynn-

Williams died after he was involved in a crash involving two vehicles near his home in Cambridge. He was the Antarctic astrobiology project leader at the British Antarctic Survey and studied the way microbes survive in harsh conditions as a model for how life might exist on other planets. He was jogging when the crash happened.

"Professor Chris Rapley, director of the British Antarctic Survey, said: 'Staff at the British Antarctic Survey are deeply saddened to hear about the tragic death of Dr David Wynn-Williams. David has worked at the survey for over 28 years as a microbiologist. He was a talented scientist who, at the early start of his career, pioneered work on the role of microbes in the Antarctic. David will be sorely missed by colleagues and friends, not only for being a brilliant and innovative scientist in the area of microbiology, but for his over-whelming enthusiasm for his work, the Antarctic and everything he did. Our thoughts and sympathy are with his family at this time,' he said.

"Dr. Wynn-Williams made 10 trips to the South Pole and collaborated with Italian, New Zealand and US colleagues. He worked with American space agency to develop and evaluate equipment for a Mars Lander and advised researchers in Britain working on the Beagle-2 Mars lander, part of the European Mars Express program.

"He was also involved in a biology experiment which is to be flown on the International Space Station. In 1980 he received a polar medal for his outstanding
contribution to polar science. The drivers of the two cars involved in the crash which killed Dr Wynn-Williams were not seriously hurt. Cambridgeshire police would like to speak to anyone who saw the crash."[28]

Then, on March 29, 2002, it was reported that MI6 (the British equivalent of the CIA) was "spearheading an investigation into the mysterious deaths of a top microbiologist, Vladimir Pasechnik. He is linked to Porton Down, Britain's ultra secret bio-defense estab-lishment. He is also one of five high-ranking scientists who have died mysteriously in the past five months. Like Pasechnik, they all worked in the doomsday world of bio-chemical weapons. Colleagues of Pasechnik had confirmed that in Russia he had been working on a 'bio-weapon that could wipe out a third of the world's popula-tion.'"

"Pasechnik had been attached to the Center for Applied Microbiology and Research in Salisbury, Wiltshire, England. He was a foremost specialist with DNA sequencing – sophisticated research that is a vital element in designing biological weapons.

"Dr. Ken Alibek, another Russian defector, who is now a consultant to the Pentagon, has confirmed China 'very probably is not yet fully advanced in that area.' Defense Analyst, David Jensen, said: 'It would be logical for China to want Pasechnik on board. When he refused it would be equally logical to eliminate him. That's how China handles competition. Kills it off.'

"On November 21, 2001, shortly after his last visit to Porton Down, Pasechnik was found dead in his village home outside Salisbury. The cause of death was certified as a stroke. 'There are a number of nerve agents that can mimic a stroke and leave no traces,' said Dr. Leonard Horowitz, a U.S. specialist in the field of toxic poisons."[29]

The next death, of Dr. Leland Rickman, a UC San Diego expert on infectious diseases and, since Sept. 11, 2001 a consultant on bioterrorism, occurred on June 24, 2003. Rickman was forty-seven and died while on a teaching assignment in Lesotho, a small country bordered on all sides by South Africa. He had complained of a headache, but the cause of death was not immediately known. The physician had been working in Lesotho with Dr. Chris Mathews, director of the UC San Diego Medical Center's Owen Clinic, teaching African medical personnel about the prevention and treatment of AIDS. Rickman, the incoming president of the Infectious Disease Assn. of California, was a multidisciplinary professor and practitioner with expertise in infectious diseases, internal medicine, epidemiology, microbiology and antibiotic utilization.[30]

On July 18, 2003, it was reported in the British press that David Kelly, a British biological weapons expert, had slashed his own wrists while walking in woods near his home. Kelly was the British Ministry of Defense's chief scientific officer and senior adviser to the proliferation and arms control secretariat, and to the Foreign Office's non-proliferation department. The senior adviser on biological weapons to the UN biological weapons inspections teams (Unscom) from 1994 to 1999, he was also, in the opinion of his peers, pre-eminent in his field, not only in this country, but in the world, too.

Biological Weapons Expert With a Reputation for Thoroughness was the obituary that appeared in the July 19, 2003 edition of Britain's *Guardian* newspaper. It also linked Kelly with none other than Vladimir Pasechnik, who had also died under circumstances that many saw as questionable. According to the *Guardian*:

"Kelly was the Ministry of Defense's chief scientific officer and senior adviser to the proliferation and arms control secretariat, and to the Foreign Office's non-proliferation department. The senior adviser on biological weapons to the UN biological weapons inspections teams (Unscom) from 1994 to 1999, he was also, in the opinion of his peers, pre-eminent in his field, not only in this country, but in the world.

"After the eviction of the Iraqis from Kuwait in 1991, the UN invited Kelly to join Unscom to force Saddam into compliance with the peace agreements. Kelly made 36 visits to Iraq, and, from New York, continued his work into the late 1990s. What made him the obvious candidate for such work was his earlier, and continuing, experience in Russia. In autumn 1989, he had been called in to assist MI6 in debriefing Vladimir Pasechnik, a leading Soviet biochemist and defector.

"Eighteen months later, armed with Pasechnik's evidence of a gross violation of the 1972 biological weapons convention, Kelly co-led the US/British delegation to inspect suspect Russian sites. His sympathetic manner was an asset: at Vektor laboratories in Novosibirsk, Siberia, a researcher mentioned that the lab was studying the smallpox virus - in contravention of WHO regulations and the biological weapons convention. This was a major discovery, which revealed the seriousness of the Soviet undertaking. Later, he was an observer on the reciprocal trip the Russians made to the US.

"The son of an RAF officer and school teacher, Kelly was born in the Rhondda Valley, but raised in Tunbridge Wells. His early interests were in agriculture - and in Oxford, he was an expert on biological pesticides. In 1984, he was appointed head of microbiology at the chemical and biological defense establishment, Porton Down.[31]

A colleague of Kelly added:

"As an environmental toxologist, I have covered chemical and biological warfare issues since the 1970s and met David Kelly at many conferences; notably the Pugwash gatherings, which brought together scientists from many countries to talk issues through as professionals, not bound by national or political rivalries.

"Pugwash, and those other meetings, simply relied on people like David. There is no Pugwash party line, it is simply a place where expertise is paramount. Meetings aside, when I needed to talk to somebody on a key issue of the moment - like the anthrax-in-the-post scare following 9/11 - David was there. There was no other person I would have gone to as such a source of unvarnished truth - and of such funny asides.

"The two key areas where his insights were invaluable were around the biological weapons inspections in Russia in the 1980s, and in Iraq in the 1990s, where, in both cases, he had an central role. He would have absolutely ensured that the weapons, and the weapons material, were dismantled. The complete professional, he had such an eye for detail that nothing got past him.

"Such talents served him less well when sucked into the controversies of the last few months. I dread to think of the pressures he must have been under within the MoD. To see him on television, before that parliamentary committee, almost inaudible, was to see him involved in a quite different process, over which he did not have control. "A week ago, I spent 40 minutes trying to get through to him at the MoD, to wish him well; they would not put me through to any of his numbers. After I finally got through by email, telling him to take care, he replied that he wanted to get back to Baghdad, and some real work."[32]

By September 2003, the British media was voicing its concerns about this strange rash of deaths. The Norwich, England newspaper, the *Evening News*, said on September 9:

"John Eldridge, editor of *Jane's Nuclear, Biological and Chemical Defense*
Weekly, told a national newspaper that Dr. [David] Kelly's and Dr [Ian] Langford's deaths were linked, and thought other microbiologists should be concerned for their
safety. The Royal Navy expert Mr. Eldridge said scientists involved in microbiology were terrorist targets and under close scrutiny from the US and Russia. He branded Dr. Langford's death 'mysterious.'"

"Conspiracy theorists have since speculated Dr. Langford could have been murdered - along with another 24 scientists - because of their links to biological or chemical weapons. Dr. Kelly is the latest death in unusual circumstances to set the theorists gossiping. The suggestion that the deaths of a string of weapons experts could be linked was first reported in the *Evening News* last year. A spokeswoman for Norwich Coroners Office today confirmed they had never received any details of Dr. Langford's death, with police listing it as natural causes. John Eldridge, editor of *Jane's Nuclear, Biological and Chemical Defense Weekly*, told a national newspaper that Dr. Kelly's and Dr Langford's deaths were linked, and thought other microbiologists should be concerned for their safety. The Royal Navy expert Mr. Eldridge said scientists involved in microbiology were terrorist targets and under close scrutiny from the US and Russia. He branded Dr. Langford's death 'mysterious', although Norwich Coroner's Office said they had no reason to suspect any foul play."[33]

In 2003, an article titled *Microbiologists With Link to Race-Based Weapon Turning Up Dead*, appeared on the Internet on this date and stated:

"Dr. David Kelly - the biological warfare weapons specialist at the heart of the continuing political crisis for the British government - had links to three other top microbiologists whose deaths have left unanswered questions.

"One of the men he was in touch with was a former Russian defector, Kamovtjan Alibekov. When he arrived in America, he changed his name to Ken Alibek. He is now president of Hadron Advanced Biosystems - a company specializing in medicines against biological terrorist attacks. Kelly was himself, considering resigning from his senior post at the Ministry of Defense to work in America. Before his death, he had been discreetly headhunted by two companies. One was Hadron Advanced Biosystems, which has close ties to the Pentagon.

"Hadron describes itself as 'a company specializing in the development of technical solutions for the U.S. intelligence community.' Hadron also has links to William Patrick, who has five classified patents on the process of developing weaponized anthrax. He is a biowarfare consultant to both the Pentagon and the CIA. The other company is Regma Biotechnologies - one that Kelly helped its founder, Vladimir Pasechnik, to set up in Britain, arranging for it to have a laboratory at Porton Down, the country's chem-bio warfare defense establishment.

"Regma currently has a contract with the U.S. Navy for 'the diagnostic and therapeutic treatment of anthrax.' Kelly had told family friends he wanted to go to America so that he could obtain the specialized treatment his wife, Janice, requires. 'He also felt that working in the U.S. private sector would relieve him of the intense pressures which came with his government work,' said a colleague in the Ministry of Defense.

"The two American scientists he had worked with were Benito Que, 52, and Don Wiley, 57. Both microbiologists had been engaged in DNA sequencing that could provide 'a genetic marker based on genetic profiling.' The research could play an important role in developing weaponized pathogens to hit selected groups of humans - identifying them by race."[34]

A paper titled *The Secret World of Dr. David Kelly*, revealed even more:

"Dr. David Kelly, the top British microbiologist and whistleblower, had close links to the dark world of secret intelligence. Dr. Kelly was not employed by MI5 or MI6 – or any other intelligence service. But he enjoyed unique access to all the world's top spy agencies. In Britain, France, Germany, North America, Japan and Australia: they all consulted him. Into his office – room number 2/35 – in the Ministry of Defense Proliferation and Arms Control Secretariat in London, came emails and phone calls asking him for his help...He had been the only outsider allowed by the CIA to question a top Chinese defector, Colonel Xu Junping, head of the People Liberation Army Foreign Affairs Office, about China's bio-warfare program."[35]

Four days later, on November 20, 2003, scientist Robert Leslie Burghoff, 45, was killed by a hit-and-run driver that jumped the sidewalk and ploughed into him in the 1600 block of South Braeswood, Texas. At the time, he was studying outbreaks of viruses on board cruise ships.[36]

On May 5, 2004, a Russian scientist at a former Soviet biological weapons laboratory in Siberia died after an alleged accident with a needle laced with Ebola. Scientists and officials said the accident had raised concerns about safety and secrecy at the State Research Center of Virology and Biotechnology, known as Vector, which in Soviet times specialized in turning deadly viruses into biological weapons. Vector has been a leading recipient of aid in an American program.[37]

Two month later, specifically on July 3, 2004, Dr. Paul Norman, 52, of Salisbury, Wiltshire, England, was killed when the single-engine Cessna 206 aircraft he was piloting crashed in Devon. He was married with a 14-year-old son and a 20-year-old daughter, and was the chief scientist for chemical and biological defense at the Ministry of Defense's laboratory at Porton Down, Wiltshire. The crash site was examined by officials from the Air Accidents Investigation Branch, and the wreckage of the aircraft was removed from the site to the AAIB base at Farnborough. The crash was ruled accidental.[38]

Six weeks after that, on August 12, 2004, Professor John Clark, head of the science laboratory that created *Dolly* the "cloned" sheep, was found hanging in his holiday home. Prof. Clark led the Roslin Institute in Midlothian, one of the world's leading animal biotechnology research centers. He played a crucial role in creating the transgenic sheep that earned the institute worldwide fame. Professor Clark also founded three spin-off firms from Roslin: PPL Therapeutics; Rosgen; and Roslin BioMed.[39]

And as a new year dawned, still the deaths continued to pile up. On January 7, 2005, Korean Jeong H. Im, a retired research assistant professor at the University of Missouri and primarily a protein chemist, died of multiple stab wounds to the chest before firefighters found his body in the trunk of a burning car on the third level of the Maryland Avenue Garage. MUPD with the assistance of the Columbia Police Department and Columbia Fire Department were conducting a death investigation of the incident. A person of interest described as a male 6' – 6'2" wearing some type of mask, possibly a painters mask or drywall type mask, was seen in the area of the Maryland Avenue Garage.[40]

Then, in May 2005, Australian scientist David Banks, a 55-year old who was the principal scientists with Biosecurity Australia, a company described as being a "quarantine authority" by the Australian newspaper on May 9, was killed in an aircraft crash at Queensland. At the time, he was undertaking a "survey for the Northern Australia quarantine strategy."[41]

Were the deaths of so many microbiologists in such a clearly delineated period simply a bizarre coincidence? Or was something stranger afoot? In today's climate of uncertainty, it should of course be recognized that any suspicious deaths in the field of microbiology

– and specifically where many of the victims had links to the Intelligence services of a number of countries – might be an indication that a terrorist-based assassination squad was at work in at least *some* of the deaths.

It should not be overlooked, however, that many of those same microbiologists who met untimely ends were intimately linked with activities at Britain's chemical and biological defense establishment at Porton Down – to where, it has been claimed, alien bodies were taken following a UFO crash in North Wales in 1974, and as has already been demonstrated. And, as has *also* been demonstrated, one of the dead scientists, David Wynn-Williams, was a key player in the study of "primitive organisms in the Antarctic environment," and had conducted theoretical work on "the existence of some form of life on Mars." Not only that: Wynn-Williams had also had "an exchange of ideas with NASA," that: "explored the behavior of life forms on the frontiers of existence."

In an earlier chapter, the large body of highly intriguing data that ties the Majestic 12 group with the deaths of countless players implicated in the JFK assassination of 1963 was revealed. It is not beyond the realms of possibility that those with intimate knowledge of the alien virus may, in the period 2001-2005, have also have been targeted for termination by Majestic 12.

* * *

Chapter 21 Notes:

1. *The Mystery of the Dead Scientists: Coincidence or Conspiracy?* Ian Gurney, 2002.

2. *Times*, November 30, 2001.

3. *Guardian*, October 8, 2001.

4. *The Very Mysterious Deaths of Five Microbiologists*, Ian Gurney, 2001: www. caspro.com. *Harvard Biochemist Don C. Wiley Disappears in Memphis*, Sophie Wilkinson, *Chemical and Engineering News*, Vol. 79, No. 49, December 3, 2001: http://pubs.acs.org/cen/topstory/7949/7949notw5.html. For details of the Japan Prize award made to Wiley as a result of his discoveries of how the immune system protects humans from infections, see: www.japanprize.jp/e_1999(s&w).htm.

5. Ibid.

6. *Dead Scientists and Microbiologists – Master List*, Mark J. Harper. See: http://rense.com/general62/list.htm.

7. *Scientist Found Slain in his Loudoun Home*, Maria Glod, *Washington Post*, December 12, 2001.

8. *SARS Virus First Discovered in 1998*, Ian Gurney. See: www.rense.com/general35/sarrs.htm.

9. *Nature*, January 2001.

10. *Times*, November 15, 1998.

11. *Va. Scientist Was Killed With Sword: Three Friends Interested in Occult and Witchcraft, Friends Say*, Maria Glod & Josh White, *Washington Post*, December 14, 2001.

12. *Body Carrying Missing Scientist's ID Found in Mississippi River*, www.courttv.com. December 21, 2001.

13. *Biologist Disappears; FBI Interested*, Associated Press, November 28, 2001.

14. *Wiley's Death Caused by an Accidental Fall*, Steve Ritter, *Chemical and Engineering News*, Volume 80, No. 3, January 21, 2002. See: http://pubs.acs.org/cen/topstory/8003/8003notw7.html.

15. *List of Dead Scientists*, Steve Quayle. See: www.stevequayle.com/dead_scientists/UpdatedDeadScientists2.html.

16. *Daughter Charged in Slaying of Scientist*, *Washington Post*, February 2, 2002.

17. Ibid.

18. *Strange Cluster of Microbiologists' Deaths Under the Microscope*, Alanna Mitchell, Simon Cooper & Carolyn Abraham, *Globe and Mail*, May 4, 2002. See: www.mold-survivor.com/microbioligists.htm.

19. *Times*, February 13, 2002.

20. *12 Microbiologists Killed Since September 11th Attacks*, *Flame Online News*, Spring 2002. See: www.fantompowa.net/Flame/news_brief_issue_ten.htm.

21. *Microbiologist Death Toll Mounts as Connections to Dynocorp, Hadron, Promis Software & Disease Research Emerge*, Michael Davidson & Michael C. Ruppert, From the Wilderness Publications. See: www.copvcia.com.

22. *A Career in Microbiology can be Harmful to Your Health – Especially Since 9-11*, Michael Davidson, From the Wilderness Publications. See: www.copvcia.com. Also see: http://www.rense.com/general20/car.htm.

23. *Guardian*, February 15, 2002.

24. *Space Daily*, February 24, 2002.

25. *Pizza Delivery May Have Been Ambush: Suspect Later Found Dead*, Sean Webby & Lisa Krieger, *San Jose Mercury News*, February 28, 2002. See: http://911research.wtc7.net/cache/post911/attacks/mercurynews_holzmayer.htm.

26. *Air Crash Victim Was Weapons Expert*, *The Scotsman*. See: http://news.scotsman.com/latest.cfm?id=3155120.

27. *Obituary*, *Times*, March 27, 2002.

28. *Space Bug Specialist Killed in Crash*, BBC, March 28, 2002.

29. *Dead Scientists*, Gordon Thomas, www.stevequayle.com/News.alert/03_Disease/031121.dead.scientists.html. See also: www.gordonthomas.ie?DEADSCIENTISTS.html.

30. *Updated List of Scientists Dead in Suspicious Circumstances Since Autumn 2001*, Global Elite. See: www.globalelite.org/modules.php?op=modload&name=News&file=article&sid=390&mode=thread&order=0&thold=0.

31. *Biological Weapons Expert With a Reputation for Thoroughness*, Guardian, July 19, 2003.

32. Ibid.

33. *Norwich Evening News*, September 9, 2003.

34. *Microbiologists With Link to Race-Based Weapon Turning Up Dead*, Gordon Thomas, American Free Press, August 9, 2003. See: www.americanfreepress.net/ 08_09_03/Microbiologists_With/microbiologists_with.html.

35. *The Secret World of Dr. David Kelly*, Gordon Thomas. See: http://www. rumormillnews.com/cgi-bin/archive.cgi?noframes;read=35765.

36. *Another Dead Scientist: Composite Released in Fatal Hit and Run*, *Houston Chronicle*, December 12, 2003.

37. *Russian Scientist Dies in Ebola Accident at Former Weapons Lab*, Judith Miller, *New York Times*, May 25, 2004. See: www.nytimes.com/2004/05/25/international/ europe/25ebol.html?ex=1400817600&en=1c279526fb60a291&ei=5007&partner= USERLAND.

38. *Air Crash Victim was Weapons Expert*, Sam Mardsen, PA News, July 4, 2004. See: http://news.scotsman.com/latest.cfm?id=3155120.

39. *John Clark: Pioneering Scientist Whose Entrepreneurial Skills Paved the Way for Dolly the Sheep*, Ian Wilmut, *Guardian*, August 25, 2004. See: http://education. guardian.co.uk/obituary/story/0,,1290063,00.html.

40. *Food for Thought – Several Dozen Microbiologists & Scientists Dead Under "Suspicious Circumstances" Since 2001*. See: www.organicconsumers.org/corp/ suspicious012805.cfm.

41. *Victim Lauded as "Brilliant Scientist,"* John Kerin, *The Australian*. See: www. theaustralian.news.com.au/common/story_page/0,5744,15223153%255E2702,00.html.

Chapter 22
The Blue Boy Revelations, 2006

In addition to the data that has surfaced suggesting an extraterrestrial link to the bacteriological, biological and viral angle of the Roswell controversy, it is intriguing to note that these same issues surface in a number of other distinctly-terrestrial theories pertaining to Roswell, all of which emanate from whistleblowers and sources within the world of intelligence, military and government.

For example, Albert Collins – who had worked in the early-to-mid 1940s at Berkeley and at Occidental College on the Manhattan Project and who died on New Year's Eve, 1990 – was interviewed by Timothy Cooper and advised Cooper that during the War, "...New Mexico was abuzz with unusual research into nuclear powered aircraft and bizarre biological experiments."[1]

Similarly, Cooper interviewed a nurse who had served within the Medical Laboratory at Los Alamos in approximately the same period. As Cooper recalled: "She casually mentioned to me over coffee that 'bodies' were being flown to Los Alamos periodically from late 1945 to sometime in 1947. I asked her if she had seen these 'bodies' and she said no, but others had. I asked her where these 'bodies' were coming from. She said she did not know, but it was rumored that they were experiments for biological and nuclear medicine research. She thought they may have come from Japan after the war, She said they were small bodies with deformed heads and limbs. The eyes were abnormally big, she was told. She said they were being flown in on special transport planes equipped with refrigerator units to keep the bodies from decomposing."[2]

On broadly a similar track, in 1991 – in his last-but-one *Status Report* on crashed UFOs – the late Leonard Stringfield revealed that a concerned informant had contacted him "to relate that he had been reliably informed of some new and nagging information that is in concurrence with the early, critical days of the foo-fighters, ghost rockets, green fireballs and the New Mexican saucer crashes, all of which may have a German World War II connection. One item of note was that a saucer had crashed in July of 1947 that had ties with a U.S. 'biological experiment'. Incongruously, another item according to my source, made reference to a retrieved saucer with artifacts exhibiting 'paleo-Hebraic' inscriptions. But, the gist of his revelations was that the reported crashes of UFOs with 'alien; bodies in 1947 was the beginning of a colossal cover-up to hide secret U.S. rocket experiments."[3]

And on a practically identical path, Nick Redfern's 2005 book *Body Snatchers in the Desert* revealed that he had been informed by a variety of elderly and retired Intelligence sources that the crashed UFO stories of 1947 were carefully orchestrated covers to hide something else – and, arguably, something more disturbing. Namely, the fact that American authorities had done a Faustian deal with elements of Japan's notorious Unit 731, that undertook all manner of terrible biological warfare research on human subjects at the height of the Second World War. According to Redfern's sources, those same Unit 731 elements were given permission to continue their research in the United States in the post-War era; and it was the crash of several experimental platforms, aboard which were guinea-pig crews supplied by Unit 731 that led to tales of UFOs and alien bodies having been found in the New Mexico desert.[4]

And, incredibly, there is *another* explanation for Roswell that has a biological warfare angle to it. And it is an explanation that has not publicly surfaced, at least, until now. In 2002, after Timothy Cooper had sold all of his UFO files to Robert Wood, Nick Redfern spent a week ensconced in an Orange County, California motel room carefully logging every one of the items contained within Cooper's vast document collection. One of those items was an 8-page extract from a longer document titled *UFO Reports and Classified Projects: The CIA Perspective.*[5]

Provided to Cooper by a source at the CIA that he referred to as the "Blue Boy," it is this document that details a further theory that links Roswell with down-to-earth (as opposed to extraterrestrial) biological warfare activities.

The document appears to be a draft of a briefing paper, and provides a concise history of the role of the United States' Government and military with respect to UFOs. According to the document, under the heading "HISTORICAL PERSPECTIVE":

"Since 1969, the United States Government has taken the official position that unidentified flying objects (UFO) do not exist and do not pose a threat to national security. This position is based on the conclusions reached by Project BLUE BOOK, the official United States Air Force UFO study program which began in early 1948 and was terminated in December 1969. According to General Charles P. Cabell USAF, and Deputy Director of Central Intelligence, this view was not accepted until the successful moon landing of Apollo 11 and several scientific studies. In January 1953, the CIA conducted its own review of the UFO phenomenon known as the Robertson Panel chaired by Dr. H.P. Robertson, a CIA employee, and its conclusions are mirrored by Project BLUE BOOK files. The only threat was of UFO reports, not UFOs. Freedom of Information Act responses by the CIA state that the only involvement by the CIA ended after the Robertson Panel submitted its report. Since then, the Agency has not authorized any intelligence collection project nor has received a mandate from the National Security Council to continue UFO intelligence and operations at the scientific level. A review of declassified CIA and NSA intelligence documents suggest that this may not be the case which in either event, a re-examination of all CIA and NSA intelligence documents dealing with UFOs since 1953 is warranted. I might also add that continued reporting of UFOs and related phenomenon across the United States and foreign countries, most noticeably in China, Korea, Australia, and Russia would require some form of surveillance as was done by the CIA up until 1991. Based on past CIA conclusions, a positive identification was never reached.

"The need for an American central intelligence and Coordinator of Information (COI) to advise the president of impending political and military developments among hostile governments arose in pre and post-World War II era through the efforts of Sir William S. Stephenson of British Intelligence, General William J. Donovan, and President Roosevelt. In this case, technological advantages in unconventional aircraft and weapons systems of Nazi Germany became the focus of Military Intelligence Division (MID), Army Intelligence (G-2), Office of Naval Intelligence (ONI) and COI (later Director of the Office of Strategic Services) shortly after Germany's capitulation in May 1945. Interest in securing all available rocket and aircraft technology was generated from earlier reports of incursions over the United States by yet unidentified aerial objects believed to have been advanced aircraft from a foreign power. This technical intelligence collection effort was carried out through a vast and comprehensive man hunt known as Operation PAPER CLIP whose purpose was to bring back to the United States leading German rocket and aircraft scientists and engineers to begin work on military defense projects while preventing the wholesale recruitment of remaining German scientists by Soviet military intelligence still in Germany.

"During the war OSS technical intelligence had secured reliable information that German advances in high speed, high altitude, long range fighters and bombers were all-wing, circular-shaped employing innovative airfoil designs capable of eliminating boundary layer restrictions achieved by their V-2 ballistic missile. Coupled with the fact that American and British intelligence were gravely concerned that such aerial machines could deliver atomic bombs anywhere in Europe and on the continental United States given the fact that Germany's atomic bomb program had a two-year head start of the Army's Manhattan Project. I January 1948, the Department of the Army circulated a classified intelligence document to all concerned intelligence chiefs that 'the German High Command indicated a definite interest in the Horten type of flying wing and were about to embark on a rigorous campaign to develop such aircraft toward the end of the war.' The report suggested that the Gotha manufacturing plant was the proposed site where such aircraft were to be built and warned: "This plant is now in the hands of the Russians." The report also indicated that such information was highly desirable and requested any additional intelligence on 'aircraft whose shape approximate that of an oval, disc, or saucer', including 'boundary layer control method by suction, blowing, or a combination of both" and "special controls for effective maneuverability at very slow speeds or extremely high altitudes.'

"The OSS had information regarding such developments as early as 1943 based on transcripts taken from the Flying Wing Seminar given by the Horten brothers at Bonn, Germany, on April 14, 1943, in which the newly created Central Intelligence Agency had classified and did not disseminate in 1947. British intelligence also had this information and provided the CIA technical specifications for delta-shaped, right-angled triangle, tailless and semi-circular aircraft. Other specifications included designs for 'boomerang' shapes under development in Britain, Canada, and the United States which are enumerated in General Nathan F. Twining's September

23, 1947 Air Materiel Command 'Flying Saucer' report to Air Intelligence headquarters after numerous UFO sightings subsided during the previous summer.

"During the ensuing 50-year development efforts of the CIA and defense contractors these designs evolved into today's delta-shaped stealth aircraft and uninhabited reconnaissance drones. Some of the reported UFO sightings of the 1960's and 1970's were classified CIA and Air Force satellites developed under high security and for national security reasons were not divulged publicly which fueled considerable speculation among the news media and civilian UFO researchers. One basic rule of military secrecy: You don't allow a rival service to gain control over a new area of operations. Two days after the Air Materiel Command released its "flying saucer" report, the Air Staff instructed the AMC to evaluate a Research and Development (RAND) study on the feasibility of putting earth orbiting reconnaissance satellites about the earth based on the opinions of German rocket experts employing state-of-the-art photographic techniques and optical imagery."

The "Blue Boy" then turned his (or perhaps her) attention to Roswell:

"Another rule of secrecy was: You always camouflage your operations from prying eyes. It was not widely known to many that the Air Force and navy were conducting classified rocket-launched reconnaissance payloads from White Sands, New Mexico, which failed to reach orbiting altitudes and subsequently crashed off range and generated considerable public interest in the United States and abroad. As part of a top secret Air Force atomic weapons detection project called MOGUL involving radiation dispersal in the atmosphere, selected monitoring sites across the United States were not acknowledged to by the Air Force and Central Intelligence Group (CIG) and as a result, wreckage from one of the payloads was accidentally discovered by a sheep rancher not far from the Air Force's Roswell Army Air Field.

"Also, another fact was not widely known among military intelligence was that CIG had planned to utilize artificial meteor strikes as decoy devices ejected from V-2 warheads at 60 miles above the earth to record dispersal trajectories and possible psychological warfare weapons against the Soviets in the advent of a war in Europe. One of the projects underway at that time incorporated re-entry vehicles containing radium and other radioactive materials combined with *biological warfare agents* [Italics mine] developed by I.G. Farben for use against allied assault forces in Normandy in 1944. When a V-2 warhead impacted near the town of Corona, New Mexico, on July 4, 1947, the warhead did not explode and it and the deadly cargo lay exposed to the elements which forced the Armed Forces Special Weapons Project to close off the crash site and a cover story was immediately put out that what was discovered was the remains of a radar tracking target suspended by balloons. In 1994 and again in 1995, the Air Force published what it considered the true account of what lay behind the Roswell story but omitted the radiological warhead data for obvious reasons. It may also be pointed out here that this kind of experiment was very similar to those conducted by the Atomic Energy Commission and the military in the late 1940's. It was known in the CIA that the Soviets were conducting the same kind of radiological and *biological warfare experiments* [Italics mine] in the early 1950's after their successful detonation of a [sic] atomic bomb based on stolen documents and materials from Los Alamos forwarded to Moscow by communist espionage agents in the United States."

Turning away from Roswell, the Blue Boy continued thus:

"Prior to the August 1949 Soviet atomic bomb experiment, Army, Navy, and FBI intelligence officers had classified flying saucer sightings in the United States as TOP SECRET as indicated in a January 31, 1949 FBI memorandum which located Los Alamos as an active area of investigation by USAF Office of Special Investigations and described the UFOs as an 'unconventional type without wings" and resembled 'rocket ship' configurations similar to the German V-2. Almost a year prior to the United States 1947 Flying Saucer wave, State Department military Attaches reported similar sightings over Sweden and other parts of northern Europe and it was assumed that the 'ghost rocket' phenomenon was of Soviet origin and was in response to U.S. atmospheric tests of atomic weapons in the Pacific.

"In March 1949, the CIA did a review of flying saucer sighting data conducted by the Office of Scientific Intelligence (OSI) and based upon submitted reports from Air Force Project SIGN did not concur with the extraterrestrial hypothesis reached by project officers. Dr. Stone of OSI drew other conclusions suggesting that 'many of the objects may be free meteorological sounding balloons' and that if the sightings were classified projects they would not be launched from many locations across the United States and would be 'closely coordinated with USAF or commercial designers.' Stone also ruled out foreign aircraft reconnaissance flights because of the great distances involved and 'guided aircraft' lacked the range required for such flights and was beyond technical capabilities of any government at that time. The CIA had the best intelligence available on Soviet capabilities and for security reasons would not discuss classified 'secret weapons' programs that were under development within secret establishments in the U.S. which would be compromised if Stone made some obscure disclosure to Project SIGN staff officers. And, for the same reasons General Twining did not elaborate on 'physical evidence' for recovered wreckage of failed rocket launches conducted at White Sands.

"The CIA paid particular attention to reports originating out of New Mexico as indicated in a April 24, 1949 CIA intelligence report detailing a theodolite track of a 'white spherical object' that was traveling too fast to be a balloon described as 'an ellipsoid about 2 $\frac{1}{2}$:1 slenderness ratio' at an altitude of 60 miles with a course heading that would have covered White Sands, Holloman Air Force Base and Los Alamos. At this point, the CIA did not comment on such reports and drew no conclusions without disclosing the existence of classified programs to un-authorized agencies.

"SCIENTIFIC INTELLIGENCE: UFO Identification And Analysis: The sharing of scientific intelligence between British and American agencies in missile and atomic weapons research was instrumental in defeating Japan and Germany in World War II. In exchange of aviation advances and electronics, the OSS supplied technical and scientific intelligence and kept General Groves appraised of German scientific activities in atomic fission. The use of atomic weapons in war and the spread of scientific knowledge was anticipated and magnified by the Soviet penetration of U.S. atomic secrets, enlarging the horror of a nuclear Pearl Harbor. With the growing possibility that some UFO sighting reports collected by the CIG were Soviet devices, Admiral Sidney Souers in 1946 undertook the task of coordinating scientific intelligence with the Office of Scientific Research and Development and directed the Central Planning Staff to look into the problem of surprise attack by unconventional means and recruited Dr. H. P. Robertson as his scientific consultant and established the Interdepartmental..."

The remaining pages of the document were not found within the files of Tim Cooper. And while the data imparted by the Blue Boy concerning the Roswell crash and biological warfare is certainly provocative, can it be substantiated?

With respect to the theory that a Mogul balloon was responsible for creating the legend of the UFO crash at Roswell, the United States Air Force firmly embraced, and still does embrace, this particular explanation. Mogul was a project that utilized balloons to carry radar reflectors and acoustic sensors aloft for the purpose of determining the state of Soviet nuclear weapons research.[6]

As far as the reference to I.G. Farben is concerned, this too is provocative: I. G. Farben was the company that made the Zyklon-B gas that was utilized in the Nazi death camps of the Second World War. Indeed, at the height of its production in 1944, I.G. Farben ran a slave labor plant at Auschwitz using no less than 83,000 people. Arguably any "biological" work undertaken at White Sands involving people allied to I.G. Farben would have created intense controversy and would have been subject to stringent security measures – particularly if a V-2 rocket with such a "deadly cargo" had indeed strayed off course and crashed near the town of Corona.[7]

And it is quite true that a wealth of tests of captured Nazi V-2 rockets *were* undertaken at the White Sands Missile Range, New Mexico in the period 1946 to 1952. Indeed, in total, sixty-seven V-2 rockets were assembled and tested at the Range, and ultimately provided the United States with valuable experience in the assembly, pre-flight testing, handling, fueling, launching, and tracking of large missiles. The scientific experiments conducted aboard the rockets also yielded significant information about the upper atmosphere. One series of tests, the Blossom Project, was responsible for undertaking the first biological experiments in space.[8]

Interestingly, in its July 1994 document titled *Report of Air Force Research Regarding the Roswell Incident*, the Air Force *did* address the question of whether or not a V-2 rocket was to blame for the monumental fuss at Roswell:

"A crashed or errant missile, usually described as a captured German V-2 or one of its variants, is sometimes set forth as a possible explanation for the debris recovered near Roswell. Since much of this testing done at nearby White Sands was secret at the time, it would be logical to assume that the government would handle any missile mishap under tight security, particularly if the mishap occurred on private land. From the records reviewed by the Air Force, however, there was nothing located to suggest that this was the case. Although the bulk of remaining testing records are under the control of the U.S. Army, the subject has also been very well documented over the years within Air Force records. There would be no reason to keep such information classified today. The USAF found no indicators or even hints that a missile was involved in this matter."[9]

As far as can be determined, the Air Force was playing it straight with regard to the V-2 theory: the table below provides a comprehensive listing of all of the V-2 launches from White Sands and none correlates with the approximated dates of the Roswell affair. Abbreviations of the organizations and terms cited within the table are listed directly below.[10]

APL: Applied Physics Lab (John Hopkins University)
ARDC: Air Research and Development Command
GE: General Electric Company
NIH: National Institute of Health
NRL: Naval Research Laboratory
PU: Palmer Physics Laboratory (Princeton University)
SCEL: Signal Corps Engineering Laboratory (University of Michigan)
UAR: Upper Atmosphere Research

V2#	Date	Time (Local)	Altitude (Miles)	Agency	Experiments
1	15 Mar 46				Static firing-no UAR experiments
2	16 Apr 46	1447	3.4	GE	Cosmic radiation (APL)
3	10 May 46	1415	70	GE	Cosmic radiation (APL)
4	29 May 46	1410	69.7	GE	Cosmic radiation (APL)
5	13 Jun 46	1640	73	GE	Solar radiation, ionosphere (NRL)
6	28 Jun 46	1203	67	NRL	Cosmic radiation, solar radiation, pressure, temp
7	9 Jul 46	1230	83.5	GE	Cosmic radiation, ionosphere (NRL)
8	19 Jul 46	1211	3	GE	Ionosphere (NRL)
9	30 Jul 46	1240	100.4	APL	Cosmic radiation, ionosphere (NRL); bio (Harvard)
10	15 Aug 46	1100	4	PU	Cosmic radiation
11	22 Aug 46	1015	0	ARDC	Pressure, density, ionosphere, sky brightness
12	10 Oct 46	1102	108	NRL	Cosmic & solar radiation, pressure, temp, bio
13	24 Oct 46	1218	65	APL	Cosmic & solar radiation, winds, photography
14	7 Nov 46	1331	0.2	PU	Cosmic radiation
15	21 Nov 46	1000	63	ARDC	Pressure, temp, ionosphere, sky brightness
16	5 Dec 46	1308	95	NRL	Cosmic & solar radiation, pressure, temp, photo
17	17 Dec 46	2218	114	APL	Cosmic radiation, meteorites; bio (NIH)
18	10 Jan 47	1413	72.2	NRL	Cosmic radiation
19	23 Jan 47	1722	31	GE	No UAR experiments
20	20 Feb 47	1116	68	ARDC	Pressure, ionosphere, sky brightness, bio, photo
21	7 Mar 47	1123	101	NRL	Cosmic radiation, pressure, temp, photo, bio
22	1 Apr 47	1310	80.3	APL	Cosmic & solar radiation, photo
23	8 Apr 47	1713	63.5	APL	Cosmic & solar radiation, photo
24	17 Apr 47	1422	88.5	GE	Pressure, temp (SCEL)
25	2 Apr 48	0640	89.5	SCEL	Density, pressure, temp, composition, cosmic & solar radiation (NRL)
26	15 May 47	1604	84	NRL	Cosmic & solar radiation, temp, ionosphere, photo
27	9 Oct 47	1215	97	GE	Solar radiation (NRL); pressure, composition (SCEL)
28	8 Dec 47	1442	65	ARDC	Pressure, temp, solar radiation, sky brightness, ionosphere, photo
29	10 Jul 47	1218	10	NRL	Cosmic radiation, pressure, temp, ionosphere, biological (Harvard)

30	29 Jul 47	0555	99.9	APL	Cosmic & solar radiation, photo
31	8 Dec 49	1214	81	ARDC	Composition, ionosphere, meteorites, solar radiation, sky brightness
32	16 Sep 49	1619	2.6	ARDC	Composition, ionosphere, meteorites, solar & cosmic radiation, sky brightness, biological
33	2 Sep 48	1800	93.6	SCEL	Density, pressure, temp, composition
34	22 Jan 48	1312	99	NRL	Cosmic radiation, pressure, temp, ionosphere
35	27 May 48	0716	86.8	APL	Cosmic & solar radiation, photo, composition (SCEL)
36	6 Feb 48	1015	69	GE	No UAR experiments
37	11 Jun 48	0322	38.7	ARDC	Pressure, temp, composition, ionosphere, sky brightness, solar radiation
38	19 Apr 48	1254	34.8	NRL	Cosmic & solar radiation, pressure, temp
39	19 Mar 48	1610	3.4	GE	Magnetic field, composition, winds, temp (SCEL)
40	26 Jul 48	1103	54	APL	Cosmic radiation, photo, pressure, temp
41	21 Mar 49	2343	83	ARDC	Ionosphere, sky brightness, solar radiation, composition, photo
42	9 Dec 48	0908	67.4	SCEL	Winds, pressure, temp; solar radiation (NRL)
43	5 Aug 48	0507	103	NRL	Cosmic & solar radiation, temp, pressure, ionosphere, photo
44	18 Nov 48	1534	90.3	GE	Bio (Harvard), solar radiation (NRL), composition (SCEL)
45	28 Jan 49	1020	37.2	NRL	Cosmic & solar radiation, pressure, temp, photo
46	5 May 49	0815	5.5	GE	Solar radiation (NRL)
47	14 Jun 49	1535	83	ARDC	Cosmic & solar radiation, temp, pressure, ionosphere, photo
48	17 Feb 49	1000	62.5	APL	Cosmic & solar radiation, photo (NRL); composition (SCEL); bio
49	29 Sep 49	0958	93.7	NRL	Cosmic & solar radiation, meteorites, pressure
50	11 Apr 49	1505	54.2	SCEL	Temp, composition, solar radiation (NRL); bio
51	31 Aug 50	1009	84.8	ARDC	Ionosphere, meteorites, sky brightness, density, bio
52	28 Jun 51	1443	3.6	ARDC	Solar radiation, air glow, sky brightness
53	17 Feb 50	1101	92.4	NRL	Cosmic & solar radiation, pressure, temp
54	18 Jan 51	1314	1.0	NRL	Cosmic & solar radiation
55	14 Jun 51	- - - - -	0	NRL	Solar & cosmic radiation
56	18 Nov 49	0803	77	SCEL	Winds, composition, temp; cosmic radiation (APL); solar radiation (NRL)
57	8 Mar 51	2016	1.9	ARDC	Composition, air glow, sky brightness, ionosphere
58	- - - - -	- - - - -	- - - - -	- - - - -	This rocket never fired
59	20 May 52	0906	64.3	SCEL	Composition, photography

60	29 Oct 51	1404	87.6	SCEL	Pressure, temp
61	26 Oct 50	1602	5	NRL	No UAR experiments
TF-1	22 Aug 51	1200	132.6		No UAR experiments
TF-2	- - - - -	- - - - -	- - - - -	- - - - -	See V-2 Rocket No. 59
TF-3	22 Aug 52	0033	48.5	NRL	Composition, pressure, magnetic field, solar radiation; cosmic radiation (NIH); sky brightness (ARDC)
TF-4	- - - - -	- - - - -	- - - - -	- - - - -	Never fired
TF-5	19 Sep 52	0849	16.8	SCEL	Temp, composition; cosmic radiation (NIH)
GE Spec.	20 Nov 47	1647	16.6	GE	No UAR experiments

Whatever the true nature of the Roswell events of July 1947, it is a curious and intriguing fact that *all* of those sources that imparted the data and documentation to Leonard Stringfield, to Nick Redfern, to Timothy Cooper, and to Robert Wood that is specifically cited within this chapter, suggested that Roswell was connected with biological experimentation. However, the fact so many conflicting theories were provided to the above-researchers is something that ensures that the question of whether that biological experimentation was alien-originated or human-originated, remains both unanswered and confusing. Some might argue that, all along, that was the exact intent of the shadowy whistleblowers that provided these accounts.

* * *

Chapter 22 Notes:

1. *The White Sands Proving Ground UFO Incidents of 1947: A Preliminary Report*, Timothy Cooper (unpublished). *The Grizzly*, January 10, 2001. *UFO Crash Retrievals: The Inner Sanctum, Status Report VI*, Leonard H. Stringfield, 1994, published privately.

2. *UFO Crash Retrievals: The Inner Sanctum, Status Report VI*, Leonard H. Stringfield, 1994, published privately.

3. Ibid.

4. *Body Snatchers in the Desert: The Horrible Truth at the Heart of the Roswell Story*, Nick Redfern, Paraview-Pocket, 2005.

5. *UFO Reports and Classified Projects: The CIA Perspective.* Source: *The Blue Boy* (date of document unknown). *Inventory of Tim Cooper's UFO Files* by Nick Redfern, for Dr. Robert M. Wood & Ryan Wood, 2002.

6. *Report of Air Force Research Regarding the Roswell Incident*, Colonel Richard L. Weaver, United States Air Force, 1994. *Results of a Search for Records Concerning the 1947 Crash Near Roswell, New Mexico*, General Accounting Office, July 28, 1995. *The Roswell Report: Fact vs. Fiction in the New Mexico Desert*, Colonel Richard L. Weaver, United States Air Force, 1995. *The Roswell Report: Case Closed*, Captain James McAndrew, United States Air Force, 1997.

7. *Wall Street and the Rise of Hitler*, Antony C. Sutton: http://reformed-theology.org/html/books/wall_street/chapter_02.htm.

8. *V-2 Rocket*: www.wsmr.army.mil/pao/FactSheets/V2/v-2.htm.

9. *Report of Air Force Research Regarding the Roswell Incident*, Colonel Richard L. Weaver, United States Air Force, 1994.

10. *V-2 Firing Tables*: www.wsmr.army.mil/pao/FactSheets/V2/v-2tab.htm.

Chapter 23
The Area 51 Revelations, 2006

The following account comes from "John," who was born in Bloomington, Minnesota and served from 1948 to 1959 in the New York Police Department.[1] He stated that from the latter part of 1957 until January 1958 he and a number of police colleagues were tangentially involved in an FBI undercover operation to locate and arrest a Soviet spy-ring that was believed to be targeting and infiltrating a defense-related company in the city. John stated that it was suspected that someone within the company had been compromised by the Soviets, although this was never ultimately proven, and that this was the area that the Police were involved in, mainly because the compromised individual also had suspected links, again that were never ultimately proven, with a money-laundering "Mob"-based operation.

John stated further that arrests of Soviet citizens were made in connection with this operation, along with two American citizens. Partly as a result of his involvement in this operation and also because he was very ambitious, John says, that after leaving the New York Police, he was involved in additional work with the FBI that began in late 1959 and that continued – albeit sporadically - until October 1970.

John declined to describe fully the nature of his work with the FBI, but stated that it centered upon Soviet attempts to obtain classified files of an intelligence-, military-, and defense-nature. In July 1970, John was approached and offered a position with Wackenhut. He began working with Wackenhut in December 1970; and in February 1971 was asked if he would be interested in doing contract work for an arm of the Intelligence community that, he was told, "operated out of Nevada."

John was told that the pay would be very good, that the contract would be for one-year only, and the work would ensure that he would develop contacts within the intelligence community and would be extremely good for his future career. Having spoken with his bosses at Wackenhut, who strongly urged him to accept the job, John elected to accept the position.

John says that he was then subjected to a very stringent background check and was interviewed on four occasions – twice by representatives of an unnamed agency, once by someone who identified himself as a representative of the National Security Agency, and once by a former senior colleague at the FBI. The interviews were apparently satisfactory, and he began working at the location in Nevada on April 13, 1971.

John stated that part of the reason for accepting the posting was because, as a bachelor, he would be required to be on-base for twenty-seven-day stints at a time and would then return to Las Vegas for three or four days - depending on whether there were thirty or thirty-one days in the month. This, John said, would not necessarily be ideal for a married man, and he speculated that his bachelor status might have had something to do with the reason why he, specifically, was approached.

John states that the location where he worked was within the confines of the location now openly described as Area 51, Nevada. He would be flown both into and out of Area 51 in a small aircraft (usually a Cessna) along with three colleagues who he got to know well. There were blinds on the windows of the aircraft that had to be pulled down after take off from Las Vegas and that had to remain pulled down after landing. Upon landing at Area 51, everyone was required to put on a pair of goggles. These were not normal goggles, however.

The goggles had split lenses, like bi-focal glasses, and the top section was so thick that it prevented any effective vision and all that one could make out was a vague blur and nothing else. The only part of the goggles that could be seen through with any real effectiveness was a small section at the bottom of each lens. As a result, the wearer was forced to look only at the floor and his shoes to see where he was going. This was without any doubt, he stated, done to ensure that the person wearing the goggles was unable to make out the details of anything that they might inadvertently view on the base. They would be guided to a bus, again with blacked-out windows, and would then be driven for a few minutes to another location. On getting off the bus they were still required to wear the goggles on and were be directed to their place of work.

The location was a small concrete building approximately sixty-feet square. Security at the door was very stringent, John adds. On entering the building, which was simply a bare concrete room, he took off his goggles and viewed two things only: the entrance to an elevator and a concrete staircase. Sometimes, John, said, they would enter the elevator and sometimes they would use the staircase to descend the two-floors to their place of work. He had no idea what work was carried out on the first floor. On arriving at the second floor, there was a second, rigorous security screening procedure - a procedure that would follow every time he returned to the base after his three-to-four days back in Las Vegas. However, he recalled that after passing the second security screening he entered, via a large pair of thick, metal doors, a long corridor that was around 180-feet in length, and that had six doors leading off it – three on the left and three on the right. His office was the second on the right and it had a simple lock, identical to a standard lock on a house door.

John was directed to his office and given a briefing by three men. He was advised that the location where he would be working was classed as the History Department. It was related to John that the overall location he was working at (he says that the term Area 51 was *never* used during his employment there) was involved in the development of prototype and radical aircraft, biological warfare, chemical warfare, exotic weaponry and "something else."

That something else, John was told, was research into "things that had happened in the 1940s." It transpired that John and his colleagues were being employed as custodians of historical files on all of the above subjects – files that would from time to time be required by base employees in the nature of their work. John stated that there were three reasons, and three reasons only, why the files that he was the custodian of were ever accessed by anyone:

- On a regular basis scientific personnel would require access to the files as part of their work;
- The files would be used to brief new employees to the base if it was required; and
- There would be regular (and random) checks on the part of security personnel to ensure that all of the files were present.

According to John, the files were never allowed out of his office: the briefings for new personnel were conducted in his office by a four-man team. And if anyone needed to access the files as part of their work, they would have to make pencil notes from the files.

Those pencil notes had to be exclusively written on a bright orange paper that John had never seen before – or since. He speculates that perhaps this curious color could somehow have been picked up on security screenings if anyone tried to smuggle the paper out of the base.

John stated that one of his colleagues was the custodian of historical files on prototype aircraft at the base, another was custodian of historical files on exotic weaponry being developed there, and another was responsible for historical files on biological weaponry. John was the custodian of historical files on UFOs. He says that the first two weeks were spent receiving briefings from personnel on the base; and, because he was the custodian, he was allowed to read the files, and acquaint himself with the file names in a fashion that would allow him to identify them with ease if they were requested by visitors to his office.

John stated that the files covered the period 1943 to 1968. He added that, "like most people" he knew from "magazines and television" that the Air Force had investigated UFO sightings via its Project Blue Book but also knew that the project had been closed down a few years earlier. However, he elaborated that the files in his office told a far more in-depth – and sinister - story of official, and highly classified, UFO investigations in the United States. He stressed several times that he never saw any UFOs, aliens or alien bodies at Area 51 – only documents that dealt with alleged UFO crashes in the 1940s. However, the fact that there were people who required access to the files led him to believe that there were crashed UFOs and alien bodies on the base.

According to John: in 1947, an incredibly well hidden group was established deep within the confines of the American intelligence community that was known as Majestic. In the late 1960s (John is unsure if it was in 1968 or 1969) Majestic was reorganized. Instead of each of the various agencies (such as the NSA, the CIA, etc.) playing a part in the Majestic program and having their own files and their own input, all of the work, data and documents were transferred to a centralized body that operated out of what is now known as Area 51.

Interestingly, the allegation that there was a big reorganization of the Majestic group in 1968 or 1969 is something that was also claimed to Timothy Cooper in 1997. On July 9 of that year Cooper received a copy of a document that has become known as the *Important Memo* - the reason being that the word "Important" is stamped across its pages. Cooper's source of the document that became known as "S-1," is described in the document, in his own words, as having an, "association with the Intelligence community."

According to the data related to Cooper by S-1: "MJ-12 does not exist as a government intelligence entity. It ceased to exist in 1969 and became a private concern financed by big money and big science. In 1969, President Nixon was briefed by MJ-12 on all aspects of UFO activity and the EBE [Extraterrestrial Biological Entity] problem since 1947. Fearing possible leaks within his NSC [National Security Council] and national security advisor Kissinger, Nixon approved a Special Classified Executive Order that required the U.S. Intelligence Community to purge all references to MJ-12 in the UFO files."

Ryan Wood expanded upon background data concerning S-1: "Source S-1 got his name because the return address and many of the documents had a '-1' on the first page. The return address is Las Vegas, Nevada, and he mailed information on three different occasions during the summer [of 1997] with postmarks of Big Bear Lake and Fort Meade, Maryland with return addresses of Las Vegas and a suspiciously torn return address. The materials supplied included some typed personal cover letters to Tim Cooper of which one [was] the IMPORTANT memo. Other photographs arrived as undeveloped film and upon developing were pictures taken of a TV displaying the [Ray] Santilli [Alien Autopsy] film."[2]

Yes, said John, the new Majestic group continued to have the same input from Intelligence personnel that it had before, and much of the membership stayed the same. The only major difference was that all of the Majestic documentation was removed from the vaults of the many and varied intelligence agencies and was transferred to Area 51. And anyone in the Intelligence field or the military that worked on the Majestic projects was required to transfer to Area 51, too.

John says that he feels that it is for this reason that noone has been able to access any Majestic related documents via the Freedom of Information Act – all of the relevant records that might have been Majestic-related were removed from agency files and vaults back in the late 1960s and, as a consequence, will never surface for declassification.

According to John, this process was not without its problems: there were people allied to the Majestic program who were considered "rogue" and who had gone way beyond their normal limit to keep Majestic hidden from the public, the press and even from the regular government. This, said John, was part of the reason for having a centralized location for the files: they referenced various controversial and highly secret activities that had been done to hide the truth and that were, in many ways, more sensational than the UFO truth itself.

If the files were in numerous locations, explained John, there was a chance they would leak out. Those rogue individuals, said John, had not complied with orders to relinquish their Majestic files; and, as a result, some files were found to be missing from secure vaults. Other files, supposedly, had been shredded (when it was strongly suspected by certain, unnamed figures in the story that they had not been), and some people with Majestic clearance simply vanished, or were found dead under questionable circumstances. No one could work out how "deep" the Majestic program ran and there were suspicions of an even deeper Majestic program than the "official" one.

John stated that, in his briefing, he was told that aside from the documents that existed in his office, all of the other Majestic papers that had been pulled from the agencies had been destroyed (because, essentially, they duplicated the files in his office); apart, that is, from files that were suspected of having been stolen by Majestic personnel with their own agendas – and more likely, says John, to cover their own tracks.

John says that the files he read all had one curious similarity – the cover page on each was missing. He explained that all of the files were stapled; however, many of the documents had a tiny piece of torn paper stuck under the staple – indicating that the cover-page had been carelessly torn off. In turn, a new cover page had been added – a blank piece of paper with a pencil-written new title that was affixed with a paperclip to the second page.

He was told that these surviving copies of the Majestic papers had come from the office of a man who had a major role to play in Majestic in the late 1950s and 1960s and that, in addition to the files that he had legal access to, the man had obtained some of these files after they had been literally "lifted" from other agencies, and he had kept them in a secure location and had assigned his own filing- and naming-system to the files. The man was also suspected of having shredded numerous Majestic files for reasons of his own – files from the mid-1940s - that were not duplicated and that told stories that were now utterly lost forever. John alluded to the possibility that that this man was none other than James Jesus Angleton, who was appointed Counter-Intelligence chief of the Central Intelligence Agency by Director Allen Dulles in 1954.[3]

The earliest document that John recalls was, he said, also the most disturbing. It dated from 1943 and was a long letter/memo of complaint from a medical man working at Los Alamos whose team had been required to carry out certain tests and experiments on a group of unusual-looking people. The doctor was complaining to a military officer about the nature of what was being asked of his team and was highly concerned about why these people looked the way they did.

John said that he remembered clearly that at some point in 1943, seventeen people of unusual appearance were brought to Los Alamos. They all looked very alike – around five feet in height, hairless, with enlarged heads, large eyes and with an appearance that made them look not unlike victims of progeria: the rapid-aging disease that afflicts a very, small percentage of children.

They were brought to the base in a covered army vehicle and were totally naked and walked in a slightly stiff fashion. He stressed that the eyes of the "people" were normal apart from their size – they were *not* the black eyes as ascribed to the stereotypical alien. The people were taken to a secure location at Los Alamos, and over the course of four months subjected to a variety of medical tests – blood was taken, skin samples were taken and several were used in radiation experiments and controversial and then-fledgling bacteriological warfare experimentation.

The doctor described all of this in truly nightmarish tones: the people never spoke and only made strange noises like a cross between a seal's bark and a hiccup that was very loud and disturb-ing. They would have to be restrained by military personnel before any of the tests could be performed. They were fed on a diet of a mashed and very condensed mixture of various fruits and drank only water or milk. According to the doctor he was told by the military that they were malformed people.

As a medical man, he said, he found this explanation highly suspicious: there was no way that seventeen people could all be afflicted in such a strange way and for the world's medical community not to know this, he considered. The doctor advised that rumors at Los Alamos suggested that no one (not even the military who brought them to Los Alamos) knew who or what these people were or where they were from; but that they had been found somewhere in the Arizona desert. All of the people died before the end of 1943 and their bodies had been removed by the military as they died, one by one. No one was ever able to communicate with any of the seventeen people and the doctor complained about the way in which he and his team were threatened by the military never to discuss this.

The file, said John, referred to additional documents on these people that, he was told in his briefing, had been destroyed by the man who the files had been taken from. Bizarrely, John was informed, no record of these experiments now existed (apart from this one solitary letter), the location of the bodies of the seventeen creatures or people was unknown, and the entire paper-trail appeared to have been destroyed by the people involved in this project. It was suspected, however, that this was linked with similar events that occurred in New Mexico in the summer of 1947.

John says that there was a *very* large file titled *Autopsies – Bodies Unknown Origin 47* that dealt with the bodies of eight people found in the New Mexico desert (there was no reference in the autopsy report to a spacecraft or vehicle – just the bodies) in the summer of 1947. All were substantially like the creatures taken to Los Alamos in 1943. There was no name on the document to identify the writer; however, John suspects that the name was probably on the missing original title page. He recalls that the file stated that of the eight bodies, four were preserved intact, two were autopsied and their remains were then disposed of, and two were dissected and their body parts and organs were preserved separately. John says the document referred to photographs; however, at no time did he ever see any photographs in any of the files in his possession. Several of the bodies were badly damaged and the rest were in good condition. The report was very detailed and covered the major body organs, brain, eyes, ears, skin (which was a sickly white-gray), fingers and toes, blood analysis, limbs, teeth.

Interestingly there was also a file that had the hand-written title of *Autopsies – Bodies Unknown Origin 47, Biological Problems and Deaths* that dealt with an unknown virus that had contaminated and killed a medical team that had examined one of the bodies. All of the personnel were dressed in protective suits; however, these were apparently useless with respect to providing adequate biological protection. Curiously, however, none of the other bodies exhibited any signs of this virus.

John stated that there was a report that interested him greatly that was titled *Suit Study 48 Armageddon* and that was a lengthy document dealing with a scientific study of the clothing that the people had been wearing. The clothing was a yellowish color and a one-piece outfit that extended from the lower neck right down to the bottom of the feet. It apparently took several hours to remove the clothing of the creatures by forcibly cutting through the material. Upon examination, it was determined that the suits were put together in what today we would term a Velcro-style fashion. However, the suits almost seemed to be alive or had an in-built memory because not only would the individual fibers re-bond when brought close together, they would re-bond with the same corresponding fibers time and again.

The most bizarre aspect of this file centered around one of the scientific personnel – the shortest member of the team - who chose to try one of the suits on. Having learned how to open the suit, his colleagues held it open for him to climb into and the suit molded itself around him. Due to his size, the suit was not comfortable but could be worn. However, something curious and ominous then occurred. The man began to get images in his mind of a dark and frightening future for the Earth – of an irradiated world, ruined cities, huge atomic mushroom clouds looming miles upwards into an ever-black sky as strange objects flew across the wrecked landscape, and perhaps most significantly, a Human Race reduced to minimal levels as a direct result of a killer virus of unknown origins that destroyed the human immune system. The man got a distinct and disturbing impression that whatever these creatures were, they hated us with a vengeance and that there was a plan on their part to spark off a nuclear holocaust between the United States and the Soviets. Interestingly, this accords well with several entries in a number of MJ-12 files about the fear of nuclear war being sparked by the Soviets misidentifying UFOs as American nuclear warheads.

Sensing he was in distress, the man's colleagues and friends ripped the suit off him and a report was referenced that stated that the man was briefed intensively by a team from the CIA that had expertise in psychological matters. The file also stated that this bizarre episode was a further clue to the fact that the suit was somehow "alive" and linked with the minds and memories of the creatures that had previously worn them. Perhaps most weird of all was a note in the file that stated that the suits were themselves kept locked away in a vault and considered an "intelligence hazard."

Most of the other files, recalled John, fell into two categories – there were dozens and dozens of very technical files on two "aircraft" that had been found in the New Mexico desert in 1947 that dealt with propulsion, structure, landing gear, internal mechanics and much more that John couldn't recall. There were also hundreds of one-page and two-page memos from and to various Majestic personnel discussing on-going Majestic-related projects, many of which focused upon biological and bacteriological issues.

John said that there was never any reference in the files to the creatures or the aircraft being alien in origin. Indeed, no one seemed to have any awareness of what they were or their point-of-origin.

John did assert, however, that there was a brief file from July 1947 speculating that this was all an ingenious hoax on the part of the Soviets – until it quickly became apparent that even they would not have the expertise to do this, much less biologically alter a number of human beings into something else - or that it was "a domestic cover" to hide Cold War atrocities undertaken on handicapped people.

John stated that among the people with who he worked, however, there were three possibilities that were considered the most viable:

- That these things were from another world;
- That they were from somewhere on the Earth (other dimensions and even the more remote parts of the world were discussed);
- And that they were, incredibly, from our future.

John adds that, in discussion with colleagues at Area 51, he learned that even by the turn of the 1970s there was still no definitive proof as to what these creatures were or where (or indeed when) they were from. He did state that there were two points in favor of the "future theory." One was that while the "aircraft" recovered in New Mexico were highly advanced technologically-speaking, several components within the craft were constructed in "feet-and-inch measurements."

Also, there were references in the files to extensive studies done on the possible existence of alien life and numerous experts had been consulted. The overriding conclusions were that there was nothing to deny the possible existence of alien life in the Universe, that it was even possible that alien life was coming here, and that this is precisely what these creatures were.

The most suspicious aspect of this whole affair, however, was that not only were these creatures apparently comfortable breathing our air but they were also perfectly synchronized for the Earth's atmospheric pressure – and this seemed to be simply too coinciden-tal. John said that this split the teams into two camps – one that favored the idea that the creatures were from the Earth (but from a time far in the future or from some location on the Earth in our present), or that they were indeed alien and had been genetically altered to allow them to comfortably operate on our planet.

John said that other files he read and was custodian over were titled:

- *White House Brief*, that was a summary of the 1947 incidents and that appeared to be a document that could have been used in various presidential briefings since there was no direct reference to any president in particular;
- *Majestic Soviet Problem 55* (that dealt with fears – unfounded, it transpired - that the Soviets had infiltrated the Majestic program);
- An empty folder with the curious (but somewhat amusing) title of *Body Of Unknown Origin: Where Is Number 5?*;
- The apocalyptically titled *Majestic Four Horseman*, that dealt with the visions of the man that donned the creature's suit;
- *Majestic Security Problems, 47-65*, that focused its attention upon people allied to – or with knowledge of – Majestic and

who, it was feared, would reveal the secrets of Majestic to the outside world;

- And one with the unusual title of *Majestic 59 – Speak to Charles P. Olivier: Is 4 Enough?* This can only be a reference to the noted astronomer Charles Pollard Olivier, an expert on meteors and comets, whose correspondence files can be found at the American Philosophical Society in Philadelphia, PA. Interestingly, the collection – of 400 items – includes correspondence with alleged MJ-12 member Donald Menzel; Lincoln La Paz (of Project Twinkle/Green Fireball fame); Otto Struve; and Gaylord Harnwell of the Research and Development Board.[4]

John stayed with the program for the prearranged one-year contract and then carved out a career for himself in the private sector, before retiring in 1981. Notably, his thoughts and theories on this curious affair and his exposure to the files at issue are intriguing. As he rightly points out: he had no expertise in the area of UFOs, and why, if this was such a huge secret, was he briefed on it at all? In addition, he asks: given the alleged magnitude and significance of the operation, is this not the type of job that a person would be drafted into for life, rather than for a mere twelve months?

Taking the above into consideration, John stresses that although the documentation at issue looked genuine, he does not dismiss the possibility that his exposure to the files could have been a part of some larger, spook-sponsored mind-game. Since his highly successful post-Area 51 career surfaced as a direct result of his FBI contacts, John speculates that his superiors exposed him to bogus materials at Area 51, and then watched his every move to see if he spoke out of turn. The fact that he did not (at least not until now) and was thereafter considered utterly trustworthy, led him to be rewarded with a near-decade long career in the private sector, that saw him move within highly influential circles in the world of U.S. Intelligence.

Whether genuine or not, the files were carefully crafted, told an astonishing story and, again, promoted the idea that alien viruses were a reality. Not only that: those same viruses were incredibly deadly, too.[5]

* * *

Chapter 23 Notes:

1. Interview with John, January 4, 2006.

2. *Important Memo*, July 9, 1997. Available at: www.majesticdocuments.com by downloading: http://209.132.68.98/pdf/important_memo.pdf.

3. For further data on James Angleton, see: www.spartacus.schoolnet.co.uk/ SSangleton.htm.

4. The files and correspondence of Charles Pollard Olivier are held at the American Philosophical Society Library at 105 South Fifth Street, Philadelphia, PA 19106. See: http://libserv.aip.org:81/ipac20/ipac.jsp?uri=full=3100001~!5497~!0&profile=new custom-icos#focus for further details of Olivier's work.

5. Interview with John, January 4, 2006.

Conclusion

This book was finished in 2006 on schedule by Nick Redfern, who applied his talents with remarkable efficiency to help create this book.

I personally feel that this book is unique because:

- It blends the British and American UFO cultures about UFOs.
- It systematically and chronologically provides a perspective of the concern about alien pathogens (such as bacteria, viruses, fungi or prions) that might cause epidemics.
- It is exceptionally systematic in referencing the sources.
- It contains summaries of documents you have never seen.
- It addresses the issue of Weapons of Mass Destruction, pertinent to all of us.
- If the aliens want to kill us all, this will be the way it's done.

Dr. Robert M. Wood

With deep appreciation to collaborator Nick Redfern, to son and colleague Ryan Wood, and to publisher Richard Dolan.

Appendix: Illustrations

The Special Operations Manual (see www.majesticdocuments.com) gives on page 6 a detailed description of EBE Type I and EBE Type II. In 2003, the author contracted with forensic artist, Bill McDonald, to use those words in the Manual to create images of what how they might have appeared on the examination table.

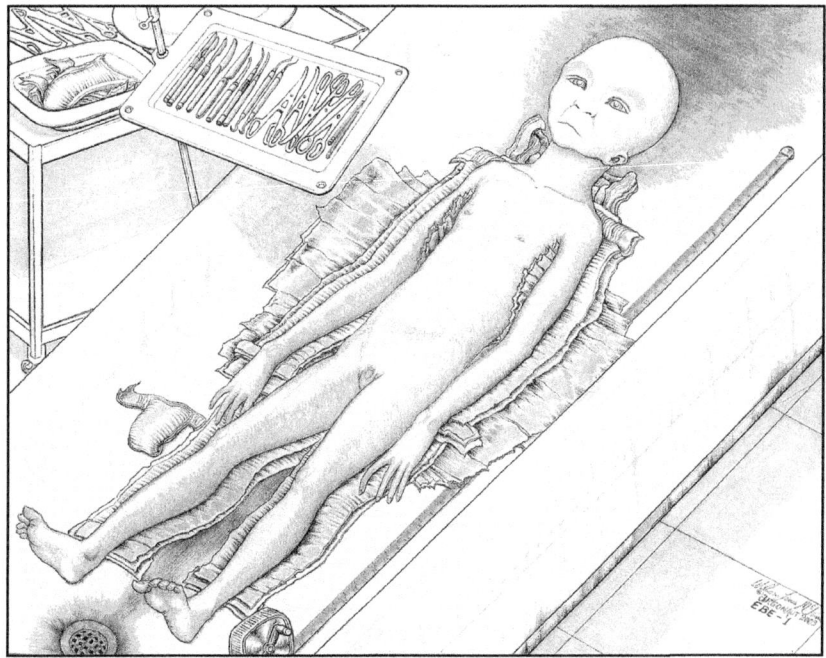

This is the result for EBE-I.
The small genitals were added at Bill's suggestion.

This is the result for EBE-II.

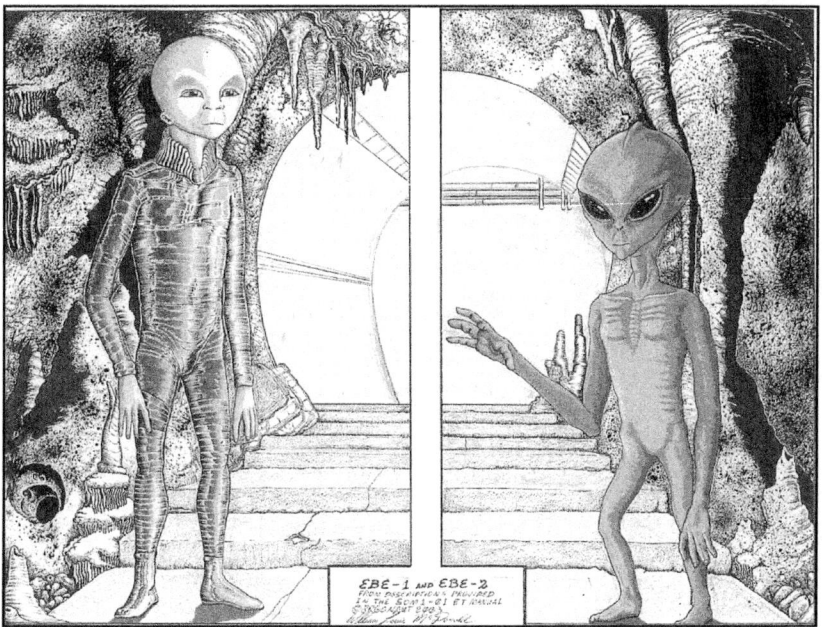

Image EBE-I and EBE-II.

The author asked Bill McDonald to create the two aliens as they would have appeared alive and well. He decided to put them in an underground environment, not exactly together in a not exactly artificial setting.

About Dr. Robert M. Wood

Bob Wood received a B.S. in Aeronautical Engineering from University of Colorado in 1949, a Ph.D. in Physics from Cornell in 1953, worked for General Electric Aeronautics and Ordnance, served in the U.S. Army at Aberdeen Proving Ground for two years, and then completed 43 years with Douglas Aircraft and its successors. A long-time Director of the Mutual UFO Network (MUFON), a Councilor for the Society for Scientific Exploration, and member of the American Institute of Aeronautics and Astronautics since 1947, he has garnered a reputation for integrity and scholarship in this field over the last two decades.

His aerospace career included the thermodynamics of keeping missiles cool; managing and selling the independent research and development projects of a couple of dozen scientists and engineers; designing radars to discriminate between Soviet ballistic missiles and their decoys; applying advanced technology to make the Space Station cheaper, better, and sooner; and finally helping to sell the Delta launch vehicle as the workhorse for NASA orbital payloads.

In the late 1960s, he ran a proprietary project to try to discover how UFOs "worked," and has been studying the UFO topic ever since. Upon retirement, he became involved in the forensics of authenticating questioned "leaked" UFO documents, collaborating occasionally with his colleague and son Ryan (author of *MAJIC – Eyes Only*). He recognized the excellence of Nick Redfern's attention to high standards and asked him to provide his international reports concerning aliens and viruses.

About Nick Redfern

Scott A. Andrews

Nick Redfern is the author of 27 books on UFOs, conspiracies, and strange creatures. His books include *A Covert Agenda*; *Contactees*; *Final Events*; *The Real Men in Black*; *Science Fiction Secrets*; *On the Trail of the Saucer Spies*; and *Strange Secrets*. He has appeared on more than 70 TV shows, including: Fox News; the BBC's *Out of This World*; the SyFy Channel's *Proof Positive*; the Space Channel's *Fields of Fear*; the History Channel's *Monster Quest*, *America's Book of Secrets*, *Ancient Aliens* and *UFO Hunters*; the National Geographic Channel's *Paranatural*; and MSNBC's *Countdown with Keith Olbermann*.

Originally from the UK, Nick lives on the fringes of Dallas, Texas. He can be contacted at: http://nickredfernfortean.blogspot.com

Index

pneumonia, 8, 237, 238
polio epidemic, 115-117
Porton Down, 3, 5, 83, 181-184, 188-190, 193-197, 232, 262-264, 266, 268, 269
Prado, Fernando Eugênio, 236
Prescott, James, 183-187, 190, 191, 193, 195, 232
Presidio, 201
Primakov, Yevgeni, 246
Prine, Richard, 223
Project 63, 57
propulsion, 40, 52, 54, 57-59, 64, 79, 100, 121, 124, 146, 202, 294
protective suits, 81, 293
provenance, 41, 92, 93, 125
Prusiner, Stanley, 9
Psychological Strategy Board, 99, 100
psychological warfare, 12, 89, 90, 93-104, 150, 245, 276
psy-op, 4, 45, 46, 99
psy-war, 90
Puget Sound, 156, 157
Pugwash, 264, 265
Putman, Forrest S., 219, 221, 228
Que, Benito, 250, 267
rabies, 6
radar, 26, 32, 64, 96, 136, 142, 143, 145, 151, 159, 199, 200, 203, 277, 279
radiation count, 216
Radiation Laboratory, 113
radio silence, 200
RAF Bentwaters-Woodbridge, 196, 197
Ramey, Roger, 25
Randle, Kevin, 28
Randles, Jenny, 181, 186
Rapley, Chris, 262
Rea, Charles E., 65, 70, 72-74
rectum, 209, 216, 218, 230
red eyes, 235, 239
red marks, 147
red rain, 22
Redfern, Nick, iii, 5, 15, 39, 42, 82, 120, 121, 124-126, 132, 146, 160, 161, 173, 194, 195, 197, 199, 273, 283, 298, 303
Regma Biotechnics, 250
remote viewing, 2, 93
Rendlesham Forest, 196, 197
Research and Development (RAND), 276
retrieval, 37, 89, 129, 132-134, 136-139, 157, 158, 167, 169, 171, 184, 240, 243, 244
Retrievals of the Third Kind, 132-134
retrovirus, 4, 9, 10, 12, 83-85, 124, 247
Reuters, 233, 254
Ricin, 7
Rickenbaugh, Kent, 259
Rickett, Lewis, 28
Rickman, Leland, 263
Riconosciuto, Michael, 159, 163
rinderpest, 108, 109

RNA, 83, 84, 216
Roberts, Andy, 178, 180, 181
Robertson Panel, 274
Roe, A.V., 125
Rommel, Kenneth M., 225-227
Roninson, Igor B., 259
Roosevelt, Franklin D., 50, 51, 120
Rosack, Theodore P., 209
Rostov, Russia, 5
Roswell, 3, 12, 15, 25-30, 32, 33, 35-39, 41, 44, 50, 53, 64, 114, 119, 126, 137, 159, 160, 164, 178, 207, 243, 272, 273, 276, 277, 279, 280, 283
Rous viruses, 84, 180
Rowe, Frankie, 29
Royal Air Force, 120, 121, 179, 181, 189, 193, 196, 197
Royall, Kenneth, 99
Ruppelt, Edward, 157
Russell, Richard, 159-160
S-2, 46, 47, 56
Sagan, Carl, 19, 20
"Salina," 46, 89, 165
Samford, John A., 68
San Augustin, New Mexico, 27
Sandia, New Mexico, 8, 64, 65, 149, 216, 225
Santos Gomes, Elaine Maria, 239
Sarbacher, Robert Irving, 30
Sarin, 7
SARS, 17, 18, 252
satanic, 105, 208, 217, 223
satellites, 142, 276
saucer, 25, 26, 28, 32, 40, 53, 54, 98, 114, 116, 122, 125, 134, 135, 137, 145, 150, 272, 277
SCEO, 165
schizophrenia, 253
Schmitt, Don, 28, 136
Schmitt, Harrison, 214, 215, 220, 225, 228
Schulgen, George F., 77
Schwartz, Clara Jane, 255
Schwartz, Robert M., 252, 253, 255
Scientific and Technical Intelligence Branch (STIB), 121-123
Scott Air Force Base, 114-116, 261
Scottish Rite, 116
scrapie, 9, 10
Sea Stallion, 201, 202
security police, 212
SED personnel, 81
"Sergeant HJ," 168
Serpo, 138, 139
serum, 236
Shandera, Jaime, 37
Shaw, Clay, 157, 163
sheep, 6, 10, 224, 268, 276
Shrinikyo, Aum, 7
Sign (Project), 58, 277, 278
Silva, Valquíria Aparecida, 235

Printed in Great Britain
by Amazon

19124244R00183